How Hume and Kant Reconstruct Natural Law

How Hume and Kant Reconstruct Natural Law

Justifying Strict Objectivity *without* Debating Moral Realism

Kenneth R. Westphal

CLARENDON PRESS · OXFORD

OXFORD
UNIVERSITY PRESS

Great Clarendon Street, Oxford, OX2 6DP,
United Kingdom

Oxford University Press is a department of the University of Oxford.
It furthers the University's objective of excellence in research, scholarship,
and education by publishing worldwide. Oxford is a registered trade mark of
Oxford University Press in the UK and in certain other countries

First Edition published in 2016

Published in the United States of America by Oxford University Press
198 Madison Avenue, New York, NY 10016, United States of America

British Library Cataloguing in Publication Data
Data available

Library of Congress Control Number: 2015957841

ISBN 978–0–19–874705–5

For Onora O'Neill
—in admiration and gratitude

Contents

Analytical Contents

Acknowledgements

I wish to express my gratitude to B. J. Diggs, who as my first instructor in political philosophy brought and commended Hume's theory of justice to our attention (cf. Diggs 1974). Ever since, I have been pondering it, natural law and, though I did not yet know its quintessential formulation, the Pyrrhonian Dilemma of the Criterion.

I first encountered Onora O'Neill's work in graduate school, when I read *Acting on Principle* (1975), very evidently the work of a superior mind and spirit, whose work I resolved then and there to follow closely. Her research and her model have amply rewarded careful, renewed attention at every step. Having studied Kant's critical philosophy extensively and intensively, I have learned more about how to read, understand, and make good philosophical sense of Kant's writings and views in moral philosophy from her research than from any other source, far more than I can make evident in this slim volume, or in my entire *oeuvre*. I know of no one who so richly deserves her splendid name!

Material contained in Chapters 3 and 4 appeared originally in 'Von der Konvention zur Sittlichkeit. Humes Begründung einer Rechtsethik aus nach-Kantischer Perspektive', in D. Heidemann and K. Engelhardt, eds, *Ethikbegründungen Zwischen Universalizmus und Relativismus*. Berlin: DeGruyter (2005), 153–80; translated with minor revisions in 'From "Convention" to "Ethical Life": Hume's Theory of Justice in Post-Kantian Perspective', *The Journal of Moral Philosophy* 7.1 (2010): 105–32.

Material contained in Chapter 5 appeared originally in 'Practical Reason: Categorical Imperative, Maxims, Laws', in W. Dudley and K. Engelhard, eds, *Kant: Key Concepts*. London: Acumen (2010), 103–19.

Material contained in Chapter 6 appeared originally in 'Kant's Constructivism and Rational Justification', in S. Baiasu, S. Pihlström, and H. Williams, eds, *Politics and Metaphysics in Kant*. Cardiff: Wales University Press (2011), 28–46.

Chapter 8 appeared originally as 'A Kantian Justification of Possession', in M. Timmons, ed., *Kant's Metaphysics of Ethics: Interpretive Essays*. New York: Oxford University Press (2002), 89–109.

I am grateful to, and thank the respective editors and publishers for permitting my using these materials here. All have been revised for the present study, often extensively. Much more than that, I am very grateful to each of these editors for their interest in my work and for their very productive invitations to contribute to their respective volumes. An anonymous reader for Oxford University Press kindly indicated some salutary improvements, as did a reading group studying the penultimate manuscript, kindly organized by Lucas Thorpe at my new home institution, Boğaziçi Üniversitesi, İstanbul (Autumn 2014). My final revisions were also facilitated by teaching closely related topics at both undergraduate and graduate levels during my first, Autumn term there—a very fortunate convergence of departmental and scholarly interests. Final preparations of the manuscript were kindly supported by the Boğaziçi Üniversitesi Research Fund (BAP; grant code: 9761). *Thank you very much, each and all!*

İstanbul
4 July 2015

Primary Sources and Citation Methods

Individual works by Hume are cited by each work's divisions into books, parts, sections (§), or paragraphs and, following a slash, by the page number of the Selby-Bigge–Nidditch editions. Essays lacking subdivisions are cited by title and paragraph number, designated '¶'; an 'Appendix' is designated 'App.'. Occasionally, non-sequential paragraphs in one § are cited thus: *T* 3.2.2 ¶¶3, 7, 9.

Similar methods are used for citing other collected works, as indicated in the bibliography under their respective entries.

Kant's works are cited by volume:page.line numbers of *Kants Gesammelte Schriften*; this pagination is provided in all recent translations of Kant's works. Translations of Kant's writings are my own, unless otherwise indicated. Minor revisions to others' translations are not noted.

Hume, David, 1898. T. H. Green and T. H. Grose, eds, *The Philosophical Works of David Hume*, 4 vols. London: Longman's, Green & Co.

——, 1932. J. Y. T. Greig, ed., *The Letters of David Hume*. Oxford: The Clarendon Press.

——, 1954. R. Klibansky and E. C. Mossner, eds, *New Letters of David Hume*. Oxford: The Clarendon Press.

ECHU, *ECPM*, SBN^{E} ——, 1975. L. A. Selby-Bigge, ed., *Enquiries Concerning Human Understanding and Concerning the Principles of Morals*, 3rd edn. Oxford: The Clarendon Press.

SBN ——, 1978. L. A. Selby-Bigge and P. H. Nidditch, eds, *A Treatise of Human Nature*, 2nd edn. Oxford: The Clarendon Press.

EMPL ——, 1987. E. F. Miller, ed., *Essays, Moral, Political, and Literary*. Indianapolis: Liberty Classics. Cited by Part.Essay.¶ numbers.

——, 1997. *The Complete Works and Correspondence of David Hume*. Charlotte, VA: Intelex Corporation. Includes: Hume (1898), (1832), (1954), (1975), (1978), and (1987), with corrections.

NHR ——, 1757. *The Natural History of Religion*, rpt. in Hume, David, 1997. *The Complete Works and Correspondence of David Hume*. Charlotte, VA: Intelex Corporation.

T ——, 2000. D. F. Norton and M. J. Norton, eds, *A Treatise of Human Nature*. Oxford: Oxford University Press.

KdrV ——, 1781. *Critique of Pure Reason/Kritik der reinen Vernunft*, 2nd ed. (1787). Cited, respectively, as 'A' and 'B'; *GS* 3, 4.

GMS ——, 1785. *Groundwork of the Metaphysics of Morals/Grundlegung der Metaphysik der Sitten*, *GS* 4.

KdpV ——, 1788. *Critique of Practical Reason/Kritik der praktischen Vernunft*, *GS* 5.

MdS ——, 1798. *The Metaphysics of Morals/Die Metaphysik der Sitten*, 2nd edn, *GS* 6.

RL ——, 1798. *The Metaphysics of Morals, Part 1: Doctrine of Right/'Rechtslehre'*, 2nd rev. edn, *GS* 6.

TL ——, 1798. *The Metaphysics of Morals, Part 2: Doctrine of Virtue/'Tugendlehre'*, *GS* 6.

GS ——, 1902–. *Kants Gesammelte Schriften*. Königlich Preußische (now Deutsche) Akademie der Wissenschaften. Berlin: G. Reimer (now De Gruyter); cited by volume:page.line numbers.

——, 1964. *Groundwork of the Metaphysics of Morals*. H. J. Paton, tr. New York: Harper & Row.

——, 1986. B. Ludwig, ed., *Metaphysische Anfangsgründe der Rechtslehre*. Hamburg: Meiner.

——, 1991. *The Metaphysics of Morals*. Mary Gregor, tr. Cambridge: Cambridge University Press.

CEWK ——, 1995–2015. P. Guyer and A. Wood, eds. in chief, *The Cambridge Edition of the Works of Immanuel Kant in Translation*. Cambridge: Cambridge University Press.

——, 1996. M. Gregor and A. Wood, eds, *Practical Philosophy*, M. Gregor, tr., Cambridge: Cambridge University Press (*CEWK*).

——, 1998. A Wood and G. di Giovanni, eds and trs, *Religion within the Boundaries of Mere Reason, And Other Writings*. Cambridge: Cambridge University Press (*CEWK*).

——, 2009. K. Worm, ed., *Kant im Kontext III: Kompleteausgabe*. Berlin: InfoSoftWare.

——, 2015. F. Rauscher ed., *Lectures, Notes, and Drafts on Political Philosophy*, F. Rauscher and K. R. Westphal, trs. Cambridge: Cambridge University Press (*CEWK*).

1

Reconstructing Moral Constructivism

1 Introduction

After rather a fallow period, both Hume's and Kant's theories of justice have recently commanded well-deserved scholarly attention. These developments are welcome, yet a philosophically decisive relation between Hume's and Kant's moral philosophies has been neglected: Hume initiated a powerful and distinctive form of moral constructivism, which Kant adopted (*via* Rousseau) and further developed. Their form of moral constructivism identifies and justifies strictly objective basic moral principles and the practices they structure (social institutions), whilst maintaining neutrality about moral realism and its alternatives.[1] Their form of moral constructivism justifies cognitivism about moral principles through its account of justification, rather than by appeal to alleged, ever-controversial moral 'truths', 'facts', or 'values'. In a word, their distinctive form of moral constructivism shows that issues about moral realism and its alternatives are subsidiary, not central, to normative moral philosophy.

The basic character and strategy of this form of moral constructivism are initiated by Hume in his theory of justice in Book 3 of the *Treatise*. Though unfashionable, I do not hesitate to include justice within the scope of moral philosophy. Both Hume and Kant, and indeed all moral philosophers through the early twentieth century, addressed moral

[1] The designation 'moral realism' has become used so broadly that any view according to which there is a definite answer whether one is or is not morally obligated in some definite way is now called 'moral realism'. This laxity is obfuscating. I use the phrase 'moral realism' to designate views according to which there are human mind-independent moral truth-makers, of whatever kind.

philosophy as a genus with two proper, coordinate species: ethics and justice (*ius*). There is much to recommend this taxonomy, not least because one of our most basic ethical duties is: Comply with the dictates of justice! As a fundamental practical matter, central ethical issues about individual action, virtue, and life-plans can be no more than theory, if even that, without a significant degree of public peace, security, and stability, which require principles and institutions basic to justice. Examining the form of moral constructivism Hume and Kant develop provides, *en passant*, some good reasons for adhering to this traditional taxonomy (fortunately still common in Europe), also because their moral constructivism forges direct and important links with philosophy of law and with economics—links which today require emphatic restatement.[2]

A central conviction underlying this study is that the genre 'business ethics' is poorly conceived and can offer little more than ineffective moralizing unless and until it is clearly recognized that the central issues in this domain are issues of justice, including the justice involved in proper accountancy. It is no secret that steady erosion of accountancy procedures and oversight in the USA in recent decades unleashed the current financial crisis.[3] To get our respective houses in order requires clarity of purpose; it is hoped that this study may contribute to regaining some of the clarity about morals, justice, law, finance, accounting, and auditing we so dearly need. (I must, however, beg forbearance of those interested in the justice of accounting and auditing, which cannot be addressed directly until the final chapter.)

In Anglophone jurisprudence there is growing consensus, more evident in North America than in the UK, that legal positivism and legal realism have run their course, though no consensus has emerged about a better successor. In the UK, jurisprudes are beginning to reconsider

[2] An important issue I cannot address in this study is the scope and grounds of obligation to non-ideal jurisdictions. Kant's unqualified obligation to obey political authority holds only within his strictly metaphysical principles of justice and so holds only of ideal, fully just states (Westphal 1992). Parallel to this analysis Kant argues that we have very strong, though not unqualified, obligations toward actual, non-ideal states, insofar as obedience to them is necessary in the long run to provide and improve compliance with fundamental principles of justice. For discussion, see Horn (2014). (The 'metaphysics' relevant to Kant's theory of justice concerns *a priori* principles, not Transcendental Idealism.)

[3] See, *e.g.*, Greenspan (2002), Morris (2008), Waxman *et al* (2008). Like Greenspan (2002), Morris (2008) appeared before the crisis broke—but see below, §46.

prospects for natural law, which has enjoyed greater attention in North America and on the European Continent.[4] On the Continent natural law theory has remained on the agenda, both in philosophy and in jurisprudence, especially in the acute formulation of its key issues by Hobbes (see §8), though Continental legal theorists have neglected Hume's theory of justice. In Anglophone circles, Hume is widely regarded as the destroyer of natural law theory. Certainly he contributed mightily to discrediting traditional natural law theory and its central appeals to moral realism and to moral teleology. His having done so, however, is compatible with his fragment of a theory of justice (in Book 3 of the *Treatise*) having inaugurated the approach I here call Natural Law Constructivism.

Accordingly, this monograph aims at concision and clarity, so that it may be read profitably by scholars and students of philosophy, law, politics, economics, business, or accountancy alike. Where needed, specialists are referred for further details to other works. In addition to setting aside interminable debates about moral realism and its alternatives, Hume's and Kant's Natural Law Constructivism sets aside debates about 'consequentialism' *versus* 'deontology'; their moral constructivism exposes this contrast as simply unhelpful.[5] Their moral constructivism further shows that Kant's moral philosophy need not appeal, as a basic value or premiss, to the purported intrinsic, incommensurable value or 'dignity' (in contrast to price) of rational agency as such.[6] Finally, their moral constructivism is independent of issues about human motivation, and so sets aside debates about 'internal' and 'external' links between reasons and motives. Let me be very clear: Hume's and Kant's moral constructivism is simply neutral about moral realism, about the contrast between 'consequentialism' and 'deontology', about the putative incommensurable value of human agency, and about intrinsic or extrinsic links

[4] On the USA, see, e.g., Haines (1965); on Canada, see, e.g., The Canadian Charter of Rights and Freedoms (1982), and judgments of the Supreme Court of Canada in the cases Roncarelle *v.* Duplessis (1952), Perka *v.* The Queen (1984), and Hofer *v.* Hofer (1992). On the German and French contexts, see, e.g., *Archives de philosophie du droit* 6 (1961): *La réforme des études de droit. Le droit naturel*, Maihofer (1962), and Schmölz (1963). An interesting contrast is provided by Chakraverti (1967), who, working within the English tradition transported to India, considers 'natural justice' only as 'fundamental principles of judicial procedure'. (My thanks to Arthur Ripstein for references to Canadian law.)

[5] In this I agree with Herman (1993), 208–40.

[6] On Kant's account of dignity, see Sensen (2009, 2011) and Waldron (2012).

between reasons and motives. These views may, in some form, be true or justified; they simply are not required by Hume's and Kant's Natural Law Constructivism. These are cardinal virtues of their method and its results, which show that persisting theoretical squabbles between Humeans and Kantians over those issues are tangential to the central issues examined here. This is also to say: I shall be forthright, even at risk of perturbing various professional sensibilities, persuasions, or habits of thought. However, fault finding has become such a professional preoccupation that a reminder is in order, that critical assessment requires reflective reading to determine whether or how the reader's doubt, query, or challenge may be answered by, or on the basis of, an author's published analysis; this alone distinguishes criticism from cavil.

2 Conspectus

2.1 Contra contemporary moral constructivisms

Famously, Hume's ethical theory is rooted in his account of human sentiments, and of how some sentiments become specifically moral sentiments. Reading Hume's theory of justice through the lens of his ethical theory, however, fails to do justice to his theory of justice because it occludes his radical recasting of natural law theory on a constructivist, though objective, basis.[7] In chapter 3, I argue that Hume's construction of the basic principles of justice is independent of his sentiment theory. In chapter 4, I argue further that Hume's theory of justice exposes some substantial flaws in his sentiment-based ethical theory. Remarkably, these flaws directly anticipate Kant's reasons for rejecting moral empiricism (discussed in §19).

Various contemporary neo-Humean ethical theories, such as Blackburn's projectivism, appeal, not to Hume's sentiments, but rather to various forms of subjective human responses, motives, emotions, manifest preferences, values, moral commitments, moral intuitions, 'validity claims' (Habermas's *Geltungsansprüche*), and so forth. These contemporary forms of moral constructivism share the weaknesses of Hume's

[7] I am not the first to take seriously Hume's natural law theory; I gratefully follow the lead of Forbes (1977), Buckle (1991, 234–5, 298), and Haakonssen (1996), though I develop Hume's constructivist approach to natural law in greater detail.

sentiment-based ethical theory, as revealed by Hume's theory of justice and by Kant's reasons for rejecting moral empiricism. These contemporary views have much to offer; this I do not deny. I contend, however—with Hume and Kant—that they cannot identify or justify the most basic, strictly objective moral principles. This concise study cannot examine the range of contemporary forms of constructivism in detail. I shall, however, explain why the inadequacies of Hume's sentiment-based ethical theory generalize to these contemporary forms of moral constructivism, and shall examine two paradigm cases: one is Hume's ethical theory (chapter 4), the other is Gauthier's refined, radical contractarianism (chapter 7). These two examples flesh out the general problem confronting contemporary forms of moral constructivism posed in chapter 2 (§§6, 9), and indicate, sufficiently for present purposes, how these difficulties generalize to other contemporary versions of moral constructivism.

2.2 Natural law constructivism

Chapter 7 examines Kant's construction of the basic principles of rightful—that is, just—acquisition, possession, and use, which proves to be a subtle and sophisticated development of the distinctive and powerful form of moral constructivism inaugurated by Hume's theory of justice (chapter 3), and developed and ascribed to Kant—rightly, I shall argue (yet again)—by Onora O'Neill. The key point of their shared form of constructivism is that the most basic principles of justice may well be literally artificial: *we* construct them, they are our artefacts—although they are *not* arbitrary: they are indispensable, non-optional, and non-negotiable because only by establishing and abiding by them is individual human action possible, under broadly met conditions of moderate population density.

Hume's and Kant's moral constructivism appeals to some basic anthropological facts about the character and conditions of human agency. This is their key to avoiding problems about *homo sapiens* who happen not to share—or not to admit to sharing—various common, morally relevant sentiments, motives, attitudes, values, or commitments (etc.). What best to make of, or how to address, such persons is an important problem, though not one lying at the core of normative moral theory. It belongs, rather, to moral education, social and psychological pathology, and to social policy, including the administration of justice.[8] The centrality of egoism in moral philosophy is not due to the overwhelming predominance of egoists in the human population. My surmise is that its centrality is due to two kinds of consideration. One concerns the extent to which individual prudential self-interest does, or can be brought to, coincide with the requirements of justice, or of right action more broadly. This is an important desideratum for any moral theory, though the agenda for its examination is not hostage to the restrictions of egoism or of egoists.

The other consideration which lends centrality to issues about egoism is a specific, often implicit model of, or approach to, justifying moral theory. The basic idea of this approach is that, to justify a theory, principle, claim, or conclusion rationally consists in justifying it *to* relevant individuals, which (it is supposed) requires justifying it solely by appeal to an individual's antecedent commitments. This is the demand of justificatory internalism. Yet egoists are to moral theory what radical sceptics are to epistemology: they demand that we theorists justify our views to them, whilst they reject all (or nearly all) relevant considerations, whether evidence, principles, or their specific use within any piece of justificatory reasoning. Within epistemology, justificatory internalism was discredited in the aftermath of Gettier's (1963) classic article, 'Is Justified True Belief Knowledge?', after which a healthy variety of externalist and mixed internalist–externalist theories of cognitive justification bloomed. Put generally, externalist theories of cognitive justification hold that at least some important factors pertaining to the justificatory status of someone's beliefs, claims, principles, or knowledge may not, or not easily, be available to that person's awareness or reflection. Such factors may include, for example, physiological conditions, such as the proper functioning of one's perceptual systems, or environmental conditions, such as the absence of *faux* objects such as movie sets or mock styrofoam garden 'rocks' from that person's environs.[9]

[8] On those who pathologically precipitate interpersonal conflict, see Vallacher, et al (2013); on the chronically obstreperous, see Prost (2009).

[9] I shall comment only briefly on coherence theories of justification, which are less plausible in moral philosophy than in epistemology, and are untenable even in this latter domain. The main reason for this is that, to distinguish themselves from foundationalist theories of justification, coherence theories must emphasize justificatory internalism, but they then are subject to the 'French novel' objection, that coherence alone cannot

Natural law approaches to moral theory have been widely unpopular amongst contemporary Anglophone moral philosophers for several reasons. One concerns the difficulty of establishing the kind of sufficiently comprehensive, yet sufficiently general account of the substance of a good or pious life from which to infer basic moral principles. Historically, this theoretical issue exploded in practice into the Thirty Years War in Europe, with rather too many subsequent recurrences. A second problem concerns the comparable difficulty of establishing sufficient and sufficiently uncontroversial claims to moral realism. A third, however, concerns the broad, if implicit commitment amongst Anglophone moral philosophers to justificatory internalism, a commitment which has occluded the very prospect of justificatory externalism in matters moral—to the extent, *e.g.*, that it is often no longer recognized that the Social Contract tradition is a branch of the Natural Law tradition.[10]

These are among my reasons to present here, clearly and concisely, the core features of Hume's and Kant's radical reconstruction of Natural Law through their distinctive, powerful reconstruction of moral constructivism. I do not assert that justificatory internalism, even when addressed to egoists, is hopeless.[11] I contend that it is not necessary, because Hume and Kant show how the most basic, strictly objective moral principles can be identified and justified without invoking justificatory internalism, and without invoking either moral realism or its alternatives.[12]

If these issues about justice may seem remote from the concerns of ethical theory, recall again that the first answer to the question, 'What ought I do?', is: 'Act justly, at least by acting in accord with the

distinguish between truth and any elaborately detailed, coherent fiction (Westphal 1989, 56–7; Bonjour 1997, 13–15).

[10] *E.g.*, Rawls (1971) sought to argue for his neo-Kantian conclusions on the basis of his opponents' empiricist, belief-desire model of (merely) instrumentally rational individual (ist) agency; Gauthier (1986) sought to argue for his contractarian conclusions on the same narrow basis.

[11] The most successful constructivist response to egoism I have found is Beyleveld's (1991) subtle, systematic reconstruction of Gewirth's Principle of Generic Consistency.

[12] Wood (2014, 41–2, cf. 65–7) assumes that, 'In general . . . *justification* is always justification *to* someone.' That assumption neglects Kant's justificatory externalism. Although it is important to Kant's view that rationally judging that an action (or an omission) is obligatory can also be motivating, Kant's interest in justifying reasons is not confined to what Wood calls 'motivating reasons'; see chapters 5 and 6.

requirements of justice.' This duty recalls two of Ulpian's maxims, *honeste vive* and *neminem laede*: live honourably, and do no one wrong. Both are cited by Kant (*MdS* 6:236) in just this connection; the first is approximated by Hume's quotation from Ariosto (Canto 5).[13] As Hume's and Kant's moral constructivism shows, so acting is required for undertaking any further, rationally justifiable actions. Conversely, acting in unjustifiable ways entitles others to constrain, sanction, or counter-act such actions so as to maintain compliance with the requirements of justice or to rectify or redress any violations.

Allow me one last caveat. My thesis is that Hume and Kant both develop the same kind of moral theory; I do not claim that Kant knowingly followed Hume in so doing. Clearly and expressly Kant had followed Rousseau, but there is no evidence that Rousseau had knowingly followed Hume in this regard, although he, too, adopts Natural Law Constructivism, and indeed developed it much further than Hume (Westphal 2013d). The central issues of this study are systematic, not historical, though historical accuracy about Hume's and Kant's views is systematically important to this study.

3 Chapter Overview

Chapter 2 details the central issues about objectivity and conventionalism by reconsidering Socrates' justly famous question to Euthyphro about the status of piety and the gods' love of piety, and indicates why contemporary forms of moral constructivism are ill-suited to address those issues. Their common weakness serves to highlight some central merits of Hume's and Kant's Natural Law Constructivism.

Chapter 3 reconstructs Hume's account of the basic rules of justice, and how they count, on his view, as natural laws. I develop significantly further Baier's (1991, 243–8) insightful suggestions about the character of Hume's analysis to show that it is a powerful fragment of, and basis for Natural Law Constructivism.

Chapter 4 argues that Hume's theory of justice reveals basic deficiencies in his own sentiment-based ethical theory. Because Hume's ethics has been widely used as a model or inspiration for many contemporary

[13] 'Of the Rise and Progress of the Arts and Sciences', ¶39; note added to the third and subsequent editions.

forms of moral constructivism, Hume's demonstration that moral sentiments are an insufficient basis for normative moral theory likewise calls deeply into question these successor forms of moral constructivism, though beyond some specific remarks I shall leave it to the reader to recognize these further implications. The findings of this chapter provide the context for characterizing and then dismissing the debate between Humeans and Kantians about whether there are intrinsic, or only extrinsic links between justifying reasons and motives for action (§17). Discounting issues about motivation also demotes game theory to secondary status—which is not to say it is insignificant, only that it is not fundamental.

Chapter 5 considers the centrality of principles in Kant's moral philosophy, their distinctively 'Kantian' character, why Kant presents—in a special, 'Critical' sense—a 'metaphysical' system of moral principles and how these 'formal' principles are to be used in practice. These points are central to how Kant thinks pure reason can be practical. These features have often puzzled Anglophone readers, in part due to focusing on Kant's *Groundwork* to the neglect of his later works in moral philosophy, in which the theoretical preliminaries of that first essay are properly articulated. In part, however, these puzzles stem, directly or indirectly, from Kant's opposition to moral empiricism, which puzzles readers whose default orientation is empiricist.[14] Accordingly, particular attention is paid to Kant's reasons for rejecting moral empiricism (§19). These reasons accord with Hume's own showing of the deficiencies of moral sentiments as a basis for normative theory (chapter 4), and also with the core problems facing contemporary forms of moral constructivism identified in chapter 2 (§§6, 9).

The broadly empiricist orientation of much contemporary Anglophone philosophy is evident in not infrequent wholesale rejections of 'the' synthetic *a priori*, 'the' noumenal, 'the' transcendental, and so forth. Kant himself fostered such reactions by contending that these features of his view all require Transcendental Idealism, which empiricists reject—as do I. The technical issues involved here merit careful consideration, though not here.[15] The most important points for present purposes are

[14] In this connection Watson (1881) and Caird (1889) remain instructive.

[15] See Westphal (2004, 2006, 2007a–c, 2010b, 2012a, 2016a). Very briefly, although coherent, Kant's central arguments by elimination for Transcendental Idealism are shown

three. First, Kant is mistaken that Transcendental Idealism is required to defend the possibility of moral freedom and responsibility. Kant's transcendental analyses of various principles necessarily presupposed in human thought, knowledge, and action stand independently of his Transcendental Idealism (see below, §27). Second, all normative matters as such are 'noumenal' because they cannot be exhaustively specified or justified empirically; in this Hume and Kant agree, namely, that normative conclusions do not follow from merely factual premises! (Kant's use of the term 'noumenal' to characterize normative relations is especially plain in his analysis of rightful possession.) Third, more vital than ever in today's philosophical context is Kant's critique of Cartesianism (Westphal 2007a–c), insofar as empiricism is an offspring of Cartesianism, as Hume all but acknowledged,[16] and as is evident even in Quine's purportedly 'naturalized' epistemology.[17]

Chapter 5 examines Kant's constructive approach to normative moral theory. I examine how Kant's universalization test serves as a criterion of morally obligatory, permissible, or prohibited actions, and what is morally wrong with actions which violate those criteria. Examining these points provides a compelling synopsis of Kant's system of moral principles, centring on the key terms 'practical reason', 'law', 'maxim', and 'Categorical Imperative'. The surprise—I hope, a welcome one—is that Kant's moral constructivism is a sophisticated, cogent development of the kind of moral constructivism initiated by Hume's theory of justice.

Chapter 6 characterizes concisely a key issue about rational justification which highlights an important achievement of Natural Law Constructivism: uniquely, it can resolve the Pyrrhonian Dilemma of the Criterion. Hume's and Kant's constructivist method is both sound and significant because it is based upon a core principle of rational justification as such within non-formal domains. Explicating this basis of Natural Law Constructivism affords an illuminating and defensible explication of four key aspects of the autonomy of rational judgment,

to be fallacious by a sound version of the 'neglected alternative' objection based squarely upon Kant's own central analyses in the Transcendental Analytic. However, Kant's semantics of cognitive judgment, including causal judgment, suffice to rebut the apparent threat of causal determinism regarding human action and to justify freedom of decision and action (Westphal 2012b).

[16] See Hume's letter of 26 August 1737 to M. Ramsey, in Mossner (1980), 627.

[17] Westphal (2015b).

including our positive moral freedom. Explicating these four aspects of autonomous rational judgment shows how, *inter alia*, Kant's constructivism is fundamentally social because it is fundamentally inter-subjective. It also shows how Kant's constructivism can readily accommodate historical factors which bear upon the appropriateness and legitimacy of social and political institutions.[18] All of these advantages are available without recourse to Kant's Transcendental Idealism; all of them respond to common complaints about or purported objections to Kant's moral philosophy.

Chapter 7 further details Natural Law Constructivism by examining the powerful response it affords to Gauthier's subtle contractarianism, according to which all moral obligations are elective. In this regard he presents a *radical* contractarianism, which itself is a form of moral constructivism. Gauthier's (1997, 134–5) contractarianism begins with an idea of a rational deliberator but 'finds no basis for postulating a moral need for the justification of one's actions to others. The role of agreement is to address each person's demand that the constraints of society be justified to him, not a concern that he justify himself to his fellows.' He contrasts his view with Scanlon's contractualism, according to which agreement with others is the core of morality and each agent has the burden of justifying his or her actions to others. Both of their views count as 'constructivist' because they reject moral realism and hold that normativity is a function of what we do, either individually or collectively. Hume's and Kant's Natural Law Constructivism is neutral regarding moral realism and yet is constructivist about moral norms. However, the relevant acts basic to Gauthier's and Scanlon's views concern voluntary agreements we make. Using agreement to establish basic norms faces some serious difficulties, indeed, those highlighted by Socrates' question to Euthyphro (§§6, 9). Natural Law Constructivism avoids these problems by showing how basic moral norms can be identified and justified independently of voluntary agreement. Moreover, it does so in a way that shows that an individual's justification of his or

[18] By saying that Kant's constructivism is fundamentally social, I do not ascribe to him any of the views commonly designated as 'social constructivism'. Natural Law Constructivism—whether in Hume's or in Kant's version—focuses upon necessary conditions of social life, through which alone individual life and action are possible for our form of finite rational agency.

her acts to others, and the justification of the acts of others to any individual, are inseparable aspects of one and the same justificatory reasoning in which voluntary agreement plays no constitutive role. (I reconsider Gauthier (1997) because the issues it addresses—and those it raises—are more fundamental than subsequent discussions.)

Chapter 8 examines in greater detail the analysis sketched in chapter 7 (§32) of Kant's justification of rights to possession and use. Kant's analysis appears to assume rather than prove the legitimacy of such rights. This apparent *petitio principii* has been recapitulated or exacerbated, but not resolved in the literature. However, Kant provides a sound justification of limited rights to possess and to use things: rights to usufruct, not to private property. Kant's argument is not purely *a priori*; it is in Kant's Critical sense 'metaphysical' because it applies the pure *a priori* 'Universal Principle of Justice' (*Recht*) to the concept of finite rational human agency.[19] Kant's 'application' implicitly involves a 'Contradiction in Conception' test, which I explicate in some detail. The limited rights to possession and use justified by Kant's argument suffice for his justification of the legitimacy of the (republican) state.

This chapter reconstructs and defends the soundness of Kant's argument to justify rights to usufruct, which he bases on human autonomy. In so doing, it defends the modal interpretation of Kant's universalization tests (advocated by O'Neill) against the objection that the modal interpretation cannot, in the end, avoid appeal to some form of consent. By developing and refining Hume's (and Rousseau's) preliminary versions of Natural Law Constructivism, Kant makes a unique and uniquely powerful contribution to a major issue in moral philosophy (generically speaking) in part by providing a revolutionary reconstruction of natural law, and in part by showing that only rights to usufruct can be defended by appeal to natural law, whereas rights to property require public legislation (positive law).

Chapter 9 concludes this study by briefly recapitulating some of its central findings and suggesting further lines of development. One central result may not be surprising, but merits clear and cogent justification and re-affirmation: proper accountancy is a fundamental matter of *justice*,

[19] '*Recht*' is the German counterpart to '*ius*', i.e. justice in its broadest and most fundamental normative sense. I render the term as 'justice'; using 'right' provides no translation.

and nothing less than a *fundamental* matter of justice, whether for individuals, businesses, or governments. The steady erosion and evasion of accountancy principles and procedures, which have unleashed yet another major international financial crisis, require proper redress and a return to fundamentals. It is too often neglected that the relevant fundamentals are matters of justice, and that instituting principles and practices of justice requires concerted public education, including centrally education for that most important public office: the office of citizen (Green 1999, chapter 7).

The Appendix shows that Hobbes does not espouse egoism in the *Leviathan* (§44), and that the simplistic moral epistemology involved in Locke's natural law theory is untenable according to grounds provided by his own account (§45). This latter finding helps to underscore why only use rights, though not property rights, can be identified and justified by natural law, specifically by Hume's and Kant's Natural Law Constructivism. That Hobbes does not espouse egoism underscores the irrelevance of human motivation to issues about identifying and justifying basic moral principles, and that identifying and justifying basic moral principles requires addressing some fundamental social coordination problems.

This brief study does not aspire to present an entire moral theory, but instead to highlight an unjustly neglected approach to moral theory, pioneered jointly by Hume and Kant, which has much to recommend it, as is evident from the central examples examined herein.

2

Objectivity, the Euthyphro Question, and Reconstructing Natural Law

4 Moral Objectivity, Social Contract Theory, and Natural Law

The branch of natural law theory inaugurated by Hume and further developed by Kant is a distinctive kind of moral constructivism which is altogether independent of moral realism and its alternatives, and yet identifies and justifies strictly objective basic moral principles. Cognitivism about basic moral principles is provided by this view through its account of justification, rather than by appeal to moral truth or truth-makers.[1] Their approach I call 'Natural Law Constructivism'.

In addition to distinguishing two kinds of natural law theories—the traditional moral realist, and Hume's constructivist varieties—I also contrast two kinds of social contract theory: those which use a social contract solely as an expository or heuristic device, and those which ascribe a constitutive role to contractual agreement in identifying or justifying basic moral principles. The former, expository use of a social contract model can be combined with a natural law theory, or may be based entirely upon one. The latter, substantive or constitutive use of a social contract model is less dependent upon a natural law theory; radical social contract theories—such as Gauthier's—deny any such dependence. I shall refer to these as 'illustrative' and 'substantive' social contract

[1] Prior studies of natural law in Rousseau's *Du contrat social* considered only traditional versions of natural law which involve moral realism (see, e.g., Herb 1989), and so have neglected the alternative presented here. I examine Rousseau's Natural Law Constructivism in Westphal (2013d).

theories, respectively. This issue is joined directly in chapter 7, on the basis of the alternative 'Natural Law Constructivism' outlined in this chapter and developed in consideration of Hume's and Kant's theories of justice in chapters 3–5.

This chapter details the theoretical context within which to reconsider natural law and the prospects for developing Natural Law Constructivism. I begin with the Euthyphro question to pose a basic dilemma in moral theory (§5), which raises an issue about the relation between artifice and arbitrariness (§6). This issue about arbitrariness highlights the significance of Hume's key insight into the prospect of Natural Law Constructivism (§7), and how this type of theory addresses Hobbes' insight that our most fundamental moral problems are problems of social coordination (§8). (Recognizing these fundamental social coordination problems need not be, and is not here, an invitation to game theory, for reasons indicated in §17.) These problems raise the issue about the extent to which any social contract theory is substantive, because contractual agreement plays a constitutive role in identifying or justifying basic normative principles, or instead is merely expository, because a theory assigns no such constitutive role to contractual agreement (§9). This latter kind of social contract theory may instead be a natural law theory.

5 The Euthyphro Question and Moral Optionality

5.1 *Socrates' question to Euthyphro*

Questions about the objectivity of moral principles have often focused on issues about moral realism, the idea that there are objective, mind-independent moral facts or standards woven into the fabric of the universe, as it were, which serve as criteria of moral right and wrong, and also as criteria of correct or adequate moral thinking. One central contrast between moral realism and moral non-realism (irrealism, anti-realism) is evident in Socrates' question to Euthyphro:

> Is the pious (τὸ ὅσιον) being loved by the gods because it is pious, or is it pious because it is being loved by the gods?
>
> (Euthyphro, 10a)

The first option represents moral realism about the pious: the pious is what it is, and the gods recognize it for what it is and love it accordingly. The second represents moral non-realism, for on this option, the gods make something pious by loving it (doubtless, in a certain way). This question is easily permuted to ask the same kind of question about the right, the virtuous, the just, or the moral good. The Euthyphro question thus highlights a fundamental dichotomy in moral philosophy:

Either: Moral realism (in some version) is true, in which case there are objective moral standards.

Or: Moral non-realism or anti-realism (in some version) is true, in which case moral standards are artificial.

A further thought—call it the 'Optionality Premise'—makes this dichotomy especially pressing:

Optionality: If moral standards are artificial, then they are relative, conventional, or arbitrary, and so are not objective but instead are optional (in some regards or others).

This triad is pervasive in moral philosophy. To the minds of many moral philosophers, the challenge of optionality, which threatens relativism, conventionalism, arbitrariness, or (in sum) lack of objectivity, has made moral realism appear mandatory. Unfortunately, articulating and justifying a tenable form of moral realism has defied the repeated attempts to do so, and indeed, for reasons quintessentially formulated in the Pyrrhonian Dilemma of the Criterion.[2] This Dilemma is discussed in chapter 6. Very briefly, the problem concerns whether or how it is possible to justify criteria of justification in disputed substantive domains, in which dispute can easily come to encompass dispute about purported criteria of justification. This Dilemma is widely regarded as insoluble (*e.g.*, Sinnott-Armstrong 2006), though it is not. However, the merits of Natural Law Constructivism do not depend upon the outcome of that dispute. It suffices to recognize that the Pyrrhonian Dilemma of the Criterion highlights key problems both for moral realism and for contemporary forms of moral constructivism, especially those modelled upon Hume's sentiment-based ethical theory, and that Natural Law

[2] Sextus Empiricus (1933), 2.4.20; cf. 1.14.116–17.

Constructivism neatly avoids those problems. It avoids the problems about moral realism through its neutrality about those debates; it avoids the problems facing Hume's sentiment-based ethics and contemporary forms of moral constructivism through its justificatory externalism (§§11, 17, 19, 31, 38). These are topics for subsequent chapters.

To begin, it suffices to recognize the key problem confronting moral realism: as a group, moral realists disagree fundamentally about what are, so to speak, 'the real moral facts', and no one has developed an adequate account of moral knowledge or moral justification to distinguish between true or false, or between better or worse justified, claims about those alleged, supposedly mind-independent 'real moral facts'.[3] Moral realism too easily falls into moral dogmatism or moral relativism, as anticipated by the Pyrrhonian Dilemma of the Criterion. In view of the Euthyphro question, the Fundamental Dichotomy, and the Optionality Premise, interminable controversy about moral realism strongly suggests to many moral philosophers that basic moral principles must instead be artificial. This option is taken seriously by contemporary moral constructivism, inaugurated in contemporary political philosophy by John Rawls' *Theory of Justice* (1971), though many constructivist ethical theories take inspiration from Hume's sentiment-based ethical theory.

5.2 Constructivism as an express philosophical method

Constructivism as an explicit philosophical method was first developed by Carnap in *Der logische Aufbau der Welt* (1928). His method is followed, unacknowledged, by all contemporary forms of moral constructivism. The constructivist strategy comprises four steps:

Within some specified domain of interest,

[3] The designation 'moral realism' has come to be used by philosophers for a plethora of views, which cannot be canvassed here. (For a good conspectus, see Sayer-McCord 1988, 1–23.) Three prominent tendencies may be briefly remarked. Here I understand moral realism to concern mind-independent moral facts or states of affairs. 'Moral realism' is now often used to label any view according to which at least some moral principles are 'objective' in the sense of holding for all human agents. Natural Law Constructivism shows that moral realism has no exclusive claim to such moral objectivity. Many contemporary moral realists adopt a Quinean approach to 'ontological commitment' and claim that their justified moral principles commit them to the existence of whatever makes their principles true. That is moral realism on the cheap; Quine's notion of ontological commitment is a very poor guide to what actually exists (Travis 2008; Westphal, 2015b).

1. identify a preferred domain of basic elements;
2. identify and sort relevant, prevalent elements within this domain;
3. use the most salient and prevalent such elements to construct satisfactory principles or accounts of the initial domain by using
4. preferred principles of construction.

This states the constructivist procedure very generally, so that it may be used in epistemology, philosophy of science, or semantics (as Carnap did), or instead in moral philosophy. According to constructivist moral theories, basic moral principles are artificial because they are identified and justified by constructing them, in whatever way a specific constructivist moral theory proposes (steps 3, 4). According to constructivist moral theories, the right or the just simply *is* whatever is identified and justified as right or as just by a specific constructivist moral theory. What, then, becomes of moral objectivity within constructivist moral theories?

6 Artifice and Arbitrariness

According to constructivist moral theories, to what extent are basic moral principles, because they are artificial, also relative, conventional, or arbitrary? Although contemporary constructivist moral theories seek to avoid such results so far as possible, *in principle* their methods are hardly able to forestall relativity, conventionality, or arbitrariness. Contemporary constructivist moral theories all appeal to basic elements (steps 1, 2) which are 'subjective', in the sense of something of which individual people are *aware*, and these *states of awareness* are taken as theoretically fundamental for identifying or justifying principles, where this is understood solely as justification of those principles *to* individuals by appeal (directly or indirectly) to those states of awareness. Examples of such basic elements include, for example, sentiments, passions, affective responses, motives, manifest preferences, individual interests, avowed 'values', moral 'commitments', particular moral intuitions, contractual considerations, or validity claims (Habermas's *Geltungsansprüche*).[4]

[4] In Habermas' discourse ethics, someone's *claiming* that something is morally valid, and if challenged, providing reasons for it which are accepted and lead to the original claim's being accepted, is theoretically, methodologically fundamental; on his view, a reason can only *be* a good (or bad) reason if someone *claims* or *holds* it to be a good (or bad) reason, and can win acceptance for it. For concise discussion, see Redding (1989).

This directly raises a key justificatory problem, one also central to contractarian strategies. Contemporary constructivist moral theories can develop and justify moral principles only in consideration of whatever group happens to share sufficiently in whatever subjective 'basic elements' (step 2) are used by any specific constructivist theory. Yet both historically and regionally (geographically) such subjective elements (of whatever preferred kind) vary significantly (cf. §15). How or to what extent can such theories address individuals who either lack or who disavow allegedly relevant, putatively basic states of awareness? A second problem lodges in disagreements about which principles of construction (step 4), and what use of those principles (step 3), are suitable or appropriate. In principle, the constructivist method cannot address those problems because it analyses justification *solely* in terms of constructive derivation of results (principles) from preferred basic elements (step 2) in accord with preferred principles of construction (step 4) and their preferred uses (step 3), in order to justify those principles to persons by (direct or indirect) appeal to their states of awareness or their motives. Ultimately, these are key shortcomings in all such theories. This broad claim cannot be substantiated here in detail, but later chapters examine two paradigm cases which clearly indicate that these failures are typical.[5] The two cases are Hume's sentiment-based ethical theory (chapter 4), which is shown to be inadequate by Hume's own theory of justice (chapter 3); and Gauthier's (1997) sophisticated, radical contractarianism (chapter 7). *Mutatis mutandis*, contemporary constructivist moral theories face serious difficulties in avoiding moral relativism, although so doing is one prime aspiration of such theories.[6] To the extent that this is the case, this is a very severe limit on a moral theory, which must solve certain basic kinds of social coordination problems, including those which arise amongst groups with, for example, differing interests, differing cultural outlooks, differing moral views, or differing moral responses. Contemporary moral constructivisms, too, are ill suited to addressing the Pyrrhonian Dilemma of the Criterion.[7]

[5] I examine the general case in Westphal (2013b).

[6] Carnap's early theory of truth (*ca.* 1930) involved a form of relativism, because it made truth dependent upon the protocol sentences uttered by scientists of 'our' scientifically minded cultural circle (Westphal 1989, 56–7).

[7] Although Morris (1996) promises 'A Contractarian Account of Moral Justification', his focus on hypothetical choice is no more than 'heuristic' (*ibid.*, 225), in part because it

7 Hume's Key Insight

It is unsurprising that some philosophers have concluded from this situation that moral theory is a chimera (e.g., Garner 1993), or that our moral beliefs can only be weakly justified (Sinnott-Armstrong 2006). These conclusions are premature. Consider first whether the Optionality Premise is true: does the artificiality of basic moral principles entail that they are arbitrary? No. Hume states this key insight directly and originally:

> Though the rules of justice be artificial, they are not arbitrary. Nor is the expression improper to call them Laws of Nature . . .
>
> (*T* 3.2.1.19/SBN 484)

This insight is fundamental to Hume's theory of justice, which inaugurates a distinctive approach to natural law theory, the approach I call 'Natural Law Constructivism'.[8] The key to providing objectivity within a constructivist moral theory is not to appeal to subjective states of the kinds mentioned above, but instead to appeal to objective facts about our form of finite rational agency and circumstances of action which are basic to the human condition. Obviously, appealing to these facts requires that those offering justification are aware of them. The key to objectivity lies in not restricting justification to justifying principles *to* individuals by appeal, however directly or indirectly, to their states of awareness or motives (etc.). In this important regard, Natural Law Constructivism develops an externalist account of moral justification.[9]

neglects the distinction drawn here between constitutive and illustrative uses of a social contract model.

[8] This statement is neglected by Snare (1991), Baier (1991, 2010) and Spector (2014); it is mentioned only very briefly in passing by Harrison (1981, 1, 12). Baier (2010, 166, 174, 255) regards Hume's use of the terminology of natural law as mockery. Her claim is instead yet another indication of the deplorable neglect of natural law amongst Anglophone moral philosophers. Spector (2014, 47) rightly observes that 'Hume developed an original and revolutionary theoretical paradigm for explaining the spontaneous emergence of the classic conventions of justice' and that Hume's theory 'still deserves careful discussion, even though it resists classification under contemporary headings'. However, Spector neglects the distinction between 'explaining' basic moral norms and justifying them normatively, and neglects just how radically searching is Hume's theory, insofar as it frees natural law from moral realism.

[9] A word may be in order about relevant facts: I continue to assume what I have argued in detail elsewhere (Westphal 2004, 2012b, 2015a), that Kant's Transcendental Idealism is fundamentally flawed, and yet is not required for Kant's moral philosophy. Accordingly,

More specifically, Hume's theory of justice focuses on physiological and geographical facts about the vital needs of human beings, our limited capacities for acting, the relative scarcity of materials required for us to meet our vital needs, and our ineluctable mutual interdependence. The principles Hume constructs on their basis merit the designation 'Laws of Nature' because for human beings they are utterly indispensable and so are non-optional and non-arbitrary (*ibid.*).[10] If successful—this study aims to show that it is—Hume's Natural Law Constructivism breaks the deadlock in moral theory between moral realists and their detractors, by showing that their debate is irrelevant to identifying and to justifying basic, objective moral principles. If indeed moral objectivity can be justified with appeal neither to moral realism *nor* to its alternatives, this is a major breakthrough: we need not settle that debate in order to identify and to justify objective, strictly universal basic moral principles. Showing that the relevant facts are endemic to the human condition requires recognizing, as both Hume and Kant did, Hobbes' insight that the most fundamental moral issues are social coordination problems.

8 Hobbes' Formulation of Two Basic Moral Problems

Anglophone discussion typically focuses on Hobbes' apparently pessimistic, egoistic psychology and its terrible implications in the non-governmental 'state of nature' for the mortally threatening 'war of all on all'. Hobbes makes a psychological claim (though not quite that psychological claim), but this is the least important of the three points made by his analysis of the non-governmental state of nature.[11] His two key points are these:

I reject the notion that the facts appealed to by Natural Law Constructivism ultimately depend for transcendental reasons upon us. Yet even if such transcendental dependence were admitted, insofar as this be *transcendental* dependence, it would be species wide, and so would not be subject to historical or regional variability.

[10] The quoted statement concludes: '. . . if by natural we understand what is common to any species, or even if we confine it to mean what is inseparable from the species' (*T* 3.2.1.19/SBN 484).

[11] Hobbes' insights are often overlooked in Anglophone discussions, which are preoccupied with Hobbes' psychology of human motivation, also amongst game theorists, whose individualist assumptions obscure Hume's points about our fundamental mutual interdependence and our relevant range of interests and motivations. Anglophone discussion of

1. Unlimited individual freedom of action is impossible due to consequent total mutual interference. Hence the fundamental moral question is not whether individual freedom of action may or must be limited, but rather what are the proper, justifiable limits upon individual freedom of action.
2. Complete though innocent, non-malicious *ignorance* of what belongs to whom suffices to generate the total mutual interference characterized in the non-governmental state of nature as the war of all upon all. Consequently, justice must fundamentally be *public* justice, to remedy such ignorance and thus to substitute social coordination for chronic, severe mutual interference.

This second point—call it 'the Innocent Problem' of mutual interference—entails that no account of (putative) rightful relations between any one individual and any one physical object—nor any account of (putative) rightful relations between any one individual, any one physical object, and the divinity—suffices *in principle* to identify and to justify basic principles of justice. Thus does Hobbes refute prior natural law theories of property, and also Locke's.[12] Hobbes' two points entail that the most basic moral problems are fundamental problems of social coordination: under conditions of total mutual interference, individual action is ineffective if not impossible, indeed fatally so. Plainly these social coordination problems are problems of justice, but they are also fundamental ethical problems, since one of our foremost ethical duties is to abide by the dictates of justice! (This initial hint of why justice belongs centrally to moral philosophy is developed in earnest in chapters 7–9).

However flawed may be Hobbes' positive solution to these two problems, his uncompromising, incisive formulation of them is crucial. Though he does not mention Hobbes—what European writing on justice in the eighteenth century needs to?—Hume's most basic social coordination problem stems directly from Hobbes: under conditions of relative

Hobbes has much to learn from Ludwig (1998). That Hobbes in *Leviathan* does not espouse egoism I argue in the Appendix (§44). Burkhard Tuschling first brought to my attention the two key problems noted here; cp. Tuschling (1998). Lloyd (2007) does much to correct Anglophone misunderstandings of Hobbes' moral philosophy, yet misses much that Ludwig (1998) highlights. (This is but one example of how primarily monoglot philosophy—a phenomenon taking root only *ca.* 1950—becomes provincial.)

[12] Basic problems with Locke's natural law theory are discussed in the Appendix (§45).

scarcity of external goods, the easy transfer of such goods from one person to another, the limited benevolence typical of human nature, our natural ignorance of who rightly possesses what, and our mutual interdependence due to human frailties, we require a system governing possession in order to stabilize the distribution of goods (and thereby avoid chronic, severe mutual interference).[13] The minimum effective and feasible solution to this social coordination problem is to establish, in principle and in practice, this convention: respect rights to possessions! This is Hume's first principle of justice. Hume's three principles of justice are 'that of the stability of possession, of its transference by consent, and of the performance of promises' (*T* 3.2.6.1; cf. 3.2.11.2). His illuminating construction of his three basic rules of justice shows that these three principles count for us human beings as 'laws of nature' because without them human social life—and hence *all* of human life, individually or collectively—is impossible. Hume's central claims and analysis are examined in chapter 3.

Hume only considers a fragment of the theory of justice, though a fundamental fragment. Two key omissions are these: Hume says nothing about personal safety and security, or about collective distribution, or collectively permissible distributions, of wealth (equity). Specifying only Hume's three rules of justice allows much arbitrariness about further principles and practices: society and human life are also 'possible' under highly unjust conditions. These issues were directly raised by Rousseau, who greatly extended the Natural Law Constructivist method for analysing justice, pioneered by Hume.[14] Rousseau's *sine qua non* for just collective distributions of wealth is that no one is to have any kind or extent of wealth or power which enables him or her to command or coerce the actions of anyone else. That kind of economic dependence upon the personal will of others Rousseau famously rules out as an unjust infringement of any- and everyone's 'original' right to be free to act solely

[13] Relative scarcity of goods: *T* 3.2.2, ¶¶7, 16, 18 (SBN 487–8, 494, 495); their easy transfer: *T* 3.2..2, ¶¶7, 16 (SBN 487–8, 494); our limited generosity: *T* 3.2.2 ¶¶6, 16, 18, 24; 3.2.5.8, 3.3.2.23, 3.3.3.2 (SBN 487, 494, 495, 498–9, 519, 586, 602); natural ignorance of possession: *T* 3.2.2.10, 3.2.4.2, 3.2.6.3–4 (SBN 491, 515, 527–8); limited powers and consequent mutual interdependence: *T* 3.2.2.2–3 (SBN 484–5).

[14] To avoid misunderstanding, I do not claim that Rousseau consciously adopted Hume's fragment of a theory of justice; important here is the systematic point that they both develop the same kind of approach to identifying and justifying basic moral norms.

upon his or her own will (*CS* 1.6.1, 1.8.2).[15] The fundamental claim to mutual independence is central to Kant's theory of justice, as we shall see in chapters 7 and 8.

9 Modern Natural Law and the Social Contract

Natural Law challenges the social contract strategy by highlighting this question:

> To what extent is a, or 'the', social contract merely an expository device, or conversely, to what extent is a, or 'the', social contract a specific, substantive method for identifying or justifying basic moral principles?

I say 'basic' moral principles, because many secondary principles are proper matters for public deliberation, legislation, convention, or custom. For such principles, express agreement based on considered reasons contributes constitutively both to identifying and to justifying such statutes, policies, or practices. Natural Law, however, purports to identify and to justify the most basic moral principles, whether in ethics or in jurisprudence, without constitutive appeal to contractual (nor to any other voluntary form of) agreement. The important issues may be posed by detailing the dichotomy above:

> *Either* the preferred social contract contributes constitutively and ineliminably to the identification, justification, legitimacy, or obligatory status of basic moral principles *or* it does not.
>
> *If* a social contract does *not* so contribute, then it merely models or expounds certain features of relevant reasons and reasoning concerning the identification, justification, legitimacy, or obligatory status of basic moral principles. If a social contract is merely an expository or heuristic device, *then*:
>
> (i) What exactly are the actual reasons which identify, justify and legitimate basic moral principles or their obligatory status?
>
> (ii) What exactly does the social contract model add to (i), other than, for example, flourish or obfuscation?

[15] Rousseau (1762), (1976), (1994), cited as '*CS*', by Bk.Ch.¶ numbers.

If instead a social contract model *does* play an ineliminable constitutive role in the identification, justification, legitimacy, or obligatory status of basic moral principles, *then*:

(iii) Exactly what role(s)?

(iv) Why, exactly, is this role, or are these roles, ineliminable?

(v) Exactly how, why, and with what justification are those basic principles dependent upon our social-contractual agreement for their content, their justification, or both?

(vi) How or to what extent do principles so justified (etc.) avoid arbitrariness?

These questions have not received sufficient attention from contractarians,[16] nor from contemporary moral constructivists. Their importance is highlighted in chapter 7, by Kant's critique of Gauthier's radical contractarianism.

The key insight of Natural Law Constructivism is to identify and to justify basic, objectively valid moral principles without appeal to moral realism or its alternatives, including (constitutive) contractual agreement. With these issues in view, I now argue that Hume's theory of justice is an exercise in Natural Law Constructivism.[17]

[16] Including, e.g., the contributions to: *Rationality, Markets and Morals* (Spector, 2013, vol. 4): 'Can the Social Contract Be Signed by an Invisible Hand?'

[17] A further reason for the neglect of this theoretical option may be briefly mentioned. The historical and systematic development of this option, beginning with Hume, greatly augmented by Rousseau and again by Kant (and also Hegel), cuts across artificial though chronically entrenched sub-specialities within the field.

3

Hume's Construction of Justice

10 Introduction

Hume's theory of justice shows that basic principles of justice are required to form and to maintain society, which is indispensable to human life, and that acting according to these principles is right, and violating them is wrong, regardless of anyone's sentiments, motives, or character. Furthermore, Hume's theory of justice shows how the principles of justice are artificial without being arbitrary. In this regard, Hume's theory of justice inaugurates an important, unjustly neglected branch of the modern natural law tradition.

Though he intimated it only in passing, Hume regarded himself as a natural lawyer.[1] Although Hume's philosophy of law is presented in the third book of his *Treatise of Human Nature*, forms a central component of his political writings, and is fundamental to his great *History of England*, after his lifetime Hume's recognition as a major legal philosopher came only late in the twentieth century.[2] Hume's moral philosophy—that is, his ethical, social, political, and legal philosophy taken together—belongs to a broad tradition, identified by J. B. Schneewind (1998), of moral autonomism, according to which practical norms derive, not from God or nature, but from human nature and activity.

The central idea of the present study is Hume's:

> Though the rules of justice be artificial, they are not arbitrary. Nor is the expression improper to call them Laws of Nature . . .
>
> (*T* 3.2.1.19/SBN 484)

[1] Buckle (1991), 234–5, 298; Haakonssen (1996).

[2] See, e.g., Harrison (1981); Haakonssen (1981), (1993) and (1996), chapter 3; Buckle (1991), Snare (1991). A good introduction to Hume's practical and legal philosophy is provided by Baier (1991), chapters 10, 11; Norton (1993), chapters 5–8; and Baier (2010).

This thesis retains its fundamental importance, because even today moral philosophers often fail to recognize how normative principles are (or may be) artificial—they may literally be made by us—without for that reason being arbitrary. Although Kant shares this important thesis with Hume, their respective understandings of the 'nature' of the 'naturalness' of such laws differ. According to Hume, this naturalness concerns human nature. Designating basic principles of justice as 'natural laws' is valid only:

> if by natural we understand what is common to any species, or even if we confine it to mean what is inseparable from the species.
>
> (*T* 3.2.1.19/SBN 484)

To understand principles of justice in this way, Hume faces two tasks. First, he sharply criticizes alternative strategies for justifying such principles normatively. Second, Hume attempts to explain scientifically our practical principles, judgments, and decisions in a way which avoids twin political dangers: (reactionary) superstition and (revolutionary) enthusiasm. Hume's analysis gives priority to understanding our principles and practices of justice through (purported) empirical-scientific explanation (see chapter 4). Justifying them normatively is a decidedly secondary undertaking of Hume's, in part because it requires revising, without notice, some of Hume's most basic moral premises. To understand why and how this is the case requires considering some key points of Hume's practical philosophy.

11 Founding Justice in Practice

11.1 Hume's procedure

Hume's theory of justice proceeds genetically. It aims to explain the character and status of the basic principles of justice by explaining how these principles are developed through human circumstances, sentiments, needs, abilities, and activities. Hume's genetic approach is also analytical because it identifies each relevant component of morality by locating its advent and reasons for its introduction within the development of morality and how each such element is then gradually incorporated into moral concepts, principles, and practices. The conceptual, analytical emphasis of his account of justice in the *Treatise* is underscored by his latter essay, 'On the Origin of Government', in which he argues that, regarded historically, government developed from military power (cf. *T* 3.2.8.2/SBN 540–1).[3]

In general, Hume establishes principles of justice by showing that they are the sole solution to several closely linked problems of social coordination. To achieve this, Hume must first explain why we cannot avoid confronting certain social coordination problems; then he must explain precisely why these problems can only be solved by instituting certain specified principles of justice which structure certain social conventions, which alone can reform our social practices so as to avoid or resolve the initial problem. Hume's explanations and justifications of the basic principles of justice are thoroughly functional, including those concerning government.[4]

Unlike most of his predecessors, Hume distinguished sharply between society and government and rejected the fiction of a non-social prehistory of humanity. Hume sought the origin of justice in the origin of property. He provisionally defines property in terms of possession:

> . . . property may be defined [as], such a relation betwixt a person and an object as permits him, but forbids any other, the free use and possession of it, without violating the laws of justice and moral equity.
>
> (*T* 2.1.10.1; cf. 3.2.2.11–12/SBN 309; cf. 490–1)

> We are said to be in possession of any thing, not only when we immediately touch it, but also when we are so situated with respect to it, as to have it in our power to use it; and may move, alter, or destroy it, according to our present pleasure or advantage. . . . property is nothing but a stable possession, derived from the rules of justice, or the conventions of men. . . .
>
> (*T* 3.2.3.7/SBN 506)

The relations in question require conventions because they are not merely physical, and hence not merely natural, relations: one's possessions need not be presently held physically or occupied. The relevant relations are ones of rights and obligations. Hume does not distinguish terminologically between 'possession' and 'property'. This distinction is important, but may be discussed later (§36), because Hume's analysis

[3] I have learnt much from Baier (1991), 220–76, but develop Hume's core analysis in greater detail. Baier (1991, 225, 250–3) recognizes Hume's having studied natural law and that his view is neither utilitarian nor contractarian, but she (2010, 166, 174, 255) dismisses Hume's own remarks about natural law.

[4] Cf. *T* 3.2.7.6–8, 3.2.8, ¶¶1–2, 5–6/SBN 537–8, 539–40, 543–4.

and (so far as he provides one) justification of 'property' rightly goes no further than to analyse and to justify rights to possess, use, and exchange, as indicated already in the provisional definition just quoted.

As a nominalist Hume sought to explain our concept of justice by explaining our use of the term 'justice' in connection with social conventions governing the distribution of goods (*T* 3.2.2/SBN 484–501).[5] To do so, Hume addressed two key questions: one 'concerning the manner in which the rules of justice are established by the artifice of men'; the other 'concerning the reasons which determine us to attribute to the observance or neglect of these rules a moral beauty and deformity' (*T* 3.2.2.1/SBN 484).

We human beings require society in order to compensate for our natural limitations: as individuals we have too many needs and too few, too limited powers and abilities to satisfy our needs reliably and adequately. Only through society can we expand our powers through cooperative work; only through division of labour can we perfect our abilities; only through cooperation can we improve our security against hazard and accident. However, we must also become aware of these advantages in order to preserve society and the social practices that structure it and thus make it at all possible. Becoming conscious of these advantages begins in childhood within our families as we become accustomed to, and prepare ourselves for, collective life. However, our self-interest and partiality work against the development of any expansive society, as does the easy transfer of external goods.

These are anthropological facts of human life, of which Hume reminds his readers with some relish, though he and his readers would have recognized that these facts are not merely matters of beneficence, nor of self-interest: they are matters of human necessity, as Seneca etched so clearly in condoling Marcia upon the death of her son. Knowing that

[5] Although Hume attempted in the first book of the *Treatise* to justify nominalism, unwittingly he also exposed all the key problems confronting nominalism, indeed so well that he implicitly refuted it (Westphal, 2013c). In the *Treatise*, Hume omits discussion of, e.g., any right to personal security; there he analyses justice solely in terms of possession. As Baier (2010) shows, Hume greatly expanded his conception of justice in later works, especially his *History of England*. For present purposes, however, Hume's initial focus on possession suffices, in part because only in this connection did Hume attempt to justify the concept of justice; Baier (2010) neglects this desideratum.

without society we human beings cannot live—hardly beyond birth—is part of knowing oneself. If such observations may strike the reader as either quaint or callous, this is not so: every bit of comfort, safety, and aid so many of us take for granted is all due to known and unknown others' efforts over generations.[6] (In chapter 7 I argue that social contractarians take for granted far too many of these social provisions of justice and of conditions for effective individual action.)

11.2 Hume's first social coordination problem

Under conditions of relative scarcity of external goods and the limited benevolence typical of human nature, we require a system of possession in order to stabilize the distribution of goods. This is Hume's first problem of social coordination; it can be solved only through a social convention. The problem is genuine, because the prime advantage of membership in society is the stability of possession, although the greatest dangers to society are the relative scarcity of external goods together with their easy transfer from one person to another.

[6] Seneca observed: 'Moreover, what forgetfulness of your own position and that of mankind is this? You were born a mortal, and you have given birth to mortals: yourself a weak and fragile body, liable to all diseases, can you have hoped to produce anything strong and lasting from such unstable materials? Your son has died: in other words he has reached that goal towards which those whom you regard as more fortunate than your offspring are still hastening. This is the point towards which move at different rates all the crowds which are squabbling in the law courts, sitting in the theatres, praying in the temples. Those whom you love and those whom you despise will both be made equal in the same ashes. This is the meaning of that command, Know thyself, which is written on the shrine of the Pythian oracle. What is man? A potter's vessel, to be broken by the slightest shake or toss: it requires no great storm to rend you asunder: you fall to pieces wherever you strike. What is man? A weakly and frail body, naked, without any natural protection, dependent on the help of others, exposed to all the scorn of Fortune; even when his muscles are well trained he is the prey and the food of the first wild beast he meets, formed of weak and unstable substances, fair in outward feature, but unable to endure cold, heat, or labour, and yet falling to ruin if kept in sloth and idleness, fearing his very victuals, for he is starved if he has them not, and bursts if he has too much. He cannot be kept safe without anxious care, his breath only stays in the body on sufferance, and has no real hold upon it; he starts at every sudden danger, every loud and unexpected noise that reaches his ears (Seneca, 1900 (hereafter *Dialogues*) [*Cons. Marc.*], 6.11.2–3). Need modern readers be reminded that long before abortion procedures, and even longer before medical birth control, unwanted infants—or those regarded as unhealthy—were exposed on Sparta's surroundings hillsides (as Hume knew; 'Of Refinements in the Arts', n. 50)?

11.3 *Justice as necessary artifice*

Hume's solution to this dilemma is artificial for two reasons: first, the dilemma can only be solved by our establishing a social convention; second, because our natural, literally uncivilized, uncultivated moral understanding (such as it is) works *against* this conventional solution because our natural moral understanding reinforces rather than ameliorates our self-interest and partiality (*T* 3.2.2.8/SBN 488–9).

Hume's point is confirmed by considering briefly a basic flaw in Locke's natural law theory. In the second of his *Two Treatises of Government* Locke ascribes to us in the non-governmental state of nature the right to punish violations of the laws of nature.[7] Yet due to our partiality, self-interest, and natural vices Locke also affirms that in the state of nature we cannot punish violations of the laws of nature legitimately.[8] However, 'illegitimate punishment' is an oxymoron; about this Locke is quite correct: '. . . force without right, upon a man's person, makes a state of war, both where there is, and is not, a common judge' (*ST* §19). To be punishment, exercise of coercion must be rightful. Calling an exercise of coercion 'punishment' does not suffice to make it punishment, no more than calling a tail a leg suffices to show that dogs have five legs.[9] Thus,

[7] Locke (1967; hereafter '*ST*'), 2.2, §§7, 8, 12.

[8] *ST* §§124–6, 128; cf. §13. These are precisely the 'inconveniences' Locke identifies within the state of nature. For specifics, see the Appendix (§45).

[9] Ordinary usage is insufficient to establish otherwise; 'ordinary usage', too, suffered grotesquely under abuses of power and authority in the previous century (see Klemperer 1947, Steiner 1960), and continues to do so in this, and not only through various forms of totalitarian 'new-speak'; see Herman and Chomsky (1988), cp. Draper (1991). The ripost that such abuses of language are not what *we* mean by 'punishment' may be correct, but does not answer questions about what we *should* mean by the term, because it cannot address such questions. That ripost invites if not invokes provincialism or relativism, insofar as it invites abusers of people and of language to re-assert what they happen to 'mean' by the term 'punishment'. To permute MacIntyre's title, appealing to ordinary usage to settle normative issues about moral concepts begs the question, whose usage? Which sense of 'ordinary'? For good reason Humpty Dumpty sat upon a wall, not a jurist's bench (Carroll 1939, 196):

> 'I don't know what you mean by "glory"', Alice said.

Humpty Dumpty smiled contemptuously. 'Of course you don't—till I tell you. I meant "there's a nice knock-down argument for you!"'

> 'But "glory" doesn't mean "a nice knock-down argument"', Alice objected.
>
> 'When *I* use a word', Humpty Dumpty said, in rather a scornful tone, 'it means just what I choose it to mean—neither more nor less.'

pace Locke, in the state of nature we can have no right to punish violations of the laws of nature: because we can have no right to what we cannot reliably do justly. In the state of nature there can only be revenge, self-defence, and their destructive anti-social consequences. Hume drew the correct conclusion:

> The remedy, then, is not derived from nature, but from artifice; or, more properly speaking, nature provides a remedy, in the judgment and understanding, for what is irregular and incommodious in the affections.
>
> (*T* 3.2.2.9/SBN 489)

This is to say, through enlightened self-interest and through socialization and habituation we come to see that we must rescind, or at least restrict, some of our occurrent though transient unsociable (if not anti-social) inclinations, in particular, our acquisitiveness, in order to satisfy the great majority of our inclinations, especially in the long term, and to enjoy, develop, and extend the sweet pleasures—and the manifold, irreplaceable advantages—of our social relations. Note, too, in this passage Hume ascribes a crucial role to 'the judgment and understanding' in regulating and modifying our sentiments. In ways examined below (§§13, 16), Hume's theory of justice integrates reason and sentiment in ways quite opposite to his official, sentiment-based ethical theory.

11.1 The founding conventions of justice

Especially important to Hume's analysis of the rules governing possession is that we do not establish them by contract, nor by promise, nor even (necessarily) by linguistic means. Rules governing possession develop rather as behavioural conventions, that is, as a social practice:

> This convention is not of the nature of a *promise*; for even promises themselves . . . arise from human conventions. It is only a general sense of common interest; which sense all the members of the society express to one another, and which induces them to regulate their conduct by certain rules. I observe, that it will be for my interest to leave another in the possession of his goods, *provided* he will act in the same manner with regard to me. He is sensible of a like interest in the

> 'The question is', said Alice, 'whether you *can* make words mean so many different things.'
>
> 'The question is', said Humpty Dumpty, 'which is to be master—that's all.'

The limited justificatory resources of ordinary language are considered further below, §§15, 16, 40–1.

regulation of his conduct. When this common sense of interest is mutually expressed, and is known to both, it produces a suitable resolution and behaviour. And this may properly enough be called a convention or agreement betwixt us, though without the interposition of a promise; since the actions [*sic*] of each of us have a reference to those of the other, and are performed upon the supposition [*sic*] that something is to be performed on the other part. Two men who pull the oars of a boat, do it by an agreement or convention, though they have never given promises to each other. Nor is the rule concerning the stability of possession the less derived from human conventions, that it arises gradually, and acquires force by a slow progression, and by our repeated experience of the inconveniences of transgressing it. On the contrary, this experience assures us still more, that the sense of interest has become common to all our fellows, and gives us a confidence of the future regularity of their conduct; and it is only on the expectation of this, that our moderation and abstinence are founded.

(*T* 3.2.2.10/SBN 490)

In this passage Hume repeatedly stresses that this convention regulating possession consists in reciprocal *actions* or behaviours over a period of time. Although we must mutually 'express' our 'general sense of common interest', Hume's example of jointly rowing a boat stresses that the relevant expression of this interest need not be linguistic. Here too, custom is the great guide in human life.[10] This common, reciprocal custom can be sufficiently expressed through our reciprocal behaviour; it requires no linguistic expression and thus no express agreement. The rules governing possession are first made possible and established merely as mutually coordinated behaviours; that is, as a behavioural convention.

11.5 Hume's second social coordination problem

However, simply because we must respect a certain distribution and possession of goods does not itself provide or entail any principle according to which goods should be distributed and possessed (*T* 3.2.3.1/SBN 501–2). This is at least analytically, if not temporally (historically), a second step. Indeed this second step can only be taken because the first step generates a distinct problem, although this second problem can only be solved on the basis of that first solution. Briefly, Hume contends that the sole principle governing the distribution of possessions that does not lead to socially destructive strife is that each person becomes proprietor of exactly whatever he or she already held

[10] *T*, Abstract, ¶16/SBN 652; *ECHU* 5.1.6/SBN^E 44.

(*T* 3.2.3.4/SBN 503–4). Only this second principle can make possessions, so far as possible, as secure as 'the fixed and constant advantages of the mind and body' (*T* 3.2.2.9/SBN 489).

11.6 Hume's third social coordination problem

However, this second principle regulating the distribution of possessions is too strict. The current distribution of possessions may not be the most advantageous; in view of the various hazards and happenstances of human acquisition and need, the current distribution is in all likelihood suboptimal (*T* 3.2.3.5/SBN 505). Thus a third problem arises on the basis of the solution to the second, which again can only be solved on the basis of that second solution, namely, by a principle regulating the exchange of possessions: 'possession and property should always be stable, except when the proprietor consents to bestow them on some other person' (*T* 3.2.4.1/SBN 514). The means of bestowal may include gift, loan, or exchange of possessions. The important point is that bestowal can only occur through the express agreement of the proprietor. This principle, Hume contends, is the only principle of exchange that can avoid causing such controversy and strife about who owns what as would destroy society.[11]

11.7 Hume's fourth social coordination problem

Due to the temporality of nature (e.g., the ripening or spoiling of foodstuffs) and of human life (we cannot work together at the same time on two at least spatially distant projects) it is often impossible to exchange goods simultaneously. Thus arises a fourth problem, which can only be solved on the basis of the previous three solutions, namely through promise and its especially explicit version, contract (*T* 3.2.5.8/SBN 519–20). Promise and contract alone enable us to exchange goods at distinct times or places.

The crucial and indispensable role of promising and contract in human life is laid bare by the previous problems and their solutions. Yet only because we have some possessions have we anything to promise. (A promise or contract to exchange services is omitted by Hume, but mere services without possessions would be pointless if not impossible,

[11] Hume's insufficient attention to issues of distributive equity are examined below, §14.2.

because most services consist in handling or processing something antecedently possessed.) Promises do not consist in the mere verbal formula, 'I promise . . . ', or in the decision, wish, will, or intention to perform or omit a future action at the designated time and place. A promise consists in expressly accepting the obligation to do something specific in the future.[12] This obligation to perform a future action arises as soon as one expresses one's promise to another, and this obligation is to regulate one's behaviour until the promised action is executed. Thus promising presupposes an understanding both of obligation (see below, §12) and of the convention which regulates, indeed structures promising, and thus makes it at all possible. Yet this convention is constructed on the basis of the conventions previously summarized. For both of these reasons promising, too, consists in a social practice regulated, structured, indeed made possible—in a word: *enabled*—by principles. Thus promising, too, is not natural, it is not independent of social institutions; it is instead an artificial construction, literally a convention, which exists and is effective only insofar as people recognize it and act accordingly.

11.8 Hume's fifth social coordination problem

One more step in Hume's analysis requires brief discussion. From the considerations summarized above Hume derives his three basic normative laws of nature, 'that of the stability of possession, of its transference by consent, and of the performance of promises' (*T* 3.2.6.1, 3.2.11.2/SBN 526, 567). Due to human nature, however, these basic laws are neither self-sufficient nor self-actualizing, not even through their overwhelming advantages for each and everyone. The problem is that the great advantages of acting in accord with these conventions, namely the preservation of society itself, through which alone we can enjoy the great advantages of these three natural laws, are indirect and temporally distant, all the more so as the size of society increases (*T* 3.2.2.24/SBN 497–8). However, the apparent advantages of present anti-conventional acquisition (e.g., theft, fraud, or extortion) are direct and temporally immediate, because the disadvantages of such acts fall upon others and are easily disregarded by whoever violates the three basic social conventions. For these reasons, people tend to favour their apparently direct and immediate advantages

[12] *T* 3.2.5 ¶¶3, 10/SBN 516, 521. This account of promising is not original to Hume; it is already developed by Hobbes; see Ludwig (1998), 235–47, 331–43.

over their genuine, though indirect and distant (long-term) advantages. In order to counteract this feature of human nature, government is instituted in order to preserve and enforce the three rules governing possession, and also contract. To this end government establishes impartial judges sitting in public courts. Only through government can the laws governing possession be executed and enforced through judicial decision. Thus government is the final condition required for the possibility of even a modestly sized human society, and of society's enormous advantages for each and for all (*T* 3.2.7.6–8/SBN 537–9).

Due to our very finite powers, both physical and intellectual, we are mutually interdependent; hence as individuals we each require society; hence as individuals we each require these fundamental principles and institutions, these conventions. Hence these conventions are non-optional, certainly not under conditions of moderate population density and consequent relative scarcity. Accordingly, the fundamental social conventions Hume identifies are for us as human beings 'laws of nature' (cf. *T* 3.2.2.22/SBN 497, quoted below, §13.2).

11.9 Interest, prudence, and morals

To this point, the 'rules' governing possession have been discussed as far as possible without considering right or justice. Hume thinks it enormously important to distinguish between interest as the basis of society and the basis of any specifically moral obligation (*T* 3.2.2.1, 3.2.2.23/SBN 484, 498). So far only interest and prudence have been at issue, in order to highlight and to clarify as well as possible the distinct, though closely linked steps of Hume's analysis of our basic practical principles. This analysis of interest provides Hume's basis for analysing the character of specifically moral obligation, to which we now turn.

4

Hume's Proof of the Insufficiency of Moral Sentiments

12 Hume's Account of the Basis of Specifically Moral Obligation

Briefly, Hume explains specifically moral approval of behaviour which accords with the rules of justice, and moral disapproval of behaviour which violates them, in this way (*T* 3.2.2.23–28/SBN 498–501). We ourselves experience that self-seeking and limited generosity makes us unsociable, to the point of making us unfit for society, and yet also that society is altogether necessary and enormously advantageous for our own lives and welfare. However, even in a modestly sized society we don't easily perceive the damages and disorder caused by our own violations of the three basic social conventions. Nevertheless, we do notice the damages and disorder caused by others' violations of those conventions. Even when those damages don't directly affect us, we find them 'unpleasant' because they damage society and because we sympathize with those who directly suffer those damages. Viewed generally for society, that which causes us 'uneasiness' about human actions is called 'vice', whilst that which causes the complementary 'satisfaction' is called 'virtue'. Thus our sympathy with the public interest is the source of our specifically *moral* approval or disapproval. Only in this way are we conscious of any specifically moral good or ill in connection with justice or injustice, according to Hume. Once we come to make them, we further extend these moral evaluations to our own actions, and we also sympathize with others' moral feelings regarding ourselves. Consequently, we come to feel morally obligated to act in accord with basic social conventions. Only thus do we feel any specifically *moral* obligation to act justly. These affective tendencies, which are rooted in human nature and indeed in our own individual self-interest, are also encouraged and increased through our upbringing, socialization, and public discourse, whether moral, religious, or political.

13 Hume's Theory of Justice *versus* Hume's Ethical Sentiments

13.1 Three questions for moral theory

Hume's theory of justice suffices, as we shall see, to identify certain acts as right, and others as wrong, and to justify these classifications, without any appeal to sentiments, whether moral or non-moral, whether first-, second-, or third-person. This finding casts grave doubt upon Hume's own sentiment-based ethical theory, and accordingly, on all recent constructivist moral theories modelled upon Hume's ethical theory. Much of Modern natural law theory aims to show that the requirements of enlightened self-interest generally, if not entirely accord with our moral obligations. This is a desideratum for any tenable theory of justice and indeed for any tenable normative social theory. Assessing such views requires carefully determining the extent to which they provide cogent answers to at least these three questions for moral theory:

1. Does the theory correctly identify genuine normative principles or judgments?
2. Does the theory properly explain our knowledge of (or beliefs about) those principles or judgments, and our capacities and abilities to use or make these reliably and accurately?
3. Does the theory provide a tenable normative justification for those principles or judgments, and our knowledge of (or beliefs about) them?

Moral theories typically try to answer the first question by answering either or both of the latter two. Yet it is important to distinguish these three questions in order to recognize that, for example, an ideal observer theory or a theory of moral sentiments may answer one of these questions without answering the others, or without answering them adequately. Hume's moral philosophy, including his theory of justice, shifts unwittingly and almost imperceptibly amongst these three questions because Hume fails clearly to distinguish them, and doesn't always abide by his own distinctions amongst them, such as he draws.[1] Typically his expositors have followed suit.

In this important and striking passage, Hume mixes these three key issues concerning the character of moral judgments, our knowledge of them, and their normative justification:

> Now, since the distinguishing impressions by which moral good or evil is known [*sic*], are nothing but *particular* pains or pleasures, it follows, that in all enquiries concerning these moral distinctions, it will be sufficient [*sic*] to shew the principles which make us feel a satisfaction or uneasiness from the survey of any character, in order to satisfy us why the character is [*sic*] laudable or blamable. An action, or sentiment, or character, is [*sic*] virtuous or vicious; why? because [*sic*] its view causes a pleasure or uneasiness of a particular kind. In giving a reason, therefore, for the pleasure or uneasiness, we sufficiently explain [*sic*] the vice or virtue. To have the sense [*sic*] of virtue, is nothing but [*sic*] to feel a satisfaction of a particular kind from the contemplation of a character.
>
> (*T* 3.1.2.3/SBN 471)

This passage begins with questions of moral epistemology, though it immediately shifts to questions of moral desert or merit—that is, to the correctness or appropriateness of such presumptive moral knowledge—and then shifts again to questions about the nature of virtue and vice, which Hume seeks to explain second person in terms of the sentiments of an observer, including whatever grounds there may be which explain that observer's sentiments. Finally Hume returns to issues of moral epistemology.

13.2 Reason versus *moral sense?*

Hume famously remarks that reason investigates and discovers natural objects as they actually are. In contrast, our moral sense cannot be ascribed to reason but only to taste, because taste is productive, it effects a new creation, so to speak, by 'gilding or staining all natural objects with the colours, borrowed from internal sentiment'.[2] For all his hyperbole, Hume here rightly recognizes that individual natural objects or events as

[1] This problem pervades Hume's *Treatise*; see Harrison (1976, esp. 110–25); and Johansson (2002).

[2] *ECPM* App. 1, ¶21/SBN^{E} 294; cf. *T* 1.3.14.25/SBN 167.

such are not of moral value. He also recognizes that moral value must consist in relations. However, his summary statement (above, §13.1) is deeply misleading because it seeks to locate moral value only in relations between individual objects (or their behaviour, including acts) and the mere sentiments of any individual human being who observes them. As Hume's own analysis of justice shows (above §§11, 12), moral value consists (at least in part) in complex relations among things, human beings, human society, and the necessary, constitutive principles and practices which structure human society. As Hume himself twice emphasizes in conclusion (in the passage just quoted in §13.1), it simply does not suffice to appeal to our sentiments of (moral) pleasure or displeasure: it is also necessary to find a 'reason' for these sentiments to occur, in order, at the very least, to 'explain' our moral feelings.[3]

However, Hume's very strong theses, central to his sentiment-based account of moral distinctions and moral judgments, that 'the external performance has no [*sic*] merit' (*T* 3.2.1.2/SBN 477[4]) and that 'no action can be virtuous, but so far as it proceeds from a virtuous motive' (*T* 3.2.1.9/SBN 480) are directly refuted by Hume's own analysis of justice (above §§11, 12). Hume himself argues cogently that acting outwardly in violation of the basic social conventions does have a demerit, both as injury to the directly affected party or parties, and as injury to the whole of society and its principles and system of justice, *regardless* of anyone's affective response to that action and *regardless* of any motive of the violator; i.e., regardless of whether he or she acts either negligently or viciously.

This result is also directly if unwittingly stressed by Hume himself, when he opts for rule rather than act utilitarianism in his account of why the whole system of justice preserves its enormous value and advantages, even though some particular instances of justice do not maximize general welfare (*T* 3.2.2.22/SBN 497). Hume's account of the justice of returning a great fortune to a miser or to a seditious bigot *disregards* the motives of whomever would return the sum, as well as those of the

[3] This aspect of Hume's moral philosophy is often disregarded in contemporary discussions, e.g., by Blackburn (1993, 1998), who attempts to construct a 'projection theory' of moral judgments on the basis of Hume's ethical theory. For an introduction to his account, see Blackburn (2002); for critical discussion see Westphal (1998c, esp. §5.3); Hale (1993a, 1993b, 2002); Harcourt (2005); and below, §15.

[4] Cf. *T* 3.2.1.9, 3.2.6.9, 3.3.1.4–5/SBN 480, 532, 575.

miser or bigot, and *disregards* the sentiments of any observer, whether ideal or human. The justice of restoring such a sum lies instead in the fact that:

> Property must be stable, and must be fixed by general rules. Though in one instance the public be a sufferer, this momentary ill is amply compensated by the steady prosecution of the rule, and by the peace and order which it establishes in society. And even every individual person must find himself a gainer on balancing the account; since, without justice, society must immediately dissolve, and every one must fall into that savage and solitary condition, which is infinitely worse than the worst situation that can possibly be supposed in society.
>
> (*T* 3.2.2.22/SBN 497)

Although this way of appreciating the value of society is purely instrumental, it is nevertheless crucial within any system of justice. Yet this value is moral, according to Hume's analysis, because such acts are (or would be) morally approved by impartial observers in view of their role within a system of justice as a whole, altogether *regardless* of the motives of the relevant agents.

13.3 Two theses about sentiments and moral judgment

Perhaps we recognize what is morally good or ill through various sentiments of pleasure or displeasure, as Hume contends. This would accord with the following, weak thesis:

> *Sentiments 1*: Sentiments are a necessary component or basis of moral judgments.

This thesis may answer, or contribute to answering, the second question posed earlier (§13.1), of how we know (or come to have appropriate beliefs about) moral principles or their use in judgments. However, even if this weak thesis is correct, and even if (additionally) it answers the second question about moral epistemology (or doxology), it does not follow that an action *deserves* praise or blame, or that someone's character *is* virtuous or vicious, merely *because* their observation arouses a certain kind of feeling of approval or disapproval in observers (*T* 3.1.2.3/SBN 471, quoted above §13.1). This would accord with a second, much stronger thesis:

> *Sentiments 2*: Sentiments form the sole and sufficient basis of moral judgments (or classifications).

Though Hume asserts and argues for this thesis, according to his own analysis of justice there are very good grounds why certain actions arouse approval and elicit praise, whilst others arouse their opposites, namely: certain actions *accord with justice*, whilst others *violate* the principles of justice, by either complying with or violating the three basic natural law rules governing possession and promise, without which society and hence individual action are impossible. Whether actions do or do not accord with or violate these rules of justice is a fact, regardless of whether we happen to respond affectively to such acts, and regardless of the motives of the agent. Human sentiment can at best be source, conduit, or signal of moral knowledge (or acknowledgment), but our sentiments cannot serve as the sole constitutive basis of morals. Hume himself confirms this in the passage quoted above (§13.1). This important sentence of Hume's,

> An action, or sentiment, or character, is virtuous or vicious; why? because [*sic*] its view causes a pleasure or uneasiness of a particular kind.
>
> (*T* 3.1.2.3/SBN 471)

does not stand alone in Hume's text, nor in his analysis. Hume continues:

> In giving a reason, therefore, for the pleasure or uneasiness, we sufficiently explain [*sic*] the vice or virtue.
>
> (*T* 3.1.2.3/SBN 471)

Hume's moral philosophy aims especially to discover and to explain such (putative) grounds of our moral sentiments. However, these grounds are for moral theorists to know. Such discoveries hardly affect daily life and activity (*T* 3.1.1.27/SBN 468). According to Hume, moral sentiments are primarily a source of moral knowledge (or acknowledgment):

> To have the sense [*sic*] of virtue, is nothing but [*sic*] to feel a satisfaction of a particular kind from the contemplation of a character.
>
> (*T* 3.1.2.3/ SBN 471)

This is to say, through the occurrence of certain sentiments we recognize (or at least come to believe) that a particular act is virtuous or vicious, just or unjust. Moral sentiments, in Hume's account, are moral indicators. However, *that* we recognize something through such sentiments is something we know theoretically only by correctly adducing their grounds, *and* by assessing the justificatory—rather than merely the explanatory—adequacy of those grounds. Thus it appears that Hume's analysis of our moral sentiments attempts to answer only the second of the three questions raised above (§13.1), which concerns our knowledge (or at least, our appropriate beliefs) about right and wrong, virtuous or vicious actions. Hume's analysis of justice repeatedly underscores how answering the first and third questions, regarding whether his theory correctly identifies genuine moral judgments and whether it provides for them sufficient normative justification, requires explicating the reasons that show why certain actions are right or wrong, virtuous or vicious, where these reasons also explain occurrences of the relevant moral sentiments. According to Hume's theory of justice, moral sentiments cannot be the basis for answering either the first or the third question (posed in §13.1); i.e., Hume's moral sentiments do not suffice to identify correctly genuine normative principles or judgments, nor do they suffice to justify moral principles or judgments normatively. This interim result is further confirmed in the remainder of this chapter.

13.4 Taste and moral discriminations

To what extent does recognizing the moral character or status of something via our sentiments count as moral knowledge, or at least genuine moral acknowledgment? Hume repeatedly compares moral sentiments with secondary qualities; that is, with subjective but nevertheless regular responses based upon fixed causal laws (both natural and physio-psychological) to objects or events in our surroundings.

Modelling sentiments on causal regularities in sensory perception is prominent in Hume's essay, 'Of the Standard of Taste', where he analyses and elaborates these analogies. At the outset of this essay Hume stresses that basing morality in human sentiments requires that human nature is predominantly uniform and stable. This essay expressly aims to show that human nature is predominantly uniform and stable by sharply contrasting the considerable, widespread, and enduring fame of outstanding works of classical art, which is altogether clear, stable, and pronounced, with the thorough variability of all speculation—that is, all reasoning—in theology, philosophy, and natural philosophy (i.e. natural science), as well as in fashions and customs and even in morality and the sense of propriety ('Taste', ¶¶12, 27, 28). By stark contrast to these sharp and frequent fluctuations it becomes evident, Hume argues, that the enormous, pervasive, and stable high regard for classical works of art can only be due to complex relations between such works of art and human nature, such that any great work of art always elicits the same kinds of strong feelings of aesthetic pleasure and approval. Anyone who enjoys art experiences such feelings. However, only very sensitive, well-informed (and articulate) critics can in addition properly judge works of art, and explain their appreciation and evaluation of a work of art to others. The overwhelming consensus among these two kinds of art lovers, sustained over the millennia, is due to the (putative) fact, which Hume reiterates five times within three pages, that even our tertiary feelings of aesthetic pleasure and displeasure, just like our sensory experiences of secondary qualities, are caused in us by the primary qualities of objects, in this case, by of works of art.[5] To this considerable extent even our aesthetic sentiments count as regular and generally reliable indicators of extra-mental states of affairs; aesthetic sentiments are, according to Hume, tertiary qualities regularly and reliably elicited by genuine, outstanding works of art.[6] To the extent that Hume's analysis of aesthetic judgments serves as his model for moral judgments—which is clearly, if implicitly, intended by Hume's introductory paragraphs of 'Of the Standard of Taste' and is mentioned in this connection both in the *Treatise* and in the second *Enquiry*[7]—our moral sentiments do

[5] The five passages are these: 'The relation, which nature has placed between the form [of the object] and the sentiment . . . ' ('Taste', ¶11); ' . . . the beauties, which are naturally fitted to excite agreeable sentiments . . . ' (*ibid.*, ¶12); 'It appears then, that, amidst all the variety and caprice of taste, there are certain general principles of approbation or blame, whose influence a careful eye may trace in all operations of the mind. Some particular forms or qualities [of objects], from the original structure of the internal fabric, are calculated to please, and others to displease; and if they fail of their effect in any particular instance, it is from some apparent defect or imperfection in the organ. . . . In each creature, there is a sound and a defective state; and the former alone can be supposed to afford us a true standard of taste and sentiment' (*ibid.*, ¶13); ' . . . some objects, by the structure of the mind, [are] naturally calculated to give pleasure' (*ibid.*, ¶14); 'Though it be certain, that beauty and deformity, more than sweet and bitter, are not qualities in objects, but belong entirely to the sentiment, it must be allowed, that there are certain qualities in objects, which are fitted by nature to produce those particular feelings' (*ibid.*, ¶17). These clear and emphatic assertions by Hume, to the effect that the beauties of art are tertiary qualities, are disregarded, e.g., by Blackburn (1993, 1998), on which see Westphal (1998c), 49 note 103. Blackburn's disregard of this key feature of Hume's view undermines the Humean credentials he claims for his own view.

[6] Here I do not limit Hume's claim to classical works of art. Classical art is his focus because the pronounced durability of its acknowledged excellence is the historian's method for factoring out cultural and individual variables.

[7] *T* 3.3.1 ¶¶8–9, 15/SBN 576–7, 581; *ECPM* 1.9/SBN^{E} 172.

indeed serve as a source of moral knowledge (or acknowledgment), or as reliable moral indicators. This is the basis of Hume's answer to the second question posed above (§13.1).

14 A Causal Theory in Moral Epistemology?

14.1. It would be a fine thing to show that Hume's theory of moral sentiments involves a causal-reliability theory of moral knowledge (or of appropriate belief). However, against any such suggestion it must be recognized that in this same essay Hume places morality amongst the cultural phenomena which exhibit stark variations through history. Despite his contention that moral principles do not exhibit the sharp swings found in 'speculation' (i.e., rational inquiry), once he insists that it is a genuine aesthetic defect to portray vicious acts or morays without artistic comment on their moral deficiency ('Taste', ¶33), Hume himself must acknowledge that the facts supposedly indicated by our moral sentiments are sensed and evaluated often quite differently in different periods and regions. This does not require rejecting Hume's attempt to model moral judgments on aesthetic judgments, but the admitted historical and geographical variability of moral sentiments and their objects directly raises the question of in what way(s) and to what extent Hume can or could normatively justify our moral sentiments as the sole basis of legitimate moral judgments. This difficult question favours, of course, the weaker first, over the stronger second thesis identified above (§13.3), namely that sentiments are a necessary component of our moral judgments (*Sentiments 1*), although they are not the sole and sufficient basis for moral judgments (*Sentiments 2*).

14.2. On Hume's analysis, the three basic moral 'laws of nature' (those constituting and regulating possession and promise) are justified and are non-arbitrary because they are indispensable to society, and because society is indispensable to each and to all of us (above §11). However, this issue is not so easily dispatched, for two reasons internal to Hume's own analysis. First, the rule of justice governing the distribution of goods, that each person should own only whatever he or she already holds (above §11.4), only generates a plausibly just result on the assumption that at the outset of any organized society, goods are already distributed with sufficient equity.[8] However, any such charitable assumption leads to a 'proper', or at least to a plausible or acceptable result only by highlighting the lack of any normative Humean justification of principles of equity, which alone could justify the charitable assumption.[9] This problem is not alleviated by Hume's third rule of justice governing the transfer of goods only upon permission of their owner(s) (above §11.4), because this third rule too makes no provision for sufficient equity in the distribution of goods. The presumed 'justice' of Hume's first two rules is easily destroyed by the effects of powerful individuals or groups within society.[10] Hume himself noted these deficiencies at least occasionally, when he observed that actual systems of justice frequently exploit women, the poor, and especially slaves.[11] Hume's later observation, that conventions, including conventions of justice, arise only among persons of roughly equal power (*ECPM* 3.1.18–20/SBN[e] 190–1) is far too weak and undeveloped even to begin to address these fundamental issues of equity. Hume's three moral 'laws of nature' do *not* suffice to specify a normatively justifiable system of justice, and thus also do not suffice to justify any such system normatively. To achieve this requires a sound strategy for normative justification, not merely an explanation of our moral sentiments or judgments. Hume's primarily explanatory aims (above, §§11.1, 12, 13.1) preclude his offering any such account of, or strategy for, normative justification.[12] (One *sine qua non* for just distributions of goods is Rousseau's independence requirement, which Kant adopts and defends; see below, §42.)

As noted above (§§7, 10), Hume insists that, although 'the rules of justice be *artificial*, they are not *arbitrary*', because they are indispensable to human life, both collectively and individually. Only due to this circumstance do the rules of justice count as normative natural laws (*T* 3.2.1.19/SBN 484). Although some version of Hume's three natural laws are indeed indispensable to, and thus necessary for any society

[8] Cf. Baier (1991), 239.

[9] This grave omission is neglected by Baier (1991). Though Baier (2010, 85) cites Hume's later appeal to some notion of equality (*ECPM* 3.1.18–19, 3.2.4/SBN[E] 190–1, 193–4), she does not consider whether or how Hume justifies, or could justify, such an appeal.

[10] Cf. Baier (1991), 238.

[11] *T* 2.1.9.10/SBN 307; *ECPM* 3.1.19, 3.2.4/SBN[E] 191, 193–4; 'Of the Rise and Progress of the Arts and Sciences', ¶11; cf. Baier (1991), 238–9.

[12] Cf. Hume, 'That Politics May be Reduced to a Science'.

(§11), we have just seen (§§13, 14) that they do not *suffice* for a justifiable system of *justice*. (This is quite aside from Hume's omission of personal security as a matter of justice.) This result comports all too well with Hume's recognition that, unlike the constant fame of great works of art, moral principles and evaluations shift markedly through history (§13.4). These two points follow directly from a fundamental feature of Hume's moral philosophy.

15 Radical Nominalism, the Vagaries of Usage, and Optionality

15.1 Is morality merely nominal?

Central to Hume's explanation of specifically moral sentiments or moral status of any sort is this claim:

> . . . every thing which gives uneasiness in human actions, upon the general survey, is called [*sic*] Vice, and whatever produces satisfaction, in the same manner, is denominated [*sic*] Virtue . . .
>
> (*T* 3.2.2.24/SBN 499)

These nominalist denominations are crucial, basic, and indispensable to Hume's 'explanation' of how and why certain of our sentiments count as specifically *moral* sentiments (above §§12, 13.3); without these premises Hume has no such explanation to offer. Hume himself confirms this by continuing thus:

> . . . this is the reason why [*sic*] the sense of moral good and evil follows upon justice and injustice.
>
> (*T* 3.2.2.24/SBN 499)

According to Hume's moral philosophy, if we did not designate some actions just and others unjust, there would *be* neither vice nor virtue, there would be no justice, no morality, no specifically moral sentiments, and no specifically moral obligation (above §12).

In this same radically nominalist vein Hume also remarks,

> Whoever recommends any moral virtues, really does no more than is implied in the terms themselves. That people, who invented the word *charity*, and used it in a good sense, inculcated more clearly and much more efficaciously, the precept, *be charitable*, than any pretended legislator or prophet, who should insert such a *maxim* in his writings.
>
> ('Taste', ¶5)

One can acknowledge the force of Hume's observation, and yet still urge that the normative problem lies, not simply with such moral classifications as 'charity' or 'respectful' or 'just', but rather with shifting moral perceptions of what counts—and conversely what fails to count—as charitable, respectful, or just. Hume's qualifying comment, 'and used it'—*viz.*, the term 'charity'—'in a good sense' is crucial, yet this phrase requires an analysis and justification neither his nominalism nor his sentiment-based ethical theory can provide. It is a very long and yet unfinished process to move from the ancient Greek principle of justice, to 'treat equals as equals, and unequals as unequals', to the declaration of the 'universal rights of man', and not only because 'other' races, tribes, and of course women (Gouges 1791), have so often and in so many ways been treated as unequals. In US courts of law, guilty verdicts in jury trials are rendered with the phrase 'you have been found guilty by a jury of your peers', though few today recall the origins and significance of this phrase within the mediaeval peerage system.

The problem with radical nominalism in moral philosophy is plain: whatever happens merely to be designated 'moral' can be designated otherwise, which has of course occurred historically, and not only in the various forms of twentieth-century totalitarianism (whether right- or left-wing).

Hume's radical nominalism about moral designations is required by his anti-rationalist thesis that sentiments provide the sole and sufficient basis for moral judgments ('*Sentiments 2*', §13.3). Were Hume to espouse only this thesis, he could at best answer only the second, but neither the first nor the third of the questions for moral theory posed above (§13.1), by explaining our knowledge of—or rather our putatively appropriate beliefs about—right and wrong, and our ability to make judgments based on such distinctions. What makes Hume's moral philosophy so rich and instructive is that he also holds the weaker, first thesis ('*Sentiments 1*'), that moral sentiments are a necessary component of our moral judgments. I have argued that Hume's theory of justice shows both the implausibility of the second, stronger thesis, that Hume also develops the first, weaker thesis in his theory of justice, and that Hume's better moral reasoning lies therein. Unfortunately, contemporary neo-Humeans strongly tend to disregard these aspects of Hume's moral philosophy and to take for granted only Hume's commitment to the stronger, though untenable second thesis (§13.3), that sentiments form the sole and sufficient basis of moral judgments (*Sentiments 2*).

15.2 Can morality be a matter of taste?

Appealing to Hume's theory of judgment, even as most explicitly developed in 'Of the Standard of Taste', is to no avail in this regard. There Hume insists that presumed expert critics must provide reasons for their critical interpretations and evaluations, though he says nothing about the character or basis of such reasons; in particular, he says nothing about whether these reasons are explanatory, justificatory, or both. At the least, these reasons would have to include explanations of why experts respond affectively to works of art—or analogously to objects of moral assessment—in ways which accord with Hume's express insistence (cited above, §§13.1, 13.3) that an adequate moral theory must provide reasons to explain why people have the moral sentiments they do. To the extent that such reasons are provided, sentiments serve neither as the ultimate nor as the sole bases of moral judgment; to the extent that such reasons are not provided, the resultant theory remains subject to the shifting historical sands of presumptive 'moral' sentiments and the merely nominal distinctions among classes of actions or of characters they purportedly found. Hume understood, for example, that the practices of friendship, public spiritedness, and generosity vary across cultures, though he held that these practices were widely (and properly) subjects of moral approbation because they reflect and answer to common features of human nature. However, what counts as 'friendship, public spiritedness, and generosity' differed significantly among ancient Athenians and Spartans,[13] even more so among the early Germanic tribes (who forbade theft within the tribe, but honoured theft from other tribes or peoples), and worse yet among racists, sexists, or fascists of any age or variety. Simply citing the widely shared value of, for example, 'friendship' fails to engage the key moral issue: friendships among bigots strongly tend themselves to be bigoted because such friendships strongly tend to support and to reinforce the bigotry of the bigoted friends, and likewise in the other cases mentioned. (Morally speaking, the world would be a far better place if bigots happened as a matter of fact either to despise or to be incapable of friendship, for such tendencies would thwart, or at least strongly counter-act, their collective action.)

[13] Compare Adkins (1963); Annas (1977); and Cooper (1980).

16 Hume's Impartial Spectator to the Rescue?

This same basic point holds about Hume's nascent account of an impartial moral observer who adopts a general point of view on humanity.[14] The impartiality of one's sentiments depends upon the breadth of one's perspective upon human affairs and human beings, but the breadth required for impartiality can be neither generated nor justified merely on the basis of one's own sentiments. Nor does an impartial spectator provide reasons to justify the correctness of his or her (its?) moral judgments; though perhaps Hume the moral theorist might do so. Hume's theory of justice shows that the moral goodness of acts of justice, allegiance, modesty, good manners, and compliance with the laws of nations lies in benefiting the generality of humankind (*T* 3.3.1.9/SBN 577), which goodness is in turn reflected in our sympathetic approbation of such acts. Their goodness is neither defined nor constituted *by* our sympathetic approbation; Hume's reasons for holding the contrary have been criticized above, on the basis of his own, much more plausible theory of justice (§13).

The moral judgments of Hume's impartial spectator, based as they are on his or her moral sentiments, at most answer the second, but neither the first nor the third, of the questions for moral theory posed above (§13.1). The key issue can be posed by permuting the Euthyphro question thus: does the ideal observer define or justify impartiality, or does impartiality define or justify the ideal observer? In an interesting and pertinent case, whether at the time of Tiberias the Roman empire was hereditary, Hume grants that 'we shall never be able to satisfy an impartial enquirer, who adopts no party in political controversies, and will be satisfied with nothing but sound reason and philosophy' (*T* 3.2.10.16/SBN 562–3). If the impartial enquirer requires 'sound reason', then much more constitutes the perspective of an impartial

[14] *T* 3.3.1 ¶¶8–9, 15–16, 28, 30/SBN 576–7, 581–2, 590–1; *ECPM* 5.2.27, 9.1.6, 9.1.9/SBN^E 228–9, 272–3, 275–6. For a good discussion of this aspect of Hume's moral theory, see Brand (1992), who greatly illuminates Hume's efforts to meld his psychological associationism with his account of critical judgment based on general rules, and the important role this plays in Hume's account of the impartial point of view. Brand's ambitious and important task, however, precludes his considering the issues raised here about the tenability of Hume's theory of moral sentiments, and likewise Hume's account of 'distinctions of reason', on which see Westphal (2013c).

enquirer than sentiments alone, however refined, adjusted, or filtered amongst themselves.

Hume famously held that 'reason' is nothing other than 'calm' passion or passions.[15] However, Hume's reasons for this contention assume that preferences, including moral distinctions, can only be based on sentiments, a thesis justified—to whatever extent it is justified—by his basic premise that outer actions have no intrinsic value, and are only valuable in relation to the sentiments of an observer, perhaps in response to the presumed motives of the actor (*T* 3.2.1.2/SBN 477[16]). However, this premise is shown by Hume's own theory of justice to be false, because there are reasons why some acts are just and others unjust, regardless of anyone's motives or sentiments (above, §§11, 13, 15).

Moreover, Hume's equation of reason with calm passion is highly stipulative and implausible for the following reason: passions can cause beliefs, decisions, or actions, and can thereby explain them psychologically. Likewise sentiments of an observer may signal virtuous or vicious, right or wrong actions, and may in this way either cause or explain the observer's judgments about those actions. Yet neither causation nor explanation suffice to justify the moral status of these judgments, unless and until the relevant passions or sentiments are shown not merely to be effective, but also to be morally appropriate. However, once these affects are shown to be appropriate, whatever shows them to be appropriate carries the weight of normative justification, rather than the mere occurrence of various purportedly moral sentiments. (This too recalls the basic contrast drawn by Socrates' question to Euthyphro.) As Hume repeatedly stressed in his account of the three principles of justice, what bears the weight of normative justification are the actual advantages or disadvantages, respectively, of right or wrong, virtuous or vicious actions, regardless of motives and regardless of whether those actions arouse anyone's sentiments (above, §13.3). Hume cannot prove the stronger, second thesis identified above ('*Sentiments 2*'; §13.3)—that sentiments are the sole sufficient basis for moral distinctions—and he can only answer the three normative questions for moral theory identified above (§13.3) on the basis of the weaker first thesis (*Sentiments 1*), that

[15] *T* 2.3.3.9, 2.3.8.13, 3.3.1.18/SBN 417, 437, 583–4; *ECPM* 6.1.15/SBN[E] 239; 'A Dissertation on the Passions', §5.2; see below, §17.

[16] Cf. *T* 3.2.1.9, 3.2.6.9, 3.3.1.4–5/SBN 479, 532, 575; and above, §13.2.

sentiments are a necessary (though not sufficient) component of an adequate account of moral judgment.

This result is confirmed by Hume's own account of how and why our own 'natural uncultivated ideas of morality' require modification and constraint—by 'judgment and understanding':

> ... our natural uncultivated ideas of morality, instead of providing a remedy for the partiality of our affections, do rather conform themselves to that partiality, and give it an additional force and influence.
>
> The remedy, then, is not derived from nature, but from artifice; or, more properly speaking, nature provides a remedy, in the judgment and understanding, for what is irregular and incommodious in the affections. For when men, from their early education in society, have become sensible of the infinite advantages that result from it, and have besides acquired a new affection to company and conversation, and when they have observed that the principal disturbance in society arises from those goods, which we call external, and from their looseness and easy transition from one person to another, they must seek for a remedy, by putting these goods, as far as possible, on the same footing with the fixed and constant advantages of the mind and body. This can be done after no other manner, than by a convention entered into by all the members of the society to bestow stability on the possession of those external goods, and leave every one in the peaceable enjoyment of what he may acquire by his fortune and industry. By this means every one knows what he may safely possess; and the passions are restrained in their partial and contradictory motions. Nor is such a restraint contrary to these passions; for, if so, it could never be entered into nor maintained; but it is only contrary to their heedless and impetuous movement. Instead of departing from our own interest, or from that of our nearest friends, by abstaining from the possessions of others, we cannot better consult both these interests than by such a convention; because it is by that means we maintain society, which is so necessary to their well-being and subsistence, as well as to our own.
>
> (*T* 3.2.2.8–9/SBN 489)

In sum, Hume's moral sentiments at most account for moral beliefs or judgments, but suffice neither to determine the correctness nor the adequacy of those beliefs or judgments, nor to justify them nor moral principles normatively. Whether the first thesis (*Sentiments 1*) is true I do not pursue here, but what has been argued concerning Hume's theory of justice suggests that it is far less evident, or far less central, than Hume and his contemporary followers recognize.[17] At the very least, Hume is right to grant that:

[17] In fact, Hume's moral philosophy offers little justification of his crucial claim that reason is nothing but calm passion or passions. Presumably, Hume believes this claim is a

in order to pave the way for such a [moral] sentiment, and give a proper discernment of its object, it is often necessary, we find, that much reasoning should precede, that nice distinctions be made, just conclusions drawn, distant comparisons formed, complicated relations examined, and general facts fixed and ascertained.

(*ECPM* 1.9/SBN^{E} 172)

Hume here recognizes—again, as in the previous passage—that in matters moral, reason and sentiment must work in tandem. On Hume's own account, therefore, reason cannot be merely the slave of the passions (*T* 2.3.3.4/SBN 414–5), and sentiments alone do not suffice for moral judgment; at most Hume can justify *Sentiments 1*, not *Sentiments 2*. Hume's own account of justice shows that some acts arouse the sense of injustice because they are unjust, and in so doing, he shows that no act is unjust merely because it arouses someone's sense of injustice (no matter how ideal an observer she or he may be). Hume's account of the three basic rules of justice (governing possession and promise) falls on the objectivist side of the Euthyphro question, as it should, if indeed Hume propounds (at least the rudiments of) Natural Law Constructivism.

Baier remarks:

Only when Hume in [*Enquiry into the Principles of Morals*] comes to prefer Cicero's four cardinal virtues over those of the 'divines in disguise' who overstress benevolence, and understress that sagacity that leads us to cooperate in the conventions of justice, does he [Hume] recognize that, without wisdom, the potential of many other virtues may have to lie dormant.

(Baier 2010, 17)[18]

Otherwise, she notes (ibid.), in the *Enquiry into the Principles of Morals* 'wisdom, indeed, is not much stressed'. In her judgment (ibid.), 'the moral wisdom of his *History* exceeds that of' the second *Enquiry*.

direct corollary of his preceding detailed effort to show that human 'understanding' just *is* 'the general and more establish'd properties of the imagination' (*T* 1.4.7.7/SBN 267). Close examination of this doctrine, however, shows that Hume failed to make his case for it (Westphal 2013c); hence he is not entitled to take this result, nor its presumed corollaries, for granted in his moral philosophy. This is a serious problem for any attempt to bring Hume's analysis of 'distinctions of reason' and its role in cognitive judgment (*T* Book 1) to bear on his moral theory, and in particular on the problem of how to construct the impartial point of view, whilst also maintaining the strong, second thesis (from §13.3) that sentiments form the sole and sufficient basis for making or analysing moral judgments.

[18] She does not indicate where Hume indicates this 'preference'; cf. *ECPM* App. 4.6/SBN^{E} 316.

Whatever wisdom may be contained in Hume's *History* and its expanded conception of justice, his concern there with justification is even less than in the *Treatise*: it is nil. Despite her attention to Hume's remark about Cicero's four cardinal virtues, wisdom makes only scant appearance in Baier's own account of Hume's moral philosophy, which she (2010, 52) recognizes includes his theory of justice. More significantly, Baier does not remark upon how much wisdom Hume already demonstrated in his fragment of a theory of justice in the *Treatise*, and how his demonstration there of what are the basic rules of justice and why they are necessary for human life, both social and individual, requires a good measure of this same wisdom amongst—well, within his theoretical and historical context, subjects in general, and not only their magistrates. Nor does she remark that Hume's 'preference', as she calls it, for Cicero's cardinal virtues is no simple, trifling, mere, or arbitrary (elective) preference or mere matter of taste.[19]

Hume's strong nominalist tenets are required by his strong thesis that sentiments alone provide the basis for moral distinction (*Sentiments 2*). However, these nominalist tenets are inconsistent with Hume's claim that the three laws of nature (those governing possession and promise) are 'not arbitrary'. Strong nominalism in moral theory simply cannot avoid the arbitrariness of our verbal tags. However, if this arbitrariness is remedied by providing any sufficient and non-arbitrary *grounds* or reasons for designating things, acts, or agents in certain ways, our conventional designations are provided a non-conventional basis, and strong nominalism in matters moral is accordingly rescinded. No tenable normative justification can be found amongst strongly nominalist moral theories, whether Hume's or any other. Less radical forms of nominalism may avoid this objection, but only by conceding much to objectivism and to (non-sentiment-based) justificatory reasoning in matters moral. Such concessions are precisely what most contemporary neo-Humean moral philosophers seek above all to avoid.

[19] The currency of 'preferences' within contemporary philosophy reflects the ever more pervasive and corrosive influence of conventionalism, whether acknowledged or otherwise. For discussion, see Westphal (2015b).

Hume adroitly notes the following requirement for criticizing or rejecting his moral theory:

> I must therefore, on this occasion, rest contented with requiring the two following conditions of any one that would undertake to clear up this system. First, as moral good and evil belong only to the actions of the mind, and are derived from our situation with regard to external objects, the relations from which these moral distinctions arise must lie only betwixt internal actions and external objects, and must not be applicable either to internal actions, compared among themselves, or to external objects, when placed in opposition to other external objects. For as morality is supposed to attend certain relations, if these relations could belong to internal actions considered singly, it would follow, that we might be guilty of crimes in ourselves, and independent of our situation with respect to the universe; and in like manner, if these moral relations could be applied to external objects, it would follow that even inanimate beings would be susceptible of moral beauty and deformity. Now, it seems difficult to imagine that any relation can be discovered betwixt our passions, volitions, and actions, compared to external objects, which relation might not belong either to these passions and volitions, or to these external objects, compared among themselves.
>
> (*T* 3.1.1.22/SBN 464)

Likewise, when rejecting the view that justice is or can be a natural virtue, Hume contends:

> If any one, therefore, would assert that justice is a natural virtue, and injustice a natural vice, he must assert that abstracting from the notions of property and right and obligation a certain conduct and train of actions, in certain external relations of objects, has naturally a moral beauty or deformity, and causes an original pleasure or uneasiness. Thus the restoring a man's goods to him is considered as virtuous, not because nature has annexed a certain sentiment of pleasure to such a conduct with regard to the property of others, but because she has annexed that sentiment to such a conduct, with regard to those external objects of which others have had the first or long possession, or which they have received by the consent of those who have had first or long possession. If nature has given us no such sentiment, there is not naturally, nor antecedent to human conventions, any such thing as property. Now, though it seems sufficiently evident, in this dry and accurate consideration of the present subject, that nature has annexed no pleasure or sentiment of approbation to such a conduct, yet, that I may leave as little room for doubt as possible, I shall subjoin a few more arguments to confirm my opinion.
>
> (*T* 3.4.6.4/SBN 527)

I submit that in his fragment of a theory of justice, Hume himself met these two challenges brilliantly. Justice can indeed consist in relations—

complex social relations—and neither in any merely natural facts, nor in any features of objects such as might be descried purely by reasoning. (That is the second challenge Hume issues to would-be critics; *T* 3.1.1.23/SBN 465.) As complex social relations, the principles justice involved in rightful acquisition, possession, and use are literally artefacts. Yet because such principles of justice are indispensable to human life, both individually and collectively, it is indeed proper to call them (normative) 'laws of nature' (*T* 3.2.1.19/SBN 484; above, §7). Moreover, these principles, practices, and relations hold (to whatever extent they do hold) and are just (to whatever extent they are just in any instantiation, i.e., institutionalization), for reasons Hume provides in his integrated solution to the five social coordination problems detailed above (§11), regardless of how any individuals or groups happen to respond affectively to any relevant instance or act. Hume's sentiment theory of morals rests on a fallacy of neglecting a cogent alternative, precisely the alternative he himself pioneered in his fragment of a theory of justice, the alternative I have designated 'Natural Law Constructivism'.

Insofar as Hume was concerned only to examine and explain morality, this is not, of itself, an objection. Unfortunately, the primary, merely descriptive and explanatory aims of Hume's moral philosophy (above §§11.1, 12, 13.1) are widely disregarded by contemporary Humean moralists, who believe they can find much more normative justification in Hume's moral philosophy than it does or can provide.

Providing cogent normative credentials for Natural Law Constructivism is a considerable task, initiated by Rousseau's *Du contrat social* (Westphal 2013d) and, as shall be detailed in the remainder, achieved by Kant. Kant's moral philosophy, too, requires a 'practical anthropology', but this anthropology has not to do with our sentiments, but with our capacities to act and to suffer, and with our corresponding incapacities as finite, embodied, incompletely rational agents. Kant's Natural Law Constructivism avoids the subjectivism and relativism latent (if not explicit) in contemporary forms of more constructivism and in Hume's sentiment-based ethics by appeal to a fundamental principle of rational justification (in non-formal domains) and shrewd, minimal appeal to practical anthropology. These are the keys to a robust justificatory externalism regarding basic moral principles, in particular, those of justice.

17 Justification and Motivation

17.1 Reasons: 'internal' and 'external'

Hume's moral sentiments can at most belong to an account of moral perception and belief; they are neither the sole nor the sufficient basis for determining whether our moral beliefs or judgments are correct, nor for justifying our moral beliefs, judgments, or principles normatively. This result provides a suitable context for setting aside another debate between Hume's and Kant's partisans: whether justifying reasons are inherently motivating. This debate concerns a bevy of issues arrayed under the heading of 'internalism' and 'externalism' about justifying reasons for action. A minimal version of 'reasons internalism' holds that any reason which can be a justifying reason for action can also motivate, or contribute to motivating, that action. Famously Kant holds that the feeling of respect for the moral law, which occurs when one recognizes that an action is obligatory because it is morally required, and ought to be done because it is so required, is the sole effect of pure practical reason upon our sensible nature and is the sole morally worthy motive (*GMS* 4:401 note, 403). Equally famously Hume denies that reason alone can motivate; that even correct and cogent reasoning about what ought to be done can only motivate by the concomitance of a sentiment favouring so acting (*T* 2.3.3/SBN 413–8). So far as reason alone can determine, Hume claims:

> It is not contrary to reason to prefer the destruction of the whole world to the scratching of my finger. It is not contrary to reason for me to choose my total ruin, to prevent the least uneasiness of an Indian, or person wholly unknown to me. It is as little contrary to reason to prefer even my own acknowledged lesser good to my greater, and have a more ardent affection for the former than the latter.
>
> (*T* 2.3.3.6/SBN 416)

Hume's contention is predicated upon a notoriously limited account of 'reason', reiterated immediately before this passage, as including only logical deduction and the ascertainment of truth. So far as only 'preferences' are at issue, as Hume here states, no issues about moral justification—right, wrong, or permissibility—are engaged, unless justification, too, is restricted in two portentous ways. First, moral justification must be restricted to justificatory internalism: the thesis that moral justification can only consist in justifying a moral claim or principle *to* some individual agent by appeal solely to that agent's acknowledged reasons or grounds for acting. Second, the agent's reasons or grounds for acting must be restricted to feelings, attitudes, or sentiments *pro* or *contra*, in a word, to his or her 'preferences' or 'motivational set'. All three restrictions—one upon the scope and character of 'reason', two upon moral justification—are required for the above passage to bear upon issues of moral justification. Contemporary Humeans have too readily accepted these restrictions, uncritically, with too little notice or reflection.

17.2 The belief-desire model of action

Sometimes these restrictions are buttressed by claiming, or at least presuming, that moral theory must use a simple belief-desire model of human action. This simple model may suffice for various branches of economic or sociological theory, but theirs is not the task of providing an adequate moral assessment of the reasoning, deliberation, or action of any individual agent. Two points should be noted. The first order of business in moral philosophy is assessing actions or character normatively; 'explaining' actions is no special prerogative of moral philosophers. Second, the fact that we behave in ways which, when aggregated across groups, can be modelled on the basis of a simple belief-desire model of action, does not prove that the belief-desire model is either correct or adequate as an account of individual human agency, quite aside from considerations of the extent to which heavily commercialized modern societies tend to train us to behave and to think as if the belief-desire model is true of us. Behaving in such ways boosts sales, of course, though it is hardly sufficient for a full human life.[20] That economic theory can be used to explain many individual choices and actions (Levitt and Dubner, 2006) shows only that many individuals are instrumentally rational rather than foolish and wasteful. That we tend on the whole to maximize our individual utility is insufficient to show that we are nothing but rational individual utility maximizers. Economic explanations of individual choices and actions do not warrant concluding that human reason is merely instrumental. That Rawls (1971) elected

[20] The old Roman maxim for prolonged rule: bread and circuses, has now been superceded by 'shop 'till you drop' and 'sex and drugs and rock n' roll'. We are unlikely ever to be rid of sexism because it is too useful to marketers.

to argue on the basis of an essentially economic, belief-desire model of human agency was a strategic concession to empiricists who were sceptical about the Kantian principles of justice Rawls advocated. He sought to derive his conclusions from their premises. This is not to endorse those premises.

17.3 Causal theories of the mental

Despite the current vogue of 'causal theories' of knowledge, of mind, of language, and of action, the belief-desire model provides no adequate basis for such 'theories'. Our use of causal locutions to describe mental processes is unexceptional, but causal theorists in philosophy neglect the important question raised by Kant, whether we are entitled to a constitutive construal of our causal locutions in connection with mental, behavioural, or linguistic phenomena. Kant argued cogently that we are not, because we are only able to make legitimate causal judgments about *spatio*-temporal objects and events, and indeed, that we can only make (candidate) cognitive judgments about particulars we have localized within space and time (Westphal 2004, §§8, 9, 36, 61, 62). For present purposes, this more general point suffices: causal description does not, of itself, suffice for casual *a*scription to any particular alleged causes (i.e., for predication or attribution), and causal *a*scription as such suffices neither for accurate nor for *justified* causal ascription. Only well-justified, accurate causal ascription counts as knowledge, and that is provided only by actual causal explanation of specified events we have specifically located in space and time. The causal descriptions considered in philosophical 'theories' of mental and behavioural phenomena are too vague to provide even determinate causal *a*scription; i.e., they do not suffice for ascription of causal characteristics *to* any purported mental events or states, and so cannot suffice for justified (or even for sufficiently accurate) causal belief about or knowledge of those events or states. They are 'theories' in name only, but so used the term verges upon a *flatus vocum*.

An important point of Kant's analysis and justification of causal judgment in the *Critique of Pure Reason* is that the causal *principle*, that every event has a cause, is not, as such, a justified causal *law* that every event has a sufficient cause.[21] The causal principle is a presupposition

[21] Yes, Kant often states the thesis of causal determinism generally, to hold of psychological as well as spatio-temporal phenomena, and he often claims to have justified this

of any and all causal inquiry. It is a regulative principle of natural science, of forensic science, and of much of common sense, always to seek causal explanations of phenomena. However, this regulative principle does not itself justify any causal description of a phenomenon, nor the ascription to that phenomenon of various causal characteristics or factors. The ascription of causal characteristics to any phenomenon is only cognitively justified by its successful causal explanation. Only an empirically justified causal explanation of a phenomenon can justify a constitutive interpretation of the causal locutions used to describe and to explain that phenomenon. Even after a truly marvellous 'decade (or two or three) of the brain' in neurophysiology, it will take many more such decades even to verge upon plausible causal explanations of mental contents, thoughts, beliefs, desires, reasonings, or decisions. Contemporary causal theories of mind, etc., are running on unredeemed and, for the foreseeable future, unredeemable promissory notes. These points, which may only be summarized here, I examine and defend in detail in Westphal (2004), §§61–2, (2012b) and (2016a). My analysis there provides good reason to concur with Strawson (1962, 1) that the first problem about freedom and causal determinism is to understand exactly what the problem is supposed to be.[22]

Insofar as Hume's own analysis of justice shows that certain actions are just or unjust, regardless of any agent's motives or preferences and regardless of any observer's sentiments (*per* above, §§10, 11), Hume's own analysis of justice shows that the three restrictions noted above (about motivation and justification, §17.1 end) are unwarranted. Most importantly, Hume's own analysis of the three rules of justice develops the rudiments of an externalist approach to moral justification, according to which the justificatory status of a moral claim or principle need

thesis. However, in these two regards Kant greatly overstated his demonstrated results. Nevertheless, he does justify his key thesis, *contra* Hume, that we human beings can only be self-conscious if we are conscious of at least some causally interacting physical objects in our surroundings. I mention this only to clarify somewhat my assertion here. Settling these issues is not required for the tenability of Hume's and Kant's Natural Law Constructivism. For the detailed examination these issues about causal judgment and causal knowledge require, see my (2004); cf. George (2007); Harper (2007); and Westphal (2007a, 2007b, 2016a).

[22] For an illuminating attempt to unravel many current confusions about 'naturalism' in these connections, see Rouse (2002). For detailed discussion of contemporary neuroscience and (putative) determinism regarding human behaviour, see Falkenburg (2012).

not depend upon an agent's acknowledged reasons or grounds for acting, so that moral justification is not limited to justifying a moral claim or principle *to* particular agents. This is central to the approach I here call 'Natural Law Constructivism'.

17.4 Game theory

Many interesting results are available through game-theoretic analysis,[23] but as in social contract theories, almost everything depends upon the presumed circumstances, capacities, and 'motivational sets' of individuals, stipulated by any particular game-theoretic analysis.[24] Rather too often, they are stipulated so as to obtain roughly the theorist's desired results. Accordingly, game-theoretic analyses, like social contract theories, contribute significantly to explicating various principles and practices, and their implications for groups of various sizes over various periods of time. Such results are significant, but they neither do nor can identify or justify the most basic moral principles. The main reason for this is that, insofar as game-theoretic analyses seek to justify moral principles or practices, they are restricted to justificatory internalism and to various forms of instrumental reasoning. I have previously averred that this restriction is an unnecessary capitulation to moral scepticism. The re-examination of Hume's theory of justice in the present chapter provides an initial articulation of, and case for, the justificatory externalism provided by Natural Law Constructivism. My case for Hume's and Kant's Natural Law Constructivism, and so also for justificatory externalism in basic matters moral, continues in the sequel.

17.5 Is philosophy motivationally competent?

Before turning to Kant's development of Natural Law Constructivism in chapter 5, one last word about motivation in moral philosophy.

[23] See, e.g., Axelrod (1984); Skyrms (1996); Hargreaves-Heap and Varoufakis (2004). These formal studies, however, should be supplemented by the substantive investigations by Becker (1986); Baier (1995); Uslaner (2002); Gintis et al. (2005); and Bowles and Gintis (2011).

[24] Hardin (2007) shows that interesting results can be obtained in this way from Hume's theory of justice. If the analysis presented here is correct, Hardin's essay presents neither the whole, nor the most important features, of Hume's theory of justice. For discussion of Hardin's approach, see Barry (2010).

Regarding allegations of the fundamentally selfish character of human nature, Hume observed:

> I am sensible that, generally speaking, the representations of this quality [*viz.*, selfishness] have been carried much too far; and that the descriptions which certain philosophers delight so much to form of mankind in this particular, are as wide of nature as any accounts of monsters which we meet with in fables and romances. So far from thinking that men have no affection for any thing beyond themselves, I am of opinion that, though it be rare to meet with one who loves any single person better than himself, yet it is as rare to meet with one in whom all the kind affections, taken together, do not overbalance all the selfish.
>
> (*T* 3.2.2.5/SBN 486)

Hume's observation is guardedly modest, and rightly so. Greater precision than this on the subject of human motivation is not to be gained by philosophical means alone, except to add that, generally speaking, we can fulfil moral (and other) obligations simply because they are our obligations. This is central to Hobbes' account of obligation, too; according to Hobbes, we are obligated to perform our covenants, even if our interests or motives happen to change in the interim.[25] In moral philosophy our circumstance is not that we must tailor our account of moral obligation to fit our antecedent presumptions about human motivation. It is rather the reverse: because human motivation is in so many ways due to human cultivation, it is human motivation which must be brought into accord—via upbringing, culture, and education—with our moral obligations.[26] And where this is not possible, this calls for various forms of support or intervention, or in unfortunate cases, social or psychopathology, or indeed restraint or incarceration.[27]

Kant, too, occasionally staked too much on moral motivation, claiming that respect for the moral law is the sole morally worthy motive, and that it is the sole effect of practical reason itself upon human sensibility. Despite his own claims that the only motive which is to the moral credit of the agent is the motive of duty, and that acting on mix motives risks moral corruption, ultimately Kant admits that mixed motives are

[25] That Hobbes does not espouse psychological egoism in *Leviathan* I argue in the Appendix (§44).

[26] See Fraiberg (1959); Winnicott (1964); Curren (2000); Green (1999).

[27] See, e.g., Rutschky (1977); Miller (1980, 1981); Baron-Cohen (2013).

inevitable for our human form of finite rational agency (see Westphal 1991a, §V.3).

Kant's concession is important, also as a reminder that, like 'the' state of nature or 'the' social contract, philosophers strongly tend to sketch theories of human motivation to suit their antecedent theoretical convictions and aims, so that philosophical accounts of human motivation are hardly fit to serve as independent premises for justifying criteria of right, permissible, or justifiable action or agreement. Once it is recognized that moral philosophy need not limit itself to internalist accounts of justification (i.e., those restricted to justifying a claim, act, or principle *to* an individual by appeal to that person's antecedent commitments), issues of moral motivation take their proper subsidiary place, which is philosophically advantageous because psychology is no special province of philosophical expertise—so much so, that one may well wonder about the motives of those philosophers who insist upon the centrality of issues of motivation to moral philosophy.[28]

17.6 Explanation, justification, and points of view

In *The Sources of Normativity* (1996), Christine Korsgaard claims that the explanation of moral behaviour is a third-person affair, whereas 'the normative question' of moral philosophy arises in the first person:

> The question how we explain moral behaviour is a third-person, theoretical question, a question about why a certain species of intelligent animals behaves in a certain way. The normative question is a first-person question that arises for the moral agent who must actually do what morality says. When you want to know what a philosopher's theory of normativity is, you must place yourself in the position of an *agent* on whom morality is making a difficult claim. You then ask the philosopher: must I really do this? Why must I do it? And his answer is his answer to the normative question.
>
> (Korsgaard 1996, 16)

This is her conclusion to her clarification of 'the normative question' and 'where in [the] enterprise [of moral philosophy]' it arises (§1.2.1; p. 10). She immediately reiterates the first-person character of 'the' normative question in the first paragraph of her subsequent sub-section:

[28] Wood (2014, 41–2, 65–7) neglects the prospects of justificatory externalism in moral philosophy, and the enormous contributions to justificatory externalism made by Kant's Natural Law Constructivism.

> To be successful, there are three conditions which the answer must meet. All of these conditions spring from the position from which the normative question arises, the first-person position of the agent who demands a justification of the claims which morality makes upon him.
>
> (Korsgaard 1996, 16; §1.2.2)

Certainly normative questions arise in the first-person singular as 'What ought I do?', yet neither the first-person nor the singular forms monopolize the normative questions of moral philosophy; they arise equally well second- and third-person, and equally well singular or plural. The question 'What is to be done?' makes equally good normative, moral sense third-person: 'What ought he, she, or they do?', second person (singular or plural): 'What ought you to do?', or first-person plural: 'What ought we to do?' The normative questions involved in identifying and justifying what persons ought to do arise in each and all of these grammatical, personal, social, and juridical forms. Likewise, so do explanatory questions about why people behave as they do or did. These arise not only in the singular or in plural forms, they arise third-person, and also second-person as one seeks to understand one's friends', colleagues', or mate's actions; or indeed also first-person, when one attempts to understand, for example, how one blundered, whether some time ago or immediately beforehand. At times we can do no more or better than to explain ourselves and apologize and compensate for our ineptitude, error, or incontinence.

It should not be necessary to etch these distinctions between explanatory and justificatory (normative, moral) questions about human behaviour, and how both kinds of question can arise in whatever grammatical or personal formulae may be germane, but for how lax philosophers have become about the use or abuse of the term 'explanation'. Earlier in that same sub-section, in the middle of her attempt to clarify 'the normative question', Korsgaard of course recognizes that 'the normative question' can easily arise second person:

> If I claim that you ought to face death rather than do a certain wrong action, I had better be prepared to back that claim up with an account of what makes the action wrong which is powerful enough to show that something worth dying for is at stake. But really this demand on moral theory is always there. Even when the claims of morality are not so dramatic, they are pervasive in our expectations of ourselves and each other. So these claims must be justified. That is the normative question.
>
> (Korsgaard 1996, 13)

This statement, I submit, is more accurate: 'the' normative question of moral philosophy concerns how our duties, prohibitions, and permissions are rightly identified and justified *as* moral obligations or permissions, whomever they may specifically concern.

Korsgaard (1996, 15) errs, however, in linking moral justification to motivation to behave morally. This is where and how Korsgaard unwittingly though unreservedly adopts justificatory internalism. This is the first condition she stipulates upon any successful answer to 'the normative question':

> First, the answer must actually succeed in *addressing* someone in that position. . . . [*Viz*., of . . .] an agent who doubts whether he must really do what morality says also doubts whether it's so bad to be morally bad, so the bare possibility of this sort of criticism settles nothing. And I think it can be misleading to try to imagine what we might helpfully say, in the second person, to some *other* agent who challenges morality's claims. After all, some other agent might refuse to listen to reason, or to listen at all. He might be insincere and contentious; he might just be looking for a way to evade his duty, rather than asking the question because he really wants to know. For this exercise to work, we have to eliminate these possibilities, and imagine that this other agent is sincere and reasonable, and does really want to know.
>
> (Korsgaard 1996, 16)

About these considerations she claims:

> . . . that just shows that the answer we need is really the first-person answer, the one that satisfies *us* when we *ourselves* ask the normative question.
>
> (Korsgaard 1996, 16–17)

Motivation is morally important, indeed crucial, but it is distinct from issues of justification, and belongs much more to the domain of moral education than to moral philosophy (Green 1999; Curren 2014). Kant recognized this in his fundamental distinction between hypothetical and categorical, moral imperatives. This is not at all to deny that reason can be practical; it is merely to deny that the practical, action-guiding capacities of moral reasoning can be identified or justified merely by philosophical analysis of moral reasons, moral reasoning, or human motivation(s).

5

Kant's Principles of Moral Constructivism

18 Introduction

Kant's *Groundwork of the Metaphysics of Morals* is justly famous, though he insisted that it is not self-contained. Kant's *Groundwork* must be considered within the corpus of his major writings in practical philosophy: *The Critique of Practical Reason*, *The Metaphysics of Morals*, and much of his *Religion within the Bounds of Reason Alone*, along with his several essays on ethics and politics.[1] Kant knew first hand that whoever inaugurates a new kind of systematic inquiry must begin with an initial conception of the proposed system, which inevitably is revised and improved through its development (*KdrV* A834/B862). This holds true of Kant's mature, properly Critical moral philosophy, first enunciated in the *Groundwork* but only completed in much later works. This chapter considers the centrality of principles in Kant's moral philosophy, their distinctively 'Kantian' character, why Kant presents a 'metaphysical' system of moral principles, and how these 'formal' principles are to be used in practice. These points are central to how Kant thinks pure reason can be practical.[2] These features have often puzzled Anglophone readers,

[1] All collected chronologically in Kant (1996) (*CEWK*); also pertinent are large sections of the Dialectic of the *Critique of Pure Reason*.

[2] Kant's central focus on moral principles has been questioned by some proponents of moral particularism. 'Moral particularism' is a genre of moral theories, rather than a specific moral theory (see Crisp 1998). At its most modest, it holds that moral principles do not suffice to guide moral perception, decision, or action. About this, Kant agrees (*KdrV* A132–4/B171–4); there is no eliminating the need for moral judgment. At its most extreme, moral particularism holds that moral principles are not at all required for moral perception, decision, and action. I argue against this extreme view, on Kant's behalf, in Westphal (2012a).

whose default orientation is pervasively empiricist. Having seen how Hume's theory of justice undermines both the centrality and the purported sufficiency of moral sentiments for moral theory, we may begin by considering Kant's criticisms of moral empiricism, which highlight those same shortcomings, which are shared by contemporary forms of moral constructivism.

19 Kant's Critique of Moral Empiricism

Practical principles aim (at a minimum) to indicate how to act rightly, in everyday life and in uncommonly problematic circumstances, by distinguishing moral right from wrong, good from bad, and permissible from impermissible. If we stipulate, as Kant does, that a purely rational agent is one who decides how to act and who acts solely on the basis of rationally justified moral principles, then moral principles, in conjunction with information about circumstances of action, simply describe how such an agent behaves (cf. *TL* 6:383). For such a being, moral principles are normative because they define or specify right action, as distinct to wrong or merely permissible (optional) action. Yet for a pure rational agent, normative moral principles are not *imperatives*, because *ex hypothesi* such an agent only acts as morality requires or permits. Notoriously, of course, human beings can and do depart from what morality requires. For us, normative moral principles are also imperatives because such principles indicate how we ought to behave, even if we fail to behave ourselves (*TL* 6:379–80).

This prescriptive character of morality, both as norms and as imperatives, is one reason Kant holds that moral principles cannot be identified or justified by empirical methods alone. Famously, Hume argued that normative conclusions do not follow from factual premises alone ('is' does not imply 'ought'), not at least without the intervention of a sentiment (*T* 3.1.1.27/SBN 469–70), which as a class Hume contrasted sharply with reason. Whether such sentiments are regarded as necessary for drawing normative conclusions, or instead as the sole and sufficient basis for drawing such conclusions (Hume espouses both views in various passages), Kant is suspicious about the purported roles of sentiments or other affective states in moral *reasoning*, especially that reasoning involved in identifying and justifying basic moral principles.

Kant's reasons for caution are highlighted by Mill's counterpart empiricist view in *Utilitarianism*:

> If the end which the utilitarian doctrine proposes to itself were not, in theory and in practice, acknowledged to be an end, nothing could ever convince any person that it was so. No reason can be given why the general happiness is desirable, except that each person, so far as he believes it to be attainable, desires his own happiness.
>
> (J. S. Mill 1861, *CW* 10:234)

This passage begins with the issue of justifying the principle of utility to particular individuals, and then makes a perhaps stronger statement about what can justify the principle of utility as such. In both regards Mill appeals to a (presumed) empirical fact, that each human being does desire his or her own happiness. Both Hume and Mill appeal directly and ineliminably to affective states, including sentiments and desires, to identify and to justify basic moral principles, and these affective states are also linked, in their views, with our motives for action (cf. Williams 1981).

These historical views recur today. For example, Zimmerman (1983) argues that moral obligation is linked to rational, though hypothetical motivation, and that this is consistent with linking justifying with motivating reasons. He states:

> If the principles generated by a rational motivation theory are going to have force for a given challenger, he must accept the rational constraints built into the derivational mechanism (like consistency and epistemic acceptability) and also whatever normative constraints might be built in.
>
> (Zimmerman 1983, 469)

> There is no chance to . . . bridge the gap between actual and hypothetical motivation, unless the challenger at least has an actual commitment to the constraints of rationality built into the derivational mechanism.
>
> (Zimmerman 1983, 472)

This minimum requirement, however, opens the gap Zimmerman seeks to close. He recognizes (464) that deriving 'obligations from actual motivations makes evasion far too easy'. Presuming 'an actual commitment to the [preferred] constraints of rationality' also makes moral evasion far too easy. This is why Kant holds that moral obligations are categorical, not hypothetical: our obligations do not depend upon our motives, etc., whether *de facto* or idealized (*GMS* 4:414).[3] It is exactly in this regard alone that moral imperatives, according to Kant, are 'categorical' rather than 'hypothetical': moral imperatives are obligatory regardless of whatever one may happen to want to do or avoid (cf. Wagner 1994).

Accordingly, one of Kant's concerns about empiricist moral theories is: what are we to make morally either of the truly apathetic—those who lack affect altogether, whether by nature, socialization, or practice—or of those whose affects lead them to act contrary to what we ordinarily and uncontroversially regard as minimum moral standards? If, say, typical human affects strongly favoured murder and mayhem, could such affects identify, justify, or motivate such actions *as* morally right? Can moral empiricism reject such scenarios without rescinding empiricism?[4] These questions are not arguments, yet they highlight Kant's concern that specifying right action, our obligations so to act, and our motivating reasons for so acting must not be hostage to something so varied and variable as human sentiments (cf. *GMS* 4:444, *KdpV* 5:158): our affects, sentiments, motives, 'commitments', or, for example, validity claims require moral assessment as much as do our decisions and behaviour. Apt feelings are of course central to proper and to virtuous action, in part because they are central to proper appreciation of morally salient features of our circumstances of action.[5] However, whether feelings *are*

[3] Zimmerman (1983, 476) acknowledges the Humean character of the various strategies for linking justifying with motivating reasons; cf. Foot (1972). He grants (1983, 476–7) that his reasons for rejecting Kantian views are 'dogmatic'; they are also under-informed and inadequate (see *infra*, §§17, 27).

[4] In this connection it is important to reject the common notion that empiricism has a monopoly on the empirical; much of Kant's decidedly anti-empiricist and anti-rationalist theory of empirical knowledge in the *Critique of Pure Reason* is sound (see esp. Westphal 2004; Bird 2006); there Kant first develops his sophisticated accounts of rational judgment and justification, which are extended and further refined in subsequent works. The important point here is that Kant's Critical philosophy is the first to provide a sound alternative to Hume's Verification Empiricism ('Hume's fork'), in part by recognizing that strict logical deduction suffices for justification only within formal or (as Kant thinks of them) analytic domains (*scientia*), so that rational justification in substantive (non-formal, non-analytic) domains, including morals, requires more than logical deduction, though it is not, for that reason, restricted to merely empirical justification (*historia*). These results stand independently of Kant's Transcendental Idealism, and sharply distinguish his Critical philosophy from empiricism and rationalism, both historical and contemporary. For discussion of these points about justification, see Westphal (2013b, 2014a).

[5] See Herman (1993, 73–93, 2007).

appropriate is not adequately specified by *feelings* of appropriateness. These issues vitiate much of Hume's ethical theory, as he made plain in his theory of justice, or so I have argued in chapters 3 and 4.

These issues also vitiate contemporary neo-Humean constructivist moral theories, which follow the model of Hume's ethical theory and its strategies. If affective states, moral intuitions, or shared commitments (etc.) are taken as the *basic* materials for constructing a moral theory (§5.2, Steps 1, 2), the principles identified and justified on such bases (Step 3) can aspire to no more than generality holding across whatever group of agents happens to be like-minded about those basics (cf. *KdpV* 5:58–9). In principle no such constructivist theory can provide resources for assessing and rationally resolving moral disputes between groups of agents who disagree about those basics, or about the proper forms of construction for moral theories based upon them. In principle such forms of constructivism are ill designed to avoid or to resolve problems about moral conventionalism, relativism, or *petitio principii*. This is to recall the point noted above (§§5, 6), in view of Hume's corroboration of the vagaries of moral sentiments and designations (§§15, 16).

Social contract models for identifying or justifying basic practical norms confront a similar basic problem: because contract models can only appeal to reasons or grounds which potential contractors avow, they are incapable of addressing anyone who disregards or denies important features of his or her circumstances, obligations, or entitlements. Hence such models are powerless against the socially obstinate, namely egoists, who are to social philosophy what radical sceptics are to epistemology. The prospect of correcting someone's understanding—or rather misunderstanding—of society and of him- or herself in relation to it directly challenges the radical contractarian strategy because grounds for correcting anyone's understanding of relevant matters may suffice to justify some basic social principles and practices, regardless of anyone's contractarian agreement. More precisely, the prospect of providing sufficient reasons to justify certain principles and practices of social interaction regardless of anyone's express recognition of those reasons would render contractarian agreement redundant, revealing it to be a dispensable epicycle on a more fundamental non-contractarian justificatory analysis, such as Hume's and Kant's Natural Law Constructivism. (This objection to contractarianism is substantiated in chapter 7; cf. O'Neill 2000b.)

If Kant's search for a fundamental moral principle, universally valid across all rational agents, may look quaint or quixotic, we must refresh our appreciation of the problems confronting the entire Modern natural law tradition—and confronting us world-wide today—of identifying sufficient, multi-laterally justifiable principles of conduct governing public life, both domestically and internationally, which, when institutionalized, provide the minimum sufficient, legitimate (morally justifiable) principles and institutions required to solve fundamental problems of social coordination and thus to establish peace and to enable prosperity, whilst acknowledging fundamental substantive disagreements between our various understandings of a good or a pious life.[6] Concretely, these problems confronted Modern moral philosophers in controversies over international maritime trade, religious schisms, and the Thirty Years War in Europe. Though neglected by Christian natural lawyers, the Crusades were another important, prior case in point. These kinds of very real problems can easily escalate into irreconcilable conflicts of interest and bi- or multi-lateral *petitio principii*, as Kant knew (*KdpV* 5:63). These conflicts thrust the issue of identifying and justifying adequate, multi-laterally acceptable criteria of right, wrong, and permissible action onto the agenda of Modern moral philosophy. They are amongst Kant's central reasons for developing a distinctive, carefully qualified kind of moral rationalism (*KdpV* 5:70–1).

20 The Objects of Pure Practical Reason

20.1 How practical is reason?

To address the concerns just indicated, pure reason must be practical: reason itself must be able to specify morally legitimate principles, aims, and actions, and not merely calculate the most effective ways of attaining ends to which we are antecedently committed (*KdpV* 5:62). This is not, quixotically, to neglect or omit our ends, nor to disregard the contexts in which we act, but rather to require us to act towards our ends only insofar as such ends and the actions we take to achieve them are morally permissible or obligatory. Kant aims to show, *pace* Hume (*T* 2.3.3.4/SBN

[6] See Schneewind (1991). This point was the downfall of pre-Modern natural law theory, which presumed general agreement about the good, pious life; cf. below, §40.

414–15), that reason is not simply the calculative slave of the passions. This independence of reason from our particular ends is fundamental to Kant's sense of the 'autonomy' of reason (*KdpV* 5:42).[7]

Kant recognized that to suppose that pure reason can be practical in this sense is strange and unparalleled (*KdpV* 5:31). To develop this prospect, Kant inquires whether the concept of the morally right can be specified by examples of (purported) morally good objects; or can morally good objects only be specified by use of an independent, antecedent concept of what is morally right?[8] If the concept of right is specified by examples of (purported) morally good objects, questions directly arise about how we identify such objects, adequately and reliably, and distinguish them from others which are morally indifferent or morally bad, along with questions posed above (§§6, 9, 15, 19) about how to achieve sufficient agreement, in theory and in practice, about which objects are which.

Kant uses a version of Socrates' question to Euthyphro (above, §5) to underscore the priority of our conception of what is morally right over any and all examples of what (purportedly) is morally good. Kant contends that conceiving the divinity as the paragon of moral perfection presupposes rather than defines our concept of moral perfection, and that we can only recognize the holiness of the Christian saviour by using our prior and independent concept of moral perfection (*GMS* 4:408–9).

This summary of Kant's reasons for seeking a basic *a priori* principle of morality suffices to understand some important points of Kant's analysis of an 'object of pure practical reason' (*KdpV* 5:57–71). An 'object' of practical reason is something to be obtained by free action. By definition *pure* practical reason omits all empirical desires, motives,

[7] That ethical egoists reject the autonomy of reason (in this sense) does not, of itself, show that Kant's project is ill conceived or mistaken, nor does the logical consistency of ethical egoism show that Kant's justification of a more robust moral philosophy fails. To suppose that it does is to presume the deductivist ideal of justification (*scientia*), to which Kant's Critical philosophy develops a cogent alternative in the non-formal domains of knowledge and morals (also see *TL* 6:386). If the reader finds §§20–3 forbidding, the basic points are recapped in chapter 6. The points summarized herein are neglected by Bittner (2010) and by Geuss (2011), whose objections to Kant's views exhibit more impatience than charity, understanding, or insight.

[8] *KdpV* 5:62. Kant's question should not be assimilated to Ross's (1930) question about which has priority, the right or the good, nor to Broad's (1930) distinction between moral 'teleology' and 'deontology'; his distinction obscures rather than illuminates Kant's view (*KdpV* 5:63–4; cf. Herman 1993, 208–40).

urges, inclinations, or preferences and all consideration of the agent's capacities and resources for achieving ends. An object of pure practical reason, accordingly, is one obtained by free action, regardless of any physical or physiological constraints on capacity or feasibility, and of any merely elective goals or motives of action. Hence the sole question regarding whether something is an object of pure practical reason is whether it is possible to will to achieve or to bring about this object, were the agent able so to do. This question has only two answers: necessarily the moral good is an object of pure practical reason; necessarily the morally evil is not.

The definition of pure practical reason, Kant's severe reservations about moral empiricism, and his aim to avoid *petitio principii* about the most basic principles of moral obligation, together entail that the most basic practical principle must concern the form, rather than the matter (i.e. the particular objects or ends) of the will's determining ground (*KdpV* 5:27). Any such principle must be a rational rather than an empirical principle because it can be neither defined nor justified (sufficiently) by empirically given ends, desires, or motives.

Furthermore, any will which can determine how to act solely on the basis of such a principle must be negatively free from the influence of such empirical factors and positively free to decide how to act and to act, regardless of such factors.[9] Because a pure will omits all such empirical factors, it can only determine how to act by using a *concept* of how properly to act; any such concept must be a principle, and indeed a law, because at issue here are the necessary objects of a pure will, the good and the evil as such. Hence considerations pertaining only to individual, actual agents do not pertain to a pure will. Thus this principle of action must be a practical law holding of all free rational agents as such.

[9] Cf. *KdpV* 5:25, 28–9, 42, 65. Both decision and execution belong to the will; merely conceiving of an action or merely wishing to act (i.e., omitting any means or efforts to achieve an end) do not suffice to specify any concept of *will*. Kant's analysis raises concerns about trans-causal freedom and about his appeal to Transcendental Idealism to defend its possibility. However, Kant's analysis of the autonomy of rational judgment suffices to justify the freedom of rational judgment, in cognition and in morals, without appeal to Transcendental Idealism (Westphal 2004, §61, 2012b, 2016a; cf. below, §27), or to Kant's purported 'Fact of Reason' (*KdpV* 5:31–2), on which see Wolff (2009). Kant's analysis also justifies important cautions against the appeal by moral philosophers to belief-desire models of individual action (cf. above, §17).

20.2 Law and maxims

A law, Kant claims, has only two aspects: its matter, i.e. the objects or states of affairs to which it pertains, and its legislative (law-like) form. Because the will as pure practical reason prescinds from such objects, only the legislative form of a practical law can provide the ground upon which the pure will can determine how to act and to act, provided the will incorporates this ground into its own maxim (*KdpV* 5:29). A maxim is an individual agent's principle of action ('I shall so act . . . '), in contrast to the universal form of a practical law ('All are so to act . . . '). In this regard maxims are 'subjective' because they are agent-specific, in contrast to practical laws, which are 'objective' because they hold for all rational agents as such (*KdpV* 5:19). Maxims are 'subjective' in this specific sense because they are first-person; they are not restricted to agent-centred reasons. Kant's basic criterion for the moral status of maxims is whether one's maxim is suited to the universal form of practical legislation and thus can serve as a universal law. This is Kant's Fundamental Law (*Grundgesetz*) of Pure Practical Reason:

> So act that the maxim of your will could also always count as a principle of universal legislation.
>
> (*KdpV* 5:30)

Obviously, this is closely related to Kant's Formula of Universal Law (*GMS* 4:221). This principle is a criterion for maxims, which are agent specific, and is stated in imperative form. This *Grundgesetz* is, Kant contends, fundamental with regard to any agent's deliberation about how rightly to act.

Kant's fundamental criterion of right action as such (i.e., objectively) is announced only in his *Metaphysics of Morals*; this is Kant's Universal Principle of Justice (*Recht*):

> An act is *right* if it, or if according to its maxim, one's freedom of will can coexist with everyone's freedom in accord with a universal law.
>
> (*MdS* 6:230)[10]

[10] This passage from Kant's Introduction to *MdS*, §C, belongs neither to *RL* nor to *TL*, though it pertains to both. The Universal Principle of Justice specifies strict duties, most of which belong to justice, some to ethics. (All references to '*MdS*' are to Kant's Preface or Introduction to the *Metaphysics of Morals*.)

I say this is Kant's fundamental criterion for two reasons. First, this criterion of outward action determines which kinds of action are strict duties, because they are in each case morally prohibited or required. Mostly these are prohibitions. Specifying which kinds of action are broad (meritorious) duties requires a subsequent test on maxims found by this first criterion to be permissible. Determining which actions have ethical worth is the third step, subsequent to the first two, because Kant's account of the ethical worth of actions (like Mill's) concerns the motivation of right actions, namely that they are performed by an agent because they are right or dutiful. Accordingly, with regard to both the ethical worth of actions and with regard to broad or meritorious duties of virtue, Kant's Universal Principle of Justice, as the fundamental criterion of rightful outward action, is fundamental.

Kant's view is consistent, though we must attend to the specific roles and aims of Kant's various principles. In particular, we must be careful with Kant's repeated claim, early and late, that 'the' Categorical Imperative is 'the' (sole) fundamental principle of his practical philosophy, if the Categorical Imperative is taken to be his criterion for testing maxims and is thus taken to contrast with Kant's Universal Principle of Justice. What is objectively right and wrong, Kant contends, is specified by the moral law; the most fundamental criterion for specifying the moral law is Kant's Universal Principle of Justice. The basic criterion for agents to use in deliberation is Kant's Fundamental Law of Pure Practical Reason, or, as it is often designated, the Formula of Universal Law of the Categorical Imperative. These principles specify right action in the form of strict or perfect duties (*GMS* 4:421 note). Secondary to this fundamental specification of right action is the further specification, amongst right actions as such, of broad or meritorious duties (whether self- or other-regarding). These are the topic of Kant's *Doctrine of Virtue* (*TL*, *MdS*, Part 2). The better wisdom is to recognize that when claiming that 'the' Categorical Imperative is 'the' fundamental practical principle, Kant often uses 'Categorical Imperative' to designate a close-knit family of principles, based upon the objective Universal Principle of Justice and its complementary, subjective or first-person criterion, the Fundamental Law of Pure Practical Reason.[11]

[11] It is common to complain that Kant is often technical without being precise; more germane is the observation that Kant often develops distinctions or terminology only to the

21 The Structure of Kant's Practical Philosophy

How can focusing upon the universal legislative form of law discriminate among obligatory, permissible, and forbidden actions? Kant answers by noting that the relevant laws are norms by use of which a free rational will can determine how to act. Willing is a species of causality; the objects of the will are goals to be achieved by acting (*KdpV* 5:65). Consequently, judging the moral status (forbidden, permissible, or obligatory) of the alternative courses of action available in any situation requires considering what kind of rational will the agent is, morally salient features of the agent's situation, and the *types* of consequences and the implications of available courses of action. These modal categories of possible free acts (forbidden, permissible, obligatory) provide 'the transition from practical principles as such to the practical principles of morals' (*KdpV* 5:67). This 'transition' is not simply a restriction of scope, focusing upon a specifically moral sub-set of practical principles. The main point of Kant's transition is to move from the purely *a priori* principles of morals considered so far (§20) to more specific principles required for a doctrine of morals. This doctrine is, in a specifically Kantian sense, metaphysical. 'Metaphysics' in general, Kant holds, is 'a system of *a priori* knowledge from concepts alone' (*MdS* 6:216). If these concepts are *a priori*, their analysis provides a general metaphysics; if a specific, contingent, empirical concept is also included, the analysis provides a 'specific' metaphysics pertaining to that concept (and its instances). In this regard, Kant's *Critique of Pure Reason* provides a 'general metaphysics' of nature. Kant's *Metaphysical Foundations of Natural Science* (*GS* 4:470.1–12) provides a 'specific' metaphysics of nature by *a priori* analysis of the contingent concept 'matter' as 'the moveable in space'. Kant's 'general' metaphysics of morals is contained in the *Critique of Practical Reason* and in the Preface and Introduction to the *Metaphysics of Morals*. Kant's

extent required by his immediate discussion, though Kant's terminological flexibility underscores that his issues and analyses are more important than his terminology. Kant's method and practice reflect and are rooted in his appreciation of the difference between conceptual definition and conceptual analysis, on the one hand, and conceptual explication, on the other. Only stipulated or constructed concepts can be defined or (strictly speaking) analysed; all *a priori* and all empirical concepts can only be explicated (*KdrV* A726–30/B754–8).

'specific' metaphysics of morals results from *a priori* analysis of the contingent concept of our finite, human form of rational agency, as developed in his *Doctrines of Justice* and of *Virtue*, the two main parts of the body of his *Metaphysics of Morals*.

In both the *Groundwork* and in the *Metaphysics of Morals* Kant insists that his pure rational principles of practical reason require 'practical anthropology' to be applied to us as human beings, to generate specific moral injunctions or permissions (*GMS* 4:388, 412, *MdS* 6:216–17). This practical anthropology is a 'proper appendix' to Kant's practical philosophy (*TL* 6:469); it provides the contingent, determinate concept of our species of finite human rational agency, including pervasive features of our worldly context of action. Though Kant never composed this 'appendix', his examples and analyses of our moral obligations provide much information about it.[12]

Kant's frequent insistence that moral imperatives are categorical rather than hypothetical expresses his view that our moral obligations are not conditional upon whatever we happen to *want* to do or to avoid; they do not depend upon our contingent motives or ends (Wagner 1994). It is not at all Kant's view that our moral imperatives are unconditioned by our circumstances of action and our capacities to act: famously, Kant contends that no one can be obligated to do whatever she or he is incapable of doing; 'ought implies can', whereas 'cannot' implies 'cannot be obligated to' (*KdpV* 5:30, 125).

Kant's universalization tests also use the following principle governing instrumental reasoning, which Kant calls the Principle of Hypothetical Imperatives:

> Whoever wills the end, also wills (insofar as reason has decisive influence on his actions) the indispensably necessary means to it that are within his power (*Gewalt*).
> (*GMS* 4:417)

This principle requires considering what *we can will*. It thereby serves to introduce relevant practical-anthropological information about our capabilities and our circumstantial resources into Kant's tests. This is the case, regardless of whether the ends in question are arbitrary because they are set by contingent inclinations, or whether the ends are either

[12] See O'Neill (1989, 74, 105–6, 114–15, 121, 133–4); Herman (1993, 122, 203, 204–6, 235); Louden (2002); and below, chapter 8.

inescapable or mandatory because they are due to our human form of finite rational embodied agency. In this latter case, the necessity of willing sufficient means to some ends extends to willing that there be sufficient ways and means to achieve those ends, or indeed to achieve any ends whatever. Later we shall see that this includes rights to acquire, possess, and use various materials (§32, and chapter 8).

22 Kant's Universalization Test

22.1 A contradiction in conception?

In the first instance, Kant's universalization test provides criteria for the moral status (obligatory, permissible, prohibited) of an agent's maxim.[13] A maxim is a principle on which an individual acts, for example, 'In order to get ahead in the world, I shall only deceive people when I will not be detected', or more positively, 'In order to be able to borrow money again, I shall repay my present loans on schedule.' A maxim can be schematically formulated as: 'I will do *x* if *y* in order to *z*', where *x* holds a place for an act description, *y* for a description of a kind of agent confronting specified circumstances, and *z* for a description of an end, purpose, or reason for acting. Kant has two tests for our maxims, which are to be used in sequence, commonly called the 'Contradiction in Conception' and the 'Contradiction in the Will' tests. The Contradiction in Conception test determines whether a certain kind of contradiction infects simply conceiving of a certain kind of act; this test specifies strict duties or prohibitions. The Contradiction in the Will test determines whether maxims found permissible by the first test can also be consistently *willed*; it specifies broad or meritorious duties. In neither test is the relevant 'contradiction' merely logical. The present discussion considers only strict duties identified by the Contradiction in Conception test.

Kant first presents these tests first-person, for any agent considering prospectively how rightly to act *now*. These tests can also be used retrospectively to evaluate past actions. They can also be used second- or third-person to assess the acts of others. They thus provide criteria of right (wrong, permissible) acts, and provide a basis for determining an

[13] This § is directly indebted to O'Neill (1975, 1989). Years of immersion in Kant's texts, issues, and analyses have convinced me that she has rightly understood Kant's view.

agent's moral credit in view of whether the agent acted rightly *because* so acting is right. This is the topic of Kant's discussion of 'moral worth' in the *Groundwork*, though it is often overlooked that Kant and Mill agree on this basic distinction between assessing the rightness of acts and assessing the agent's moral character.[14]

The Contradiction in Conception test determines whether there is a contradiction between a maxim and its universalized counterpart. Kant's test relies upon a very specific kind of universalization, one often misunderstood or neglected by critics. The Contradiction in Conception test uses the first two of the three descriptions comprised in a full maxim; it omits the description of the agent's ends, purposes, or reasons (z). This test works with two partial maxims; schematically these are the schema of a maxim of action, *viz.*:

I shall do x if (agent + circumstances) y

and its universalized counterpart maxim,

All shall do x, if (agent + circumstances) y.

By assuming the fiction, expressed in Kant's formulae of the Categorical Imperative, that an agent's will is universally legislating, as if for the entirety of nature (including all rational agents), an agent can confront two intentions: an intention expressed in his or her own (first-person, 'subjective') maxim and an intention expressed by its universalized counterpart, constructed by an agent in his or her putative membership in a universal realm of ends, as legislating for all agents. As noted, willing rationally to do something requires willing sufficient means for success. Using means partially distinguishes willing from mere wishing; using sufficient means partially distinguishes rational from irrational willing. Empirical information about sufficient means is relevant to testing the moral status of maxims, for the conditions under which we as rational agents must act and how we are able to act belong to the information about our finite kind of rational agency. Such information pertains to Kant's (unwritten) 'practical anthropology'.

[14] See *GMS* 4:398–9, 401, 411; *KdpV* 5:127–9, 147–8, 151, 159–60; cf. Mill (1861, *CW* 10:219–20, note). For discussion of Kant's account of moral worth, see Herman (1993, 1–22). Note that Mill thus rejects Hume's claim that outward actions as such have no moral character (cf. above, §13).

A certain wrinkle must be accommodated to avoid obvious, trivial counter-examples. Strictly, this step is not expressed by Kant, though the relevant kinds of reciprocity are central to his analysis and justification of rights to acquire, possess, and use things (see below, §38). The wrinkle arises in cases of optional actions involving optional forms of coordination between agents (O'Neill 1975, 75–7; Herman 1993, 138–43). Consider the maxim, 'Whenever I reach a door at the same time as another, I shall always pass through second.' If universalized, this maxim would have neither party willing to pass through the door first, resulting in an indefinite, comical stand off. Using Kant's universalization test twice over avoids such silliness (fit for Monty Python). The first step is to test the agent's maxim against its universalized counterpart; the second is to test the *negation* of the agent's maxim against *its* universalized counterpart.

In two cases, this paired use of Kant's Contradiction in Conception test finds for permissible (optional) maxims: if the intention expressed in one's maxim is consistent with that expressed in its universalized counterpart, *and* if the intention expressed by the negation of one's maxim is consistent with *its* universalized counterpart, then the original maxim is permissible. Likewise, if the intention expressed in one's maxim is *in*consistent with that expressed in its universalized counterpart, *and* if the intention expressed by the negation of one's maxim is *inconsistent* with *its* universalized counterpart (this can occur in cases of optional coordination maxims), then the original maxim is permissible.

If instead the intention expressed in one's maxim is consistent with that expressed in its universalized counterpart, *but* the intention expressed by the negation of one's maxim is *in*consistent with *its* universalized counterpart, then the original maxim is strictly obligatory.

If the intention expressed in one's maxim is *in*consistent with that expressed in its universalized counterpart, *but* the intention expressed by the negation of one's maxim is *con*sistent with *its* universalized counterpart, then the original maxim is strictly prohibited. These outcomes are presented in Figure 1 (p. 84).

22.2 Is Kant's criterion empty?

Mill (1861, *CW* 10:207; cf. 249) charged that Kant's *Metaphysics of Morals* fails to demonstrate any contradiction, whether logical or physical, by using the criterion of the Categorical Imperative, instead

A maxim and its universalized counterpart are mutually consistent: + .
A maxim and its universalized counterpart are mutually inconsistent: ~.

A. Your Maxim / U. Counterpart	+	~	+	~
B. Opposite Maxim / U. Counterpart	~	+	+	~
Moral status of act:	Ought!	Ought not!	May (2 cases).	

Figure 1 Chart of Universalization Test Results

succeeding only in demonstrating that the consequences of certain acts are such as none 'would choose to incur'. His objections have been echoed repeatedly since.[15] However, neither logical nor physical impossibility, nor actual consequences of the sorts Mill considers, pertain to Kant's test. Kant's test is a test of *kinds* or *types* of acts, based on their intentions (as expressed in maxims), not directly of particular acts nor of their actual consequences. Expectable consequences of kinds of acts are important to Kant's universalization test, though only under the expressly hypothetical *fiction* of *universal* action by all upon the same maxim to perform the same kind of act. A host of criticisms of Kant's universalization test seek to devise maxims which, though stated 'universally', *de facto* pertain only to one agent (or perhaps to very few agents). Such 'tailored maxims' do not generate counter-examples to Kant's universalization test because they fail to engage in the kind of universalization Kant's test requires. (Merely inserting a universal quantifier somewhere into an act description does not satisfy *Kant's* universality requirement.) In considering the preconditions of my own act and of the same kind of act committed by everyone, I consider what is involved in *willing* my act *together with* the same kind of act by all agents, for I *intend* these preconditions in intending to act rationally at all. In considering whether I can consistently will the 'universalized counterpart' of my maxim, I am considering whether I can consistently will or intend the preconditions for the same kind of act by all—consistent, that is, with my intention to execute the act expressed in my maxim.

[15] E.g., Baier (2010, 51). The charge of 'empty formalism' is associated with Hegel, though his discussion has a very different point and purpose: to highlight and to fill out the role Kant assigned to practical anthropology; see Westphal (2005).

Kant's universalization test determines whether performing a proposed act would involve treating any other persons only as a means, and not at the same time also as a free rational agent. The key point of Kant's method for identifying and justifying moral duties (prescriptions and proscriptions) is to show that sufficient justifying grounds for a proscribed act can*not* be provided to all concerned (i.e., affected) parties. Conversely, sufficient justifying grounds for omitting positive moral obligations cannot be provided to all concerned parties. By contrast, morally legitimate kinds of action are ones for which sufficient justifying reasons *can* be given to all concerned parties, also on the occasion of one's own act, such that all others can think or act on the basis of those same reasons. Kant's basic criterion of right action is *modal.* The modality of Kant's basic criterion is nicely formulated by O'Neill:

> When we think that others *cannot* adopt, a fortiori *cannot* consent to, some principle we cannot offer them reasons for doing so.
>
> (O'Neill 2000b, 200)[16]

'Adopt' here means, to be able to follow consistently the very same principle in thought or action on the same occasion as one proposes to act on that maxim. This is an issue of capacity and ability, not a psychological claim about what someone can or cannot bring him- or herself to believe or to do. The possibility of adopting a principle thus differs fundamentally from 'accepting' one, in the senses of 'believe', 'endorse', or 'agree to'. Kant's tests rule out any maxim which cannot possibly be adopted by others on the same occasion on which one proposes to act on that maxim. The universality involved in Kant's tests includes the agent's own action, and extends (hypothetically) to all agents acting the same way at that time and over time. What we can or cannot adopt as a maxim is constrained by the form of behaviour or its guiding principle (maxim), by basic facts about our finite form of rational agency, by basic features of our worldly context of action, and most centrally by whether the maxim of the proposed action cannot be adopted by others because that action neglects, evades, or overpowers their rational agency. Kant's Contradiction in Conception test directly rules out maxims of extortion, deception, fraud, and exploitation. In principle, such maxims *preclude* offering to relevant others—most

[16] Cf. Westphal (1997, §§4, 5).

obviously to victims—reasons sufficient to justify *their* following the agent's maxim (or the course of action it guides) in thought or action, especially as the agent acts on his or her maxim (O'Neill 1989, 81–125).[17] This is signalled by the lack of the very possibility of consent, which serves as a criterion (an indicator, not a justificatory principle) of illegitimacy. Obviating the very possibility of consent on anyone's part obviates the very possibility of offering sufficient justifying reasons for one's action to all concerned (affected) parties. Any act which obviates the possibility of others acting upon sufficient justifying reasons cannot itself be justified, and so is morally proscribed.

Because any maxim's (or course of action's) passing his universalization test requires that sufficient justifying reasons for that maxim or action *can* be given to *all* concerned (affected) parties for acting on that maxim on that very occasion, Kant's universalization test embodies at its core equal respect for all persons as free rational agents, that is, as agents who can determine what to think or to do by rationally assessing the merits of the case. *This* is the relevant 'universalizability' required, and identified, by Kant's tests of the Categorical Imperative.

Those who think moral justification can dispense with this condition ought carefully to rethink the Pyrrhonian Dilemma of the Criterion (below, §25). The equal respect for all persons as free rational agents built into Kant's universalization tests is a *conditio sine qua non* for rational justification in non-formal domains; it is not, however, any claim or premise about value or about values (below, §26).[18]

[17] A maxim such as one by which you and I agree now that 'I shall exploit you at one time and you me at another' may satisfy minimal requirements on the generality of reasons for action (namely, that a reason for one agent can also be a reason for others), but such examples only underscore that such generality does not suffice for Kant's specific universality requirement, which expressly rules out making an exception for oneself from an otherwise universal rule (*GMS* 4:424, 440 note, *RL* 6:321). Anglophone criticisms of Kant's universalization tests typically substitute some other, presumptive notion of universalization for Kant's, and then infer that the resulting fault is Kant's. Such problems result from the common tendency to consider Kant's sentences (in translation) piecemeal, which inevitably leads to considering them within the context of the commentator's own philosophical predilections, rather than within the context of Kant's systematic philosophy. Examples of these problems include Baier (2010, 51) and Parfit (2011, 1:275–377), whose methods occlude Kant's view; see Herman (2011a).

[18] Like too many others, Besch (2008, 2009); Budde (2009); Parfit (2011); Baron (2013); and Barry (2013) neglect the full scope of O'Neill's publications on this point, and so fail to understand how specific, detailed, and cogent her analysis is. The embeddedness of equal respect for all persons as free rational agents within Kant's universalization test shows that

22.3 Universalisability, respect for persons, and Kant's formulae of 'the' Categorical Imperative

This requirement, that sufficient justifying reasons for one's maxim or action *can* be given to *all* concerned parties for acting on that maxim on that very occasion, links Kant's formulae of 'the' Categorical Imperative:

> Formula of Universal Law (FUL): Act only in accord with that maxim through which you can at the same time will that it become a universal law.
>
> (*GMS* 4:221)

> Formula of a Law of Nature (FLN): Act as if the maxim of your action were to become by your will a *universal law of nature.*
>
> (*GMS* 4:421)

> Formula of Autonomy (FA): . . . act only so that the will can regard itself at the same time as giving universal law through its maxim.
>
> (*GMS* 4:434)

> The Humanity Imperative (HI): So act in that you use humanity, whether in your own person or in the person of any other, always at the same time as an end, never merely as a means.
>
> (*GMS* 4:429)

> Formula of the Realm of Ends (RE): . . . every rational being must act as if he were by his maxims at all times a lawgiving member of the universal kingdom of ends. The formal principle of these maxims is, act as if your maxims were to serve at the same time as a universal law (for all rational beings).
>
> (*GMS* 4:438)[19]

The relevant 'universality' in Kant's test is that sufficient justifying reasons can be given to all rational agents, so that they can adopt for themselves by considering sufficient justifying reasons for thinking or

the fallacy in Kant's argument for the incommensurable worth or 'dignity' of free rational agency (*GMS* 4:434–5) does not have the dire consequences for his moral theory which 'Kantian consequentialists' (Kummiskey 1996) seek to exploit, in part because a key premise in the consequentialist appropriation of Kant's theory is Broad's (1930) distinction between 'deontology' and 'teleology', which ill suits Kant's moral theory. Insofar as Kant holds that persons have an incommensurable worth called 'dignity' (in contrast to price and any exchange value), he espouses a kind of moral realism. This I do not deny, but I argue that he simply does not need this premise to identify and to justify the most basic moral norms. This is very important; far too much effort has been misdirected into debating whether there are any incommensurable values.

[19] These translations by Gregor. These Formulae are identified, designated, and documented by Paton (1947, 129–98).

acting as one proposes on the occasion one so proposes to act, and on all such occasions of human action. The requirement is that others *can* adopt one's maxim; Kant's test does not require that they *do* adopt it.[20] To provide sufficient justifying grounds for one's act, and to act only upon such grounds as can be addressed to all others (*per* the formulae of Universal Law and of a Law of Nature) *is* to respect all persons as rational agents and to treat none merely as a means to one's own ends, *per* the Humanity Imperative and the Formula of the Realm of Ends; and so to conduct oneself *is* to think and act autonomously, *per* the Formula of Autonomy. (Kant's account of autonomy is examined in §27.) Kant's distinct formulae of 'the' Categorical Imperative are indeed distinct formulae of one and the same principle. Ruling out maxims which fail to pass Kant's universalization test establishes the minimum necessary conditions for resolving the fundamental problems of conflict and social coordination which generated the central concern of Modern natural law theories with establishing normative standards to govern public life domestically and internationally, despite deep disagreements among various groups about the substance of a good or a pious life.[21]

22.4 Kinds of duties

Kant contrasts strict or perfect duties with broad or imperfect duties as duties of justice in contrast to duties of virtue, and as duties regarding overt actions in contrast to duties regarding maxims (*TL* 6:388). In the *Groundwork* (4:440 note 8 to 4:421), Kant expressly reserves the proper division of duties to his then projected *Metaphysics of Morals*. Duties of justice typically involve omissions of proscribed actions, which can be enforced because any violation of the proscription is wrong and, because it involves an overt outward action, at least in principle it can be prevented by external constraint. Behaviour rather than intention is primary in most duties of justice. In contrast, duties of virtue typically involve positive actions, for example, to assist others; if such duties were unrestricted, fulfilling them would be self-destructive of the agent. Accordingly, Kant contends that duties of virtue are broad or imperfect

[20] Kant's test raises issues about how to determine our responsibilities towards those who are mentally compromised. For discussion of patient autonomy and related matters, see Manson and O'Neill (2007).

[21] For further discussion, see O'Neill (2003a), Westphal (2016c).

because they require us to adopt a maxim to act on such duties whilst allowing latitude for agents to determine when, how, and to what extent to fulfil them (cf. *TL* 6:390).

Kant's distinction between outward and inner duties is, however, distinct from his distinction between strict duties of justice and broad duties of virtue. Two examples make this plain: both murder and lying involve not only outward action but also intention; killing someone is manslaughter, so doing with the intent to kill may count as murder, except in cases, for example, of legitimate (and proportional rather than excessive) self-defence. Likewise lying is distinct from both mis-speaking and from stating falsehoods about which one is ignorant, because lying involves the intent to deceive one's audience. The proscriptions upon murder and lying are strict duties, though they also involve the agent's character and intentions. Accordingly, Kant begins the *Doctrine of Virtue* by analysing the possibility and legitimacy of duties towards oneself, before analysing the character and grounds of the duty not to lie and of our obligations to assess and to improve our own moral character.[22]

23 Conclusion

Kant develops a theory of moral judgment, guided by his basic principles and universalization test. He does so, in part, because using rules ineliminably requires judgment (*KdrV* B171–4); hence no moral algorithm, metric, nor fully determinate decision procedure is forthcoming. Mill's observation remains germane:

> There is no difficulty in proving any ethical standard whatever to work ill, if we suppose universal idiocy to be conjoined with it...
>
> (1861, *CW* 10: 224)

The phrase 'moral judgment' has regained prominence in contemporary Anglophone moral philosophy, though often without due consideration of the logical forms of thought and judgment.[23] These considerations are

[22] *TL* 6:417–20, 429–31, 437–42, 444–7, respectively. Because duties of virtue are not directly germane to the present topics, I omit Kant's second universalization test for broad duties. For broader discussion of Kant's ethical theory, see Uleman (2010).

[23] Like Kant, Sellars examined the logical forms of thought, the sense of which he finds, prior to Kant, in Ockham's disciples and in Leibniz, though it is 'almost totally lacking in Descartes and his British successors' (1968, 35).

often neglected by Kant's critics. Obviously, full understanding and appreciation of Kant's principles and methods require further development and examples of their use. Kant's examples, however, often are only illustrative and cannot be understood properly without appeal to Kant's systematic moral philosophy, as presented in his *Metaphysics of Morals*.[24] Indeed, Kant's mature moral philosophy presented there *is* the proper explication and exemplification of his principles of pure practical reason and their proper use in identifying and justifying our moral obligations.

One central case in point is developed in chapter 8: rights to possess and use. Before examining that case in detail, in chapter 6 I indicate how Kant's moral theory can address the Pyrrhonian Dilemma of the Criterion. This highlights key features of the Natural Law Constructivism of Hume and Kant, including its justificatory externalism. In chapter 7, I argue that Kant's moral constructivism is a sound development of Hume's Natural Law Constructivism by showing how Kant's moral constructivism provides a trenchant critique of Gauthier's subtle form of radical contractarianism, which itself is a form of moral constructivism.

[24] For a careful study of Kant's own examples of using the tests of the Categorical Imperative, see Schnoor (1989); a preçis is provided in Westphal (1995), §2. Several of Kant's examples presuppose various social, political, or legal norms, the identification and justification of which belong to his *RL*, beginning with his analysis and justification of rights to possession (below, chapter 7). I examine more fully the aims, character, and success of Kant's specifically Critical methods, and how they support his moral philosophy, in Westphal (2015a).

6

Natural Law Constructivism and Rational Justification

24 Introduction

This chapter characterizes concisely a key issue about rational justification which highlights an important achievement of Kant's constructivist method for identifying and justifying basic norms: uniquely, it can resolve the Pyrrhonian Dilemma of the Criterion. Kant's constructivist method is both sound and significant because it is based upon core principles of rational justification in non-formal domains. Explicating this basis of Kant's Natural Law Constructivism affords an illuminating and defensible explication of four key aspects of the autonomy of rational judgment, including our positive moral freedom (§27); it shows how Kant's constructivism is fundamentally social (§26), and it shows how Kant's constructivism can readily accommodate historical factors relevant to the appropriateness and legitimacy of social and political institutions (§28). All of these advantages are available without recourse to Kant's Transcendental Idealism; all of them respond to common complaints about or purported objections to Kant's practical philosophy. Taken together they provide explicit justification of basic normative principles and practices, thus remedying a serious shortcoming of Hume's incomplete, fragmentary theory of justice. First, a *caveat*: the following brief discussion of the Pyrrhonian Dilemma of the Criterion cannot present its full solution, which I have detailed elsewhere (Westphal 2013b). It suffices to sketch that solution here, and to show that, by recourse (in part) to justificatory externalism, Natural Law Constructivism solves the problem infecting contemporary forms of moral constructivism which appeal to subjective basic elements and are committed to justificatory internalism (above, §§5, 6).

25 The Pyrrhonian Dilemma of the Criterion

The Pyrrhonian Dilemma of the Criterion has haunted philosophy, implicitly or explicitly, from Pyrrho to the present day. The modern natural law tradition within which Hume and Kant worked was no exception. Although Grotius is one of few who explicitly cited Sextus' Dilemma of the Criterion, the twin problems of enabling and regulating international commerce, especially by sea, by regulating international relations, and of achieving and maintaining peace domestically and internationally following the Thirty Years War in Europe, demonstrated that such problems cannot be solved by appeal to particular sectarian faiths. This presented the Dilemma of the Criterion *in concreto*, even to thinkers who preferred to neglect Sextus' writings. The Pyrrhonian Dilemma of the Criterion states:

> [I]n order to decide the dispute which has arisen about the criterion [of truth], we must possess an accepted criterion by which we shall be able to judge the dispute; and in order to possess an accepted criterion, the dispute about the criterion must first be decided. And when the argument thus reduces itself to a form of circular reasoning the discovery of the criterion becomes impracticable, since we do not allow [those who claim to know] to adopt a criterion by assumption, while if they offer to judge the criterion by a criterion we force them to a regress *ad infinitum*. And furthermore, since demonstration requires a demonstrated criterion, while the criterion requires an approved demonstration, they are forced into circular reasoning.
>
> (Sextus Empiricus, *PH* 2.4.20; cf. 1.14.116–17)

The Dilemma of the Criterion is a serious problem for any theory, method, or criterion of rational justification, yet in practical philosophy the only normative justification we can have is by reasoning. This Dilemma cannot be solved (in non-formal domains) by foundationalist or coherentist theories of justification, or by 'reflective equilibrium'.

The so-called method of 'reflective equilibrium' suggested by Goodman (1965, 64) and popularized by Rawls (1971) does nothing to guide different philosophers to the same equilibrium between principles and intuitions, even if they share substantially the same sets of each. Goodman's formulation expressly concerns what we (purportedly) *do*, namely, that we trim data to fit our theories, and trim our theories to fit data. Nothing in his observations shows that we *ought* to do this, or *how* we ought *best* to do this. Thus his remarks neither provide nor suggest any justificatory *method*. About rules of inference and inferential practice, whether deductive or inductive, he claims:

> *A rule is amended if it yields an inference we are unwilling to accept; an inference is rejected if it violates a rule we are unwilling to amend.* The process of justification is the delicate one of making mutual adjustments between rules and accepted inferences; and in the agreement achieved lies the only justification needed for either.
>
> (Goodman 1965, 64)

Perhaps this may be germane with regard to empirical knowledge, where our claims, principles, theories, and explanations must contend with natural fact and circumstance, but this advantage has no sufficiently evident or robust counterpart in the moral domain. Goodman's claim does nothing to link what we are willing or unwilling to accept, reject, or amend to what we *should* be willing or unwilling to accept, reject, or amend, or to explicate how we ought best to make such adjustments. Hence Goodman's remarks provide no *method*.

Furthermore, intuitions are insufficiently well ordered to ground stable equilibria (Perlmutter 1998), and there are deeply and apparently irreconcilable 'intuitions' (if that is indeed what they are) amongst (schools of) philosophers.[1] Thus reflective equilibrium as such can scarcely avoid (sub-)cultural or historicist relativism; indeed, it may instead be a source—if not an instance—of this. 'Reflective Equilibrium' simply is not a method; it may be the best for which we can initially strive in highly problematic domains, it may be a *conditio sine qua non* for any tenable view, but even in fraught domains our goals must include devising genuine justificatory methods or criteria for the domain in question. 'Reflective equilibrium' is a minimum benchmark of consistency amongst intuitions and principles; that alone does not suffice for justification because, as Griffin (1996, 124–5) notes, it says so very little. (Rawls' *method*, properly speaking, lies in his elaborate use of the veil of ignorance and its progressive removal.)

Other methods or bases of normative justification—such as an authority, a founding text, a tradition, intuitionism in its various forms, the feelings of pleasure and displeasure, or other such inclinations—are equally subject to the Dilemma of the Criterion. Briefly, appeals to

[1] On Rawls, see O'Neill (2003a) and Reidy (1999, 2000).

these suffer the same problem as foundationalist approaches to justification: because such approaches understand 'justification' solely in terms of deduction or derivation of claims unilaterally from those first or basic claims or principles (foundations), they cannot justify those first, basic foundational claims or principles, nor can they justify their preferred 'basing relations' (deduction or derivation rules or principles), because foundationalist models understand justification solely in terms of unilateral derivation from the preferred foundations (basic elements; §5, Steps 1, 2).

Coherence theories of justification cannot adequately or reliably distinguish between elaborate, systematic, well-integrated (hence 'coherent' and, according to such theories, hence justified) webs of belief and (in cognitive domains) truth or (in matters moral) correct or appropriate beliefs, judgments, or principles. Recent and continuing historical experience should make this sufficiently evident.

Contractarian forms of justification falter (*inter alia*) because they too easily allow contractors to neglect or to deny or disavow their responsibilities—their *duties*—by refusing to recognize or (hence) to negotiate about them, or by insisting upon negotiating non-negotiable issues. (I argue for these latter claims in chapter 7.) Contractarianism can neither avoid nor resolve dogmatism.[2]

In a phrase, in matters moral we require a counterpart to what Haack (1993) characterizes as 'foundherentism'. Natural Law Constructivism is that counterpart.[3]

[2] The Pyrrhonian Dilemma is distinct to, and more fundamental than, either Chisholm's 'Problem of the Criterion' or what Williams calls the 'Agrippan Trilemma'; see Westphal (1998a, 76–81), and (2013a, §3). The Pyrrhonian Dilemma of the Criterion is widely regarded as insoluble; it is solved by combining three analyses: of the possibility of constructive self-criticism, of the possibility of constructive mutual critical assessment, and of the fact that merely logical possibilities can only defeat or undermine justification in strictly formal domains, though not in non-formal, substantive domains, including both morals and empirical knowledge. These three analyses were provided by Hegel in the 1807 *Phenomenology of Spirit* (Westphal 2009a, 2010–11, 2013b), building directly upon Kant's analyses of rational judgment, autonomy, cognitive semantics, and Natural Law Constructivism (though not Kant's Transcendental Idealism; Westphal 2009b).

[3] Griffin (1996) takes seriously the need for, and the process of, improving our moral beliefs. His analysis is important, though the issues he addresses ought to be considered, and can indeed only be considered, within the context of the principles and practices of justice identified and justified by Natural Law Constructivism.

26 Kant's Constructivism

To understand how Kant's moral theory is constructivist, recall that the crux of Kant's universalization test (§22) is to show that sufficient justifying grounds for an impermissible (wrong) act can*not* be provided to all concerned (affected) parties. Conversely, sufficient justifying grounds for omitting positive moral obligations cannot be provided to all concerned parties. By contrast, legitimate principles are ones for which sufficient justifying reasons *can* be addressed to all concerned parties. Instead of consent, Kant's theory of normative justification relies upon *possible* consistency of human maxims or forms of outer action. Kant's basic criterion of right action, along with its various instances, is *modal*:

> When we think that others *cannot* adopt, a fortiori *cannot* consent to, some principle we cannot offer them reasons for doing so.
>
> (O'Neill 2000b, 200; cf. Westphal 1997, §§4, 5.)

'Adopt' means, to be able to follow consistently the very same principle in thought or action, including the occasion one proposes to act on that maxim. This is an issue of capacity and ability, not a psychological claim about what someone can or cannot bring him- or herself to believe or to do. Kant's test rules out any maxim which cannot possibly be adopted by others on the same occasion on which one proposes to act on that maxim. It focuses on whether others *can* adopt our very maxim, on the basis of sufficient justifying reasons, on that occasion—not on whether they might adopt the same kind of maxim. What we can or cannot adopt as a maxim is constrained by the form of behaviour or its guiding principle (maxim), by basic facts about our finite form of rational agency, and by basic features of our worldly context of action. This latter information is brought into Kant's universalization tests by using the Principle of Hypothetical Imperatives, that 'Whoever wills the end, also wills (insofar as reason has decisive influence on his actions) the indispensably necessary means to it that are within his power (*Gewalt*)' (*GMS* 4:417). A detailed, central example of Kant's universalization test—rights of possession—is examined in chapter 8.

Though minimal, Kant's test directly rules out maxims of coercion, deception, fraud, and exploitation. In principle, such maxims *preclude* offering to relevant others—most obviously to victims—reasons sufficient to justify their following those same maxims (or the courses of action they guide) in thought or in action (O'Neill 1989, 81–125). Maxims of coercion, deception, fraud, or exploitation in principle make irrelevant some others' capacity to think or to act upon sufficient justifying reasons—whether by condoning, allowing, or cooperating—with regard to the actions of perpetrators based on those maxims; namely, the victims. The incapacitation of their rational agency (in the sense of making their rationality irrelevant to the perpetrator's act, except insofar as they may be duped or misled) through such actions is signalled by the lack of the very possibility of consent, or by its irrelevance, which serve as criteria (indicators) of illegitimacy. Consent itself, whether implicit, explicit, or hypothetical, plays no constitutive role in Kant's test, or in Kant's justifying either the basis or the results of that test. Kant's test uses the possibility of consent to signal the crucial justificatory possibility of providing sufficient justifying reasons to all concerned parties. Obviating the very possibility of consent on anyone's part obviates the very possibility of offering sufficient justifying reasons to all concerned parties. Because any maxim's (or any course of action's) passing his universalization test requires that sufficient justifying reasons for that maxim or action *can* be given to *all* concerned parties for acting on that maxim on that very occasion, Kant's constructivism embodies at its core equal respect for all persons as free rational agents, that is, as agents who can determine what to think or to do by rationally assessing the reasons for so acting.[4]

[4] The modal formulation of Kant's test, its focus upon the very possibility of consent, and my stress on maximizing the autonomy of one's own rational, justificatory judgment raise two subsidiary issues I mention here in order to set them aside. One concerns our frequent use of expert opinion (e.g., of medical doctors, accountants, or lawyers) precisely because they, unlike we their clients, are experts in the areas in which we seek advice. In such cases, there are very important issues about how we can best distinguish genuine from lesser or merely presumed experts to which the present analysis of rational justification by rational judgment directly pertains. The other concern is whether in some cases it may be justifiable to submit to certain forms of coercion or deception. The most obvious examples of such cases are medical: how and under what circumstances might it be justifiable to remain ignorant of one's own diagnosed, fatal disease? Or likewise, for seriously obese patients to have their jaws wired together in order not to eat for a planned period of time under medical supervision? (There have been such cases in the USA.) Such cases also involve crucial issues about how such patients can most justifiedly select the expert treatment they require, or at least receive. Issues about patient autonomy in medicine are intricate and important, though I do not believe they raise genuine objections to the present analysis. For discussion of patient autonomy and related matters, see Manson and O'Neill (2007). (I thank Rüdiger Bittner for raising this point with me.)

Kant's constructivism and his universalization tests incorporate equal respect for all persons as rational agents as a *conditio sine qua non* for rational justification and for rationally justified or justifiable claims or judgments in any non-formal domain. Hence Kant's method need not and does not appeal to any alleged value of rational agency, whether commensurable or not. Kant's and O'Neill's critics have failed to notice this cardinal virtue of Kant's method because they have been too quick to link morals to values, and have neglected that basing morals on values is an open invitation to *petitio principii* and to the Dilemma of the Criterion.[5]

Ruling out maxims which fail to pass this universalization test establishes the minimum necessary conditions for resolving the problems of conflict and social coordination that generated the central concern of Modern natural law with establishing normative standards to govern public life, despite deep disagreements among various groups about the substance of a good or a pious life (Schneewind 1998).

Kant's method for identifying and justifying basic moral principles is constructivist because it makes no appeal to any antecedent source or kind of normative authority. Thus Kant's constructivist justification of practical principles and actions at its core embodies the autonomy of reason, as being both a necessary and a sufficient basis for identifying and justifying legitimate basic moral norms. This is a key dimension of the autonomy of rational judgment: Kant's justificatory strategy appeals only to a fundamental principle of rational justification as such (in non-formal domains), that justifying a principle, policy, belief, institution, or action requires that its proponent can provide sufficient justifying reasons to all other concerned parties, such that these parties can consistently adopt or follow the very same proposal and its justifying reasons in thought or action. Therefore, at its core Kant's constructivist justification of practical principles is fundamentally social, intersubjective, because it is addressed to *all* concerned parties.[6]

[5] E.g., Kummiskey (1996); Baron (2013); Barry (2013). O'Neill's (2013) replies are concise and conciliatory, though also incisive. Their cogency is more apparent when understood within the context of Kant's Critical constructivist methodology.

[6] The key question about Kant's constructivist strategy is thus not whether it is individualist or collectivist, but rather what kind of collectivism or intersubjectivity is built into Kant's universalism. Kant distinguished 'disjunctive' (i.e., distributive) and 'collective'

Our behaviour, both verbal and physical, is not coordinated naturally, or transcendentally, or transcendently. Consequently, any stable social practices or constructions, whether communicative, intellectual, political, or physical, can only be based upon principles which all parties can consistently follow (in the indicated sense) in thought and in action. To identify and to justify such principles, Kant contends, requires us to follow these maxims:

always to think actively,
to think consistently,
to think (so far as possible) without prejudice, and
'to think from the standpoint of *everyone* else'.

(*KdU* 5:294, *GS* 8:145)

These maxims are not algorithms, nor are they specific methods, but they are *conditiae sine qua non* for rationally cogent and justifiable thought, judgment, and action. O'Neill (1989, 24–7, 42–8) notes that these maxims are equally ones of communication, required so that we can communicate with everyone, not just our own partisan camp. Kant's development of this important point at the end of 'What does it Mean to Orient oneself in Thinking? (1786) merits closer reconsideration.[7]

Responding to sceptical attacks upon reason mounted by Jacobi (1785, 1786), who followed Hamann's (1784–8) and Herder's (1799) attempts at a 'meta-critique of pure reason', all of which, including Wizenmann (1786), prefigured much of today's post-modern and neo-pragmatist cant,[8] Kant admonishes:

Men of intellectual ability and broad-minded disposition! I honour your talents and love your feeling for humanity. But have you thought about what you are doing, and where your attacks on reason will lead? Without doubt you want to preserve inviolate the *freedom to think*; for without that even your own free

forms of universality (cf. *GS* 23:320.22–3). Presently I surmise that Kant's constructivism involves distributive, not collective, forms of universality.

[7] The entire essay is highly significant, though especially the final pages. Only some of the most important points may be considered here. I thank Cinzia Ferrini for recalling Kant's essay and its relevance. Allen Wood's translation (*CEWK* 1998) is very good, and is used here with only minor revisions.

[8] On Hamann's (mis-)use of Hume, see Berlin (1980); on Herder, Hamann, Jacobi, and Wizenmann, see Beiser (1987, 16–91, 109–58). (I mention Wizenmann because Kant expressly refers to his, at the time anonymous, publication; *GS* 8:134.6; mis-identified in *GS*.)

flights of genius would soon come to an end. Let us see what would naturally become of this freedom of thought if a procedure such as you initiate should get the upper hand.

(*GS* 8:144)

Kant then contrasts freedom of thought to compulsory censorship and comments:

Of course it is said that the freedom to *speak* or to *write* could be taken from us by a superior power, though the freedom to *think* cannot. Yet how much and how correctly would we *think* if we did not think as it were in community with others to whom we *communicate* our thoughts, and who communicate theirs with us! Thus one can very well say that this external power which wrenches away people's freedom publicly to *communicate* their thoughts also takes from them the freedom to *think*...

(*GS* 8:144)

The close interdependence of thinking and public communication Kant here highlights may not be self-evident, but consider that whatever cognitive capacities are innately ours, we only develop and learn to use through education—both formal and informal—by others who provide information, skills, methods, practice, and critical assessment. To 'communication' belong all publications and social sources of information. Kant further stresses that thinking cogently (*mit welcher Richtigkeit*; 'correctly') requires more than just thinking: for us fallible, limited human cognizers, distinguishing between genuinely cogent and merely apparently cogent thinking is vital, and requires communicating with others. Communicating with others is vital for assessing whether our thoughts, as we happen to have formulated and integrated them into judgments which we affirm or deny, are formulated and integrated as they *ought* to form a proper, accurate, and rationally justifiable judgment (*KdrV* A261–3/B317–19).[9]

Kant's third point about freedom of thought is that:

...freedom in thinking signifies the subjection of reason to no laws except *those which it gives itself*; and its opposite is the maxim of a lawless use of reason (in order, as genius supposes, to see further than one can under the limitation of laws).

(*GS* 8:145)

[9] Wood (2014, 65–9) neglects these fundamentally intersubjective, social aspects of Kant's constructivist account of rational justification in non-formal domains.

This lawless use of reason naturally leads, Kant contends, to this situation:

> . . . if reason will not subject itself to the laws it gives itself, it must bow beneath the yoke of laws given by another; for without any law, nothing—not even nonsense—can play its game for long. Thus the unavoidable consequence of *declared* lawlessness in thinking (of a liberation from the limitations of reason) is that the freedom to think will ultimately be forfeited, and because not misfortune but arrogance is to blame, it will properly speaking be foolishly *trifled away*.
>
> (*GS* 8:145)

Lawful, that is *regular*, rule-governed use of reason, is required simply to make sense; to make statements, claims, or judgments; to refer intelligibly and intelligently to any subject matter under discussion; to make any justified or justifiable claims or judgments; and to assess their accuracy and justification. These points likewise hold for innovations, their identifiability (recognizability), their rational assessment and, in favourable cases, their justification.

Lawlessness in reasoning instead generates:

> . . . an *unbelief of reason*, a precarious state of the human mind, which first takes from moral laws all their force as incentives to the heart, and over time all their authority, and occasions the way of thinking one calls libertinism, i.e. the principle of recognizing no duty at all. At this point the authorities intervene, so that even civil arrangements shall not fall into the greatest disorder; and since they regard the most efficient and emphatic means as the best, this does away with even the freedom to think, and subjects thinking, like other trades, to the country's rules and regulations. And so freedom in thinking finally destroys itself if it tries to proceed in independence of the laws of reason.
>
> (*GS* 8:146)

The authorities Kant has in mind are civil and religious authorities, at a time and in a place in which religious authorities were civil authorities, but today those authorities may belong not only to government but also to academic administrations or 'business leadership', such has become the demand for economic 'impact' within the academy, to the ever-increasing neglect and detriment of moral, political, and social competence and concern. Kant's emphatic conclusion is as important today as it was in 1786:

> Friends of the human race and of what is most sacred to it! Accept what appears to you most worthy of belief after careful and sincere examination, whether of

facts or rational grounds; only do not dispute that prerogative of reason which makes it the highest good on earth, the prerogative of being the ultimate touchstone of truth.* Otherwise you shall become unworthy of this freedom, and you will surely forfeit it too; and besides that you will bring the same misfortune down upon the heads of other, innocent parties who would otherwise have been well disposed and would have used their freedom lawfully and hence in a way which is conducive to what is best for the world!

(*GS* 8:146–7)

Now why, exactly, should reason be the ultimate touchstone of truth? Kant answers in his footnote to his emphatic conclusion:

**Thinking for oneself* means seeking the supreme touchstone of truth in oneself (i.e. in one's own reason); and the maxim of always thinking for oneself is enlightenment. . . . To make use of one's own reason means no more than to ask oneself, whenever one is supposed to assume something, whether one could find it feasible to make the ground or the rule on which one assumes it into a universal principle for the use of reason. This test is one that everyone can apply to himself; and with this examination he will see superstition and enthusiasm disappear, even if he falls far short of having the information to refute them on objective grounds.

(*GS* 8:146–7n)[10]

The 'enthusiasm' Kant here censures is the view that reason's legislation is invalid, whereas 'superstition' is 'the complete subjection of reason to facts', whether real or alleged (*GS* 8:145). A 'universal principle for the use of reason' is a principle any and everyone can use to judge some subject matter. This reflects Kant's observation in the Canon of Pure Reason, that 'all knowledge (if it pertains to an object of pure reason) can be communicated' (*KdrV* A829/B857). This possibility of communicating one's knowledge is a necessary condition constitutive of knowledge of any and every public object, event, structure, or phenomenon. The critical question Kant poses for any and everyone's use of reason in this footnote is a clear and important step forward from Kant's Transcendental Doctrine of Method to the universalizability tests first presented in

[10] Kant's note concludes by remarking: 'Thus it is quite easy to ground enlightenment in *individual subjects* through their education; one must only begin early to accustom young minds to this reflection. But to enlighten an *age* is very slow and arduous; for there are external obstacles which in part forbid this manner of education and in part make it more difficult.' Indeed so! Our commercially driven media-marketing societies are obstructing ever more forcefully and thoroughly the aims, means, and provisions of enlightened education and responsible, informed social participation.

the *Groundwork of the Metaphysics of Morals*. The key to Kant's universalizability tests is that universal communicability is a necessary condition for rational justification in all non-formal domains. Consequently, any claim or principle—together with its purportedly sufficient justifying grounds—which cannot be universally communicated cannot, accordingly, be rationally justified. This holds independently of the character, content, or erstwhile cogency of the claims, principles, or grounds at issue. Kant's insight into the moral assessment or justification of actions is this: no omission of strict moral duties, and no commission of morally prohibited actions, can be justified to all others by communicating the principles and purported justifying grounds for so acting (or omitting to act).

Because universal communicability of principles and their (purported) justifying grounds is a *conditio sine qua non* for the rational justification of those principles, together with any thought or action based upon or guided by them, Kant's Natural Law Constructivism circumvents, or at least circumscribes, debates about 'values', especially when used as premises in moral assessments or justificatory moral reasoning. Of course there are important issues to be settled jointly—whether locally, domestically, or internationally—about values, aspirations, policies, legislation, and their often competing recommendations, but those debates can only occur, can only be effective, and can only be resolved for cogent reasons, within the scope of the strict duties of justice identified by Kant's universalization tests, independently of such contingent and diverse material premises. Consequently, moral or political debates about 'values', aims, and aspirations can only pertain to elective, in principle justifiable policies, procedures, laws, customs, or conventions. Debate about 'values', aims, and aspirations as material premises in moral reasoning does not pertain to the most fundamental principles of justice, which are the most fundamental principles of morals, identified and justified by Kant's Natural Law Constructivism.

The justificatory strategy central to Kant's Natural Law Constructivism is thus fundamentally social, because it concerns necessary conditions—principles, institutions, and practices—of collective life required for our form of finite rational agency, for we are a kind of finite rational agent for whom individual life and action requires collective life and social coordination. Coordinating our actions conjointly makes our actions other-regarding. The social coordination problems fundamental to morality—Hobbes' 'Innocent Problem' of mutual interference (above, §8)—show that sufficiently other-regarding action is a necessary condition for any and every effective self-regarding action. Sufficiently just other-regarding action is a necessary condition for the moral justifiability of individual actions, whether these consist in omissions or commissions, and whether these latter be permissible or obligatory. The problem addressed by Natural Law Constructivism is to determine whether or how the basic social principles and practices required by, and required for, our form of finite rational agency can be just, and so can in both regards be justified. The nerve of Kant's constructivist strategy is to show that the modal capacity to provide justifying reasons to all relevant others is a very stringent requirement. One great advantage of Kant's minimalist strategy of justification is that it avoids familiar problems regarding agreement or acceptance, whether implicit, explicit, or hypothetical.[11] (The insufficiency of agreement or acceptance as a basis for identifying or justifying basic moral principles or judgments is examined in chapter 7.)

On the basis of this modal principle regarding justifying reasons addressable to all affected persons Kant develops a powerful kind of constructivism in normative theory, not in the sense popularized by Rawls (1971), but in the sense explicated by O'Neill.[12] Kant's constructivism articulates the content of a natural law theory, though it moots the issues of ontology (moral realism, natural teleology) and motivation that confront traditional natural law theories. Kant's constructivism justifies the objectivity and legitimacy of practical, action-guiding principles, without appeal to moral facts, whether natural or non-natural. Kant's

[11] This paragraph summarizes some thoughts from O'Neill (2000b; cf. 1996, 2003b, 2004a, 2004b; Westphal 1997, §§4, 5). The term 'rational justification' is in these contexts a pleonasm. In moral philosophy, justification by anything other than reasons is out of place. Aside from simple perceptual knowledge, providing justifying reasons is the sole mode of justification in matters moral, for reason giving is the only form of justification that can avoid dogmatism, question begging, infinite regress, or the Dilemma of the Criterion.

Kant's constructivist procedure does raise issues—to be sure, absolutely general ones—about how to distinguish cases in which sufficient justifying reasons can be and have been addressed to all relevant parties, though some of these parties refuse to accept these reasons, whether due to inability, incomprehension, or bias. This important issue is addressed by Hegel's phenomenological method; see Westphal (1989, 126–8), and (2013b). (The brief remarks on the point in my 1989, please note, are rooted in the entire analysis.) Hegel's analysis shows that Kant's constructivist procedure does not relapse into a consent theory.

[12] See O'Neill (1989, 1996, 2000, 2002b, 2004a, 2004b).

constructivist principle addresses neither a particular society with its norms (communitarianism), nor an 'overlapping consensus' of a pluralistic society (Rawls), nor the multitude of voices aspiring to communicate in accord with the requirements of an 'ideal speech situation' (Habermas), nor a plurality of potential contractors (e.g., Gauthier or Scanlon). These latter considerations are important, but are secondary to the basic framework principles of justice identified and justified by Kant's Natural Law Constructivism, which articulates the most basic rational principles of human thought and action as such. The principles required for legitimate contract cannot themselves be established by contract, because, as Hume recognized,[13] any such contract presupposes rather than defines or justifies those principles. Conversely, requiring consent to establish basic norms too easily allows for negligence or back sliding through refusal to consent, including refusal to acknowledge relevant considerations and obligations (see chapter 7).[14] Kant's constructivism establishes key norms to which we are committed, whether we like it or not, by our rational requirements to act in justified ways, on the one hand, and by the limits of our very finite form of human agency and our worldly context of action (see §§32, 37–8). According to Kant, there is no public use of reason without this constructivist principle, which uniquely avoids presupposing any authority, whether ideological, religious, socio-historical, or personal.

In this regard Kant's constructivism solves a problem found in 'Moral Point of View' theories, which seek to identify, characterize, and differentiate sound from inadequate moral reasons and reasoning within moral practice, and which affirm the centrality of equal moral regard for all others.[15] By affirming the centrality of equal moral regard for all other persons, these theories provide, not analyses of moral reasoning of whatever kind, but specifically of liberal moral reasoning (Nielsen 1999). This same constellation recurs in Rawls' theory of justice (1971), as was confirmed by Rawls' later article, 'Justice as Fairness: Political, not Metaphysical' (1985). Rawls (2005, 32) holds that Kant's innate right to freedom (*RL*, Einl., 6:237–8) is a 'self-originating and self-authenticating'

[13] *T* 3.2.2.10, 3.2.5.1–4/SBN 490, 516–17. Hume's observation is corroborated in chapter 7.

[14] And see O'Neill (2000b, 185–91).

[15] E.g., Toulmin (1953); Baier (1958); Singer (1961); Nielsen (1989).

claim of reason. Likewise moral freedom consists in regarding oneself and others as 'self-originating and self-authenticating sources of valid [moral] claims'. Bohmann (2009) rightly notes that the moral and legal standing of persons must be more fundamental than republican legal standing. However, the positions of Rawls and Bohmann share the instability noted by Nielsen with Moral Point of View theories. Their points may well be 'Fundamental Ideas' of 'The Political Conception of the Person'—to use Rawls' chapter and section titles—but Kant's Critical philosophy does not appeal to the alleged self-evidence of such synthetic propositions. Why should or does regarding oneself as a 'self-originating and self-authenticating' source 'of valid [moral] claims' involve or require regarding anyone else as such a source?[16] Neither Bohmann nor Rawls recognize how Kant justifies these fundamental moral claims by reason on behalf of rational persons by showing that they are required as *conditio sine qua non* for the rational justifiability of our claims, judgments, or actions within non-formal domains. These bold theses are central to Kant's Critical method and strategies of rational justification; they should be noted here, though their character, justification, and use remain central topics throughout the sequel.[17]

Saying that Kant's constructivism does not appeal to moral facts may invite a misunderstanding. Unlike most contemporary 'constructivist' programmes, Kant's constructivism is not committed to generating or 'constructing' the entire moral domain by appeal solely to empirical facts and non-moral principles. Facts about human finitude, such as our liability to injury, coercion, or deceit, are empirical facts. They are partially constitutive of our finite form of rational agency. They are *morally relevant* facts because as agents there is so much we can, and either should or should not do, to produce, avoid, exploit, avert, or minister to them. The point of departure of Kant's constructivism is not the alleged rights of others, but rather our own *obligations* towards others (and ourselves), given that each of us is a free, rational, and finite agent. *Ab initio* this version of constructivism moves within the moral domain because it begins with the problems

[16] This is a version of the basic question posed by Gauthier's radical contractarianism, examined in chapter 7.

[17] Please note that I have sought to present only the necessary minimum of Kant's Critical methodology, to keep my discussion as exoteric as possible. For more complete analysis and defence, see Westphal (2013b, 2015a). I discuss Moral Point of View theories and Kant's sole innate right to freedom below (§§41, 43, respectively).

of social coordination (if not conflict; above §8) and because restricting ourselves to those principles for which we can provide all persons sufficient justifying reasons is as much a principle of morals as it is a principle of rational justification *per se* (in non-formal domains). It is a (broadly) moral principle because it requires us to act only on those principles that can be rationally justified, and because it requires us to respect ourselves and all other persons as rational agents, as agents who can understand, develop, assess, and act upon rationally justified principles because we can recognize and understand their justificatory grounds.[18]

27 Rational Judgment, Autonomy, and Spontaneity

27.1 'I think' and 'I judge'

The self-conscious 'I think' that matters most to philosophy is the 'I judge' that is central to rational thought and action in any of its

[18] Kant primarily formulates 'respect' as respect for the moral law (*GMS* 4:400, 401 note, 403, 424, 426, 436, 440, *KdpV* 5:73, 74–6, 78–86, 128, 132, 151, 157). Respect for the moral law is constituted by recognizing the Categorical Imperative as the fundamental moral principle and following what the Categorical Imperative requires *because* it is the fundamental principle of morals. Kant's Categorical Imperative is the fundamental principle of morals because it provides the fundamental criterial procedure for distinguishing legitimate from illegitimate types of action by distinguishing between prohibited, permissible, and obligatory types of action. To use Kant's Categorical Imperative and to follow its dictates thus requires using the constructivist method explicated here for identifying and justifying legitimate maxims. Kant is emphatic that only insofar as we use the Categorical Imperative and follow its dictates can and do we treat each and every person as an end in him- or herself, and not merely as a means. Doing this requires that we think and act only on the basis of justifiable, and indeed rationally justified principles. A necessary and sufficient criterion of rationally justifiable or justified principles is that only for such principles can we offer all concerned parties sufficient justifying reasons to think or act as we do or propose to do.

Kant also speaks of respect for persons, not just for the moral law; this is central to his formulation of the Humanity Imperative (*GMS* 4:429, above §22.3). Hence on Kant's view it is proper to speak of respect for persons, although human beings merit respect as persons only due to their 'personality' (*KdpV* 5:87), which is their capacity to perform their duties by using and following the dictates of the Categorical Imperative: 'All respect for a person is actually only respect for the [moral] law (of moral integrity, etc.), of which the person provides us the example' (*GMS* 4:401 note; cf. 4:428, 435, 436, 439, 440, *KdpV* 5:87, 93). Kant's Categorical Imperative is a principle of reason. To use the Categorical Imperative requires that we each exercise our own capacity for rational judgment. For reasons developed herein, exercising our capacity for rational judgment requires constructive self-criticism and mutual critical assessment (§28).

forms. Only a strong sense of 'I judge', which involves critical assessment, makes possible justifiable and justificatory thought and reasoning. Conversely, anyone who can or does engage in genuine inquiry and debate instantiates (more or less adequately) this strong sense of the term. In the *Critique of Pure Reason* Kant sought to uncover the transcendental, *a priori* conditions which make possible self-conscious human experience (Westphal 2004). Presently my focus is the kind of self-conscious judgment required to understand, to appreciate, and to *assess* the point of any substantial piece of justificatory reasoning.

27.2 Autonomy and assessment

To judge rationally is not merely to decide. To judge rationally is to make whatever judgment is best warranted in view of all available relevant considerations, including evidence, counter-evidence, relevant principles of inference, relevant (as contrasted to irrelevant or less relevant) analogies with other examples, cases, or domains, as well as alternative accounts or assessments of the issue, whether historical, contemporaneous, or heretofore unconsidered cogent alternatives. To judge rationally is to assume responsibility for the warrant or justificatory status of one's conclusions. To assume responsibility for making judgments and for making any and every particular judgment is to exercise autonomy. The autonomy of rational judgment consists in regulating one's own thinking, deliberation, assessment, judgment, and conduct in view of the various factors (including those just mentioned) which bear upon the identification and justification of the correct, or at least the best justified, conclusion about the matter at hand. This kind of 'self-regulation' of one's own thinking literally is a form of 'auto-nomy', of self-guided, self-motivated, voluntary, and self-assessing use of rules, principles, laws, and evidence, where the relevant 'laws' are the principles, guidelines, and methods of cogent justificatory reasoning by use of which one regulates one's own thinking. Thus one basic sense in which judgment is autonomous is that one forms one's own judgment, rather than merely adopting anyone else's judgment, advice, or recommendation (much less, command).

27.3 Autonomy and proper function

A second significant sense in which rational judgment is autonomous is that it is guided by the normative considerations of appropriate assessment and use of both evidence and principles of reasoning. If judgment, as a physiological or psychological process is in some way causal, nevertheless it counts as *judgment* only insofar as it responds to such normative considerations, rather than merely to its causal antecedents as such. Judgment is a response to, not merely an effect of, its proper evidentiary and inferential antecedents. If justificatory processes turn out to be causal, they are justificatory not because they are causal, but because they satisfy sufficient normative constraints—defining or at least including *proper* functioning, *proper* inference, and *proper* assessment—to provide *inter alia* rational justification. For this reason, Kant held that reason, rational judgment (a pleonasm), is spontaneous (Allison 1997). This point merits closer consideration.

27.4 Autonomy and 'spontaneity'

Only rational spontaneity enables us to appeal to principles of inference and to make rational judgments, both of which are normative because each rational person considers whether or how well available procedures, evidence, and principles of inference warrant a judgment or conclusion. In the theoretical domain of knowledge, *having* adequate evidence, proof, or (in sum) justification requires *taking* that evidence, proof, or justification to be adequate; in the practical domain of deliberation and action, *having* adequate grounds for action requires *taking* those grounds to be adequate. We *act* only insofar as we take ourselves to have reasons, even in cases of acting on desires, where we must (*ex hypothesi*) take those desires as—by judging them to be—appropriate and adequate (at least permissible) grounds of action. Otherwise we abdicate rational considerations and absent ourselves from what Sellars (1963, 169) calls 'the space of reasons' and merely behave. In that case, as McDowell (1994, 13) says, we provide ourselves only excuses and exculpations, but neither reasons nor justifications, for acting or believing as we do.[19] Kant's conception of rational spontaneity opposes empiricist accounts of beliefs and desires as merely causal products of environmental stimuli,

[19] Note that I do not say that taking evidence to be adequate suffices for that evidence to be adequate! Some epistemologists bridle at the notion that having adequate evidence or grounds for belief requires taking that evidence or those grounds to be adequate. Yet there are many examples of people having memories or perceptions that in fact bear evidentially on a certain belief they hold, though they fail to recognize this evidential relation and so fail to base their belief on that evidence. Basing (or, *mutatis mutandis*, rejecting) beliefs on evidence requires taking that evidence to be both relevant and adequate.

and it opposes empiricist accounts of action, according to which we act on whatever desires are (literally) 'strongest'. We think and act rationally only insofar as we judge the merits of whatever case is before us. This is the third aspect of the rational autonomy of judgment.[20]

28 Reason, Justification, and History

28.1 Rational justification and fallibilism

Rational judgment is fallible because it involves one's own, as it were, 'perspectival' assessment of the relevant evidence, principles, and the interrelations among these. Due to our fallibility and limited knowledge, both factual and inferential, any particular judgment anyone makes is justified only to the extent that one does one's utmost to exercise informed judgment on that occasion, *and* to the extent that one's judgment survives critical scrutiny by all concerned parties (including oneself). In this important regard, because we are finite, fallible reasoners and cognizers, the justification and the justificatory status of our conclusions is a social phenomena. Because informed judgment is socially based, so is rational justification.[21] We are each responsible for the critical assessment of our own and of others' rational judgments. Genuine and fully rational judgment requires constructive mutual critical

[20] The first two aspects of rational autonomy are the self-regulation of one's own thinking (§27.2) and the autonomy of proper functioning, which is normatively specified, from whatever may prove to be the causal basis of our capacities for judgment (§27.3). All three of these aspects of rational autonomy can be, as they are here, specified and justified without appeal to Transcendental Idealism. Kant's 'Incorporation Thesis' (Allison 1990, 5–6, 39–40), that no inclination is a motive unless and until it is incorporated into an agent's maxim by being judged to be at least permissible (*Religion*, 6:24), is an instance of the more general principle (and third aspect) of autonomous judgment identified here. Kant's Incorporation Thesis has been challenged by McCarty (2009, 64, 71–87), but his objections are unpersuasive because he disregards Kant's theory of judgment, of which the Incorporation Thesis is an instance; see Westphal (2012b, 2015a). On the belief-desire model of agency, see above, §17.

[21] 'Judgment' has largely fallen by the wayside in analytic epistemology, except for an innocuous sense of identifying common-sense objects in one's environs. Kant insisted that rules require judgment for their application (*KdrV* A132–4/B171–3). In effect, Wittgenstein's scepticism about rule-following makes the same point, that principles are not algorithms, and indeed that their use requires social training and context (von Savigny 1991; Will 1997, 121–92). Further support for the social basis of constructive self-criticism is discussed in Westphal (2003, esp. §§20, 24, 28, 35; 2012a, 2013b). Elgin (1999) and Thiele (2006) discuss related issues.

assessment of each and everyone's judgment. This is the point of Kant's four maxims of judgment cited previously (§26), and of his strategy for vindicating reason in the *Critique of Pure Reason* (O'Neill 1992).

Because constructivist rational justification is fallibilist, it dispenses with the illicit tendency to unilateral judgment embedded in foundationalist models of justification. The 'one size fits all' notion of universalization for which the Enlightenment has been so often criticized is simply foreign to Kant's views and analysis. Kant's constructivist, fallibilist, social theory of rational justification is inherently a pragmatic and historical theory of rational justification because the justification it provides is fallible, because it is based on the present state of knowledge, because it is inherently provisional, and because the list of relevant alternative accounts of any issue and the relevant considerations bearing on it can (and often tend to) increase historically. Thus rational justification is also fundamentally historical, and indeed, only thereby can it resolve the Dilemma of the Criterion because fallibilism provides a rigorous alternative to the foundationalist regress of justifying reasons.

The Dilemma of the Criterion puts paid to the sceptical regress inherent in foundationalist models of justification and to the circularity involved in standard coherence theories. Critical self-assessment and mutual critical assessment can be constructive by enabling us to assess, to revise, or to replace any particular claim within any piece of justificatory reasoning, as well as any link among such claims. For this reason, rational judgment is not trapped in vicious circularity, *pace* the Dilemma of the Criterion.

28.2 Chisholm, the problem of the criterion, and particularism

Roderick Chisholm (1982, 65–7, 75) erred profoundly when he contended that there are only three possible solutions to what he formulated as the 'Problem of the Criterion', none of them satisfactory because each commits a *petitio principii*. According to Chisholm, one can start with universal principles (Methodism), or instead with particular claims (Particularism), or one can deny that one could start legitimately with either universal or particular claims (Scepticism). Chisholm neglected the very possibility of constructive self- and mutual criticism of the kind enabled by Kant's account of the autonomy of reason and the autonomy of rational judgment. Kant's account of these forms of autonomy (summarized above) involves and justifies a pragmatic, social, and historical account of rational justification within which even our presumed 'first principles' are subject to on-going assessment as they are used again and again in new situations. Yet Kant's account of rational justification maintains strict objectivity about the identification and justification of our principles and particular claims because on Kant's account their justification must be addressed to all concerned (that is, all affected) parties in view of all relevant facts (such as those belonging to Kant's practical anthropology): this is central to respecting all persons as ends in themselves, that is, as rational agents who can and ought to judge for themselves what is right. And when individuals unfortunately fail so to do, this too can only be identified and established by careful critical scrutiny of our own and of their reasonings. The alleged Dilemma of the Criterion is defeated by pragmatic fallibilism of precisely the kind Kant was the first to identify and develop.[22]

28.3 Fallibilism and objectivity

Pragmatist and fallibilist accounts of justification are widely thought to be insufficient for, if not inimical to, realism about the objects of knowledge or strict objectivity about basic norms. Fortunately, this is not the case. In chapter 7 I further support the modal interpretation of Kant's universalization test by showing that agreement or acceptance cannot play a constitutive role in identifying or justifying basic moral norms, by showing how Kant's Natural Law Constructivism provides a direct, cogent refutation of Gauthier's subtle version of radical contractarianism, which claims that only contractarian agreement can play such a role. Gauthier's contractarianism is itself a form of moral constructivism. Kant's rejoinder to it underscores the superiority of Natural Law Constructivism to contemporary forms of moral constructivism. In particular, contractarianism in any form is committed to justificatory internalism. Kant's rejoinder to Gauthier's contractarianism underscores the role and the importance of the justificatory externalism central to Natural Law Constructivism. These features of Kant's view, sketched in chapter 7, are augmented in chapter 8.

[22] I believe Barry's (2013) criticisms of O'Neill's interpretation of Kant's moral philosophy fail to recognize the full Critical resources of Kant's philosophy to which O'Neill rightly appeals.

7

Constructivism, Contractarianism, and Basic Obligations

29 Introduction

In 'Political Contractarianism', David Gauthier (1997) presents a succinct, self-contained, sophisticated statement of his contractarian method of justifying social norms and practices, which he significantly refined over many years to avoid recurrent objections to contractarianism, because traditional versions of contractarianism neglected the family and child-rearing, reduced all social relations to contractual relations, or required that life-plans and values be pre-social and hence non-social. In these regards, this later analysis improves upon his previous monograph, *Morals by Agreement* (1986). Its concision lends itself to focused discussion here. Examining Gauthier's radical contractarianism will underscore the importance, especially today, of moral constructivism. However, the problems confronting even Gauthier's carefully refined form of contractarianism are also manifest in other, including more recent versions of contractarianism. The fundamental issues addressed in—and those raised by—his (1997) analysis are conspicuously absent from current contractarian proposals.[1]

[1] E.g., Buchanan (1975); Höffe (1995, 1996); Stemmer (2000, 2002); Southwood (2010); Chwaszcza (2013); de Jasay (2013); Frederick (2013); Gaus (2013); Gauthier (2013); Lahno (2013); Narveson (2013); Sugden (2013); and Vanderschraaf (2013). For discussion of Höffe's contractarianism, see Kettner (1997); on Southwood see below, §34.3. Contemporary philosophers should disabuse themselves of the notion that 'the latest' is also 'the greatest'. The calibre of philosophical contributions, and indeed their status as contributions to the field, requires comprehensive knowledge and understanding of the relevant issues and their discussions from whatever period or tradition. Fixation upon 'the newest' is

Gauthier claims his contractarianism is:

> the only [form of moral constructivism] available to persons who may neither expect nor require their fellows to share their own orientation to values and norms. (132; cf. 133, 142)[2]

According to Gauthier's contractarianism, social institutions and practices are justifiable only in terms of an hypothetical agreement among mutually independent agents rationally deliberating about their conditions of interaction to the effect that it would make sense for each of them to agree to certain such conditions (132, 133, 141). He stresses that his sole concern is with justification, that his contractarian model of justification is compatible with a wide range of non-contractual forms of social interaction (141), and that it does not require constituting social authority solely by transferring the normative, justificatory resources of individuals to such an authority (142), as in Hobbes' view (Gauthier 1986). Gauthier's express focus upon justification contrasts with his acknowledged previous failure to distinguish justificational from definitory aspects of a contractarian model of society (141–2).[3] (This distinction corresponds to that drawn here between constitutive and heuristic or expository uses of a social contract model.)

Gauthier's contractarianism identifies some stringent conditions a society must meet to be justifiable. His contractarianism rules out patterns of interaction which tend to provide net over-all benefits to some individuals rather than others; the life plans of net social malefactors are ruled out (136, 137). Gauthier's contractarian justificatory agreement thus requires that:

> . . . the actual social structure be . . . mutually beneficial [. . . and ensure] that the proportion between benefits and the contribution each chooses to make be roughly the same for all. (140)

Furthermore, '. . . social norms . . . give rise to practices that enlarge the horizon of ends . . .' (138). Hence, '. . . the life-plans available to an agent . . . depend on the social practices of her society' (138). Therefore:

unwarranted self-congratulation. The long-standing neglect of the very possibility of Natural Law Constructivism is one cardinal case in point.

2 Gauthier (1997) is referred to parenthetically in the text of this chapter by page number.

3 For critical discussion of Gauthier's previous contract theory, see Vallentyne (1991); Morris and Ripstein (2001).

The contractarian supposes . . . that social practices are to be justified . . . by showing how they permit and encourage the formations of life-plans for which they offer the prospect of satisfying fulfilment. (138)

More explicitly, Gauthier states:

The society must be so structured that, first, for each normal person, there is a range of social roles effectively available, each of which demands a productive contribution from its holder, and rewards the holder appropriately to her marginal contribution to the joint social product. Second, each of these roles must be compatible with a set of life-plans, any of which could in normal circumstances be chosen by and satisfyingly pursued by someone occupying the role, and having at her disposal that share of the joint social product which rewards effective occupancy. (139)

About these conditions I believe Gauthier is correct, so far as he develops them. The critical question, posed by Gauthier's own claim (in the first quotation above) is whether these provisions, among others, can be justified solely by contractarian agreement, indeed, of the kind he specifies.

Gauthier clarifies the justificatory character of his contractarianism by contrasting it with Scanlon's contractualism. On Scanlon's contractualist view, achieving agreement by justifying one's acts to others is fundamental to morality. On Gauthier's view, it is others who must justify their acts to oneself, especially as their acts impinge upon or restrict one's own (134–5). Gauthier formulates this important contrast in these terms:

. . . on Scanlon's [contractualist] view, the direction of justification is from the individual to others. The role of agreement is to gain the acceptance of others for one's actions. But in the contractarianism I espouse, the direction of justification is quite the reverse. Beginning from the idea of a rational deliberator, the contractarian finds no basis for postulating a moral need for the justification of one's actions to others. The role of agreement is to address each person's demand that the constraints of society be justified to him, not a concern that he justify himself to others. (134–5)[4]

[4] Unlike Gauthier's contractarianism, Scanlon's (1998) contractualism expressly considers only a significant portion of the moral domain; it claims neither to be the sole nor the fundamental domain. Gauthier cites it only to clarify the character of his own view. I omit discussion of Scanlon's contractualism because this concise study focuses upon identifying and justifying some of the most basic moral principles and the institutions they structure.

The scope of contractarian agreement is restricted to social practices and institutions which are optional, and thus can either be agreed to or rejected as one chooses. If contractarianism is to be the sole and sufficient form of rational justification for basic social practices and institutions, then all basic social provisions must be optional in order to be proper candidates for elective, contractarian choice. Accordingly, Gauthier recognizes that his contractarianism is incompatible with Kant's view, which holds that complying with the dictates of the Categorical Imperative is not optional, and thus cannot be subject to contractarian agreement (143).[5]

Gauthier's concern to develop a method to identify and to justify principles of justice without presupposing substantial agreement in normative outlook is vital in today's multi-cultural context, just as it was in the early Modern period which spawned the Modern natural law tradition.[6] Gauthier is also right that identifying and justifying legitimate social principles must involve showing that it is rational to accept and to abide by them. Moreover, to address both of these desiderata requires a constructivist approach to identifying and justifying principles of justice, because only constructivism avoids presuming that there are some such norms, a presumption which cannot avoid a fundamental *petitio principii* against any and all who dissent. The key question raised by Gauthier's contractarianism is whether hypothetical contractual agreement is the sole and sufficient basis for rationally justifying basic social principles and practices. Here I argue, briefly, that Kant is right that such radical contractarianism is neither the sole nor the sufficient basis for identifying or justifying legitimate principles of justice, and that Hume's and Kant's Natural Law Constructivism—itself a radical form of constructivism—is decidedly superior to Gauthier's contractarianism. Hence Gauthier's claim that his is the only viable form of constructivism (132; cf. 133, 142) is mistaken.[7]

5 This general point also holds of utilitarianism (143), but this kind of view is not presently germane.

6 This holds true, although the 'multi-culturalism' confronting Modern natural lawyers concerned politically irreconcilable Christian schisms and international commerce on the seas; cf. Schneewind (2001, 730).

7 The brief case for this point made here (§32) is detailed in chapter 8.

Here I focus on four key questions:

1. whether all fundamental social practices and institutions are optional, and so can be objects of elective choice, in the way required by Gauthier's contractarianism; (§30)
2. whether contractarianism confronts the problem of relevant descriptions; (§31)
3. whether grounds for justifying basic social arrangements require acceptance in the form of contractarian agreement; (§§32, 34)
4. whether the asymmetrical directions of justification identified by Gauthier in his own and in Scanlon's view are tenable. (§33)

30 Are all Fundamental Social Practices and Institutions Optional?

The first problem is that the contractarian model of rational justification itself requires provisions which are not and cannot rightly be understood by that model to be optional for any prospective contractor. This problem lodges in at least three provisions of Gauthier's analysis; the first concerns one's own upbringing, the second concerns one's responsibility to reciprocate for the benefits of one's own upbringing, whereas the third concerns the key social proviso of non-exploitation.

30.1 Contractarianism, children, and adulthood

The contractarian model of justification is only available to, and only addresses, individual rational deliberators. As Gauthier recognizes, human beings can become rational deliberators only through and on the basis of an economically and emotionally secure and stable upbringing. He states:

> ... an economically and emotionally secure and stable upbringing is a basic demand enshrined in the social contract ... (146)

Accordingly Gauthier further holds that this basic demand imposes important constraints both on parents and on society (146). Gauthier's use of the term 'enshrined' obscures an important ambiguity. Such an upbringing is required to become a mature adult capable of engaging in rational deliberation so that one is able to engage in the deliberations, make the proposals, and conclude the agreements required by the contractarian model of justification, on the basis of which alone one has (according to his account) any social obligations or entitlements. Such an upbringing is a pre-condition of engaging in contractarian forms of justification. Furthermore, such an upbringing is required even to anticipate the benefits and to estimate one's share of the burdens of the social practices to be established by contractarian deliberation, negotiation, and agreement.[8] Hence having had such an upbringing is not optional for such forms of justification, nor for any potential contractor. Hence such an upbringing is not and cannot be a matter of elective contractarian agreement. Certainly it is not something anyone can opt out of in any relevant sense: to understand appropriately the relevant social or non-social options and to opt in or out of any of them on the basis of an adequate understanding of them requires that one has reached a considerable degree of emotional and intellectual maturity, which is thus non-optional for any potential social contractor.

It will not do to say that one's own upbringing simply belongs to the *de facto* historical and social conditions of one's life, which of course antedate any hypothetical contractarian deliberations or choice (cf. 133). Gauthier is clear that his contractarian model of justification is to be available, indeed central, to and within the social practices and institutions justified by his contractarian justificatory model (cf. 140). Having had such an upbringing is not optional for persons within such a society either, precisely because contractarian justification is to be central to that society and within its members' self-understanding as voluntary participants in mutually beneficial social arrangements.

30.2 Upbringing and contractarian reciprocity

More directly, by the time one has matured enough to engage in contractarian, counter-factual deliberations about whether membership in a (purportedly) contractarian society is worthwhile, one has already benefited enormously from one's society, without yet having much reciprocated by contributing to it (146). Gauthier's contractarian principles require providing benefits to others proportional and indeed at least roughly equal to the benefits one receives from them (140). Consequently,

[8] Gauthier states: 'It would be pointless to afford individuals opportunities for productive and satisfying lives if they were unable to take advantage of these opportunities for want of realized skills and developed sensibilities' (148).

someone who comes of contractarian age is already obligated to provide benefits to his or her society, regardless of whether he or she happens to 'find value in society'. In this important regard, hypothetical contractarian agreement can at best ratify grounds of obligation already established by one's already having had an adequate upbringing, yet this 'ratification' really amounts to recognizing the significance of benefits one has already received and one's reciprocal obligations to contribute to the society from which one has benefited so fundamentally, indeed, without which one would fail to be a sufficiently mature human being. In view of this, it is very difficult to see what contribution merely hypothetical 'contractarian' agreement could make to *justifying* obligations already incurred on the basis of actual circumstances and the general principles of reciprocity required for legitimate, cooperative interaction as such.[9]

This point deserves closer consideration. Someone who did not 'find value in society', Gauthier says,

> ... would have no reason to agree to its conditions of interaction. (135)

The problem here is that, although such a person may not acknowledge, or may refuse to acknowledge that she or he has obligations to society, this does not—on Gauthier's own contractarian principles of reciprocity—settle the question whether that person *does* have obligations to society. This question is settled—on Gauthier's contractarian principles—by the fact that the person in question has already and substantially benefited from society, together with at least an acceptable degree of compliance of that society with the contractarian requirements of justice (see §31).

To block this objection by stressing the purely hypothetical nature of contractarian agreement and justification can only sever the presumed link between such hypothetical contractarian agreement and our actual obligations and entitlements. As Gauthier stresses, his contractarian method only justifies actual obligations and entitlements within an actual society that meets several very stringent—indeed 'revolutionary' (148)—conditions, mentioned above (§29) and discussed further below (§31).

[9] Cf. Becker (1986).

Notice, too, that like 'enshrined' Gauthier's term 'find' is ambiguous: it could mean simply 'acknowledge' or it could mean 'discover'. If one of Gauthier's social contractors *discovers*—that is, *recognizes*—the value of social interaction or the value of her or his prior education, then the *values*—that is, the normative significance—of those social provisions carries the constitutive justificatory burden, which the contractor duly recognizes. In that case, 'contractarian' agreement is merely heuristic, not constitutive, of justification. (This is not at all to deny the significance of agreement *qua* acknowledgement or ratification of sufficient justifying reasons.) To maintain his radical contractarian account of the justification of the most basic normative principles, according to which contractarian agreement plays an ineliminable constitutive role in their justification, Gauthier must construe 'find', not as 'discover', but merely as 'affirm' or 'admit'. Taken in this merely subjective sense, however, 'find[ing]' value in society—or *not* finding value in society—belies the facts of social cooperation and of social upbringing and education, together with their normative implications—even those implications identified by appeal to Gauthier's own contractarian principle of reciprocity, his contractarian 'proviso'.[10]

30.3 The contractarian proviso revisited

Previously Gauthier maintained that the key proviso which 'prohibits bettering one's position through interaction worsening the position of another' is non-optional: 'Although a part of morals by agreement, it is not the product of rational agreement' (1986, 16). This same proviso is equally central to Gauthier's (1997) analysis considered here. The fact that this proviso is not optional shows that it cannot be justified by any constitutive (justificatory) contractarian agreement, precisely because 'it is a condition that must be accepted by each person for such agreement to be possible' (Gauthier 1986, 16). Gauthier previously argued that 'it is rational for utility-maximisers to accept the proviso' (1986, 193; cf. 200–32). However, his argument relies, as it must, on reasons which show that it is rational to accept this proviso. Therefore the proviso does not require actual, elective acceptance for its justification, much less does it require specifically contractarian agreement.

[10] I thank Lucas Thorpe for noting the ambiguity of Gauthier's use of 'find'.

Hence Gauthier's contractarian form of rational justification, which focuses solely upon reasons actually accepted by individual contractors, cannot be the sole and sufficient method of moral justification it is proposed to be, because on this model, the conditions required to become a rational contractarian deliberator are not themselves optional for any prospective contractor: contractarian agreement to undertake social obligations and to receive social benefits presupposes rather than justifies these conditions for anyone's own hypothetical agreement, including centrally the conditions of one's own proper maturation as a (putative) rational contractor. Gauthier's improved version of contractarianism still does not properly recognize the profound, non-negotiable importance of upbringing and education, which begins in the family and continues within one's community. This form of human finitude and interdependence is central to Hume's analysis of the basic principles of justice, and if it is not expressly mentioned by Kant within his *Metaphysics of Morals*, that is because it belongs to what he called 'practical anthropology', whereas he focused primarily upon his Critical 'metaphysics' of morals as a system of rational principles.[11]

31 Contractarianism and the Problem of Relevant Descriptions

The three problems just discussed raise an important version of the problem of relevant descriptions. Gauthier's justificatory strategy requires at several points that we correctly conceive ourselves and our societies. Regarding ourselves, we are required by Gauthier's model to recognize that as human beings we require proper upbringing in order to become capable of understanding and undertaking contractarian reasoning and agreement. His model also requires us to recognize that, due to our inherent human limitations, the character and quality of our individual life is greatly improved (to say the least) through social cooperation. Regarding our societies, Gauthier's model requires that an actual society is, and is recognized to be, a cooperative scheme for mutual benefit within which a roughly equal balance of the proportion of

[11] Kant has a good deal to say about education and its moral significance; see Herman (2007, 130–53), Westphal (2016c).

benefits and burdens prevails for all (135, 140; cf. 148) and which provides for a range of life-plans which can be pursued with reasonable expectations of satisfying fulfilment (139–40). It is insufficient that anyone merely *believe* she or he is both a social benefactor and beneficiary; to justify membership within Gauthier's contractarian society requires that 'each *must be* both beneficiary and benefactor' (135, emphasis added).

Once correct descriptions of ourselves as rational deliberators and of our societies as fulfilling a series of stringent justificatory conditions are recognized to be central to Gauthier's contractarianism, two issues arise:

1. What, if anything, within the contractarian model provides for correct descriptions of the relevant kinds, or for correcting misdescriptions of contractually relevant factors?
2. Is the justificatory burden born by our contractarian agreement, or is it rather born by the relevant factors and their normative (justificatory) implications, whereby contractarian 'agreement' merely models our understanding and acceptance of these factors and their normative implications?

These restate my second and third key questions (§29, end); they are best pursued in this order.

Central to Gauthier's contractarian understanding and justification of social institutions and practices is the idea that society is, *inter alia*, a 'cooperative venture for mutual advantage'—an idea as central to Hobbes', Hume's, or Rousseau's theories of justice (not to mention Aristotle's or Smith's) as it is to Kant's, or Rawls', or Gauthier's.[12] The problem of relevant descriptions gains purchase on Gauthier's contractarianism in connection with his observation that:

> Someone who did not find value in society would have no reason to agree to its conditions of interaction. Someone who did not contribute value to others would give them no reason to accept her within the scope of society's conditions of interaction. Each then must be able to draw from society some of what she seeks but could not gain on her own, and each must contribute to society some of what others seek but would lack without her. Or, put simply, each must be [*sic*] both beneficiary and benefactor. (135; cf. 148)

[12] Oddly, Gauthier only mentions Rawls in this regard (135).

The problem is this: social contract models or strategies of moral justification must and can only rely upon whatever explicit considerations individuals bring to their deliberations, because voluntary decisions can only be based upon considerations of which an agent is aware and which she or he regards as relevant and rationally compelling. Hence the relevant question for contract models of agreement is not only whether someone *in fact* contributes to as well as benefits from the activities of others (in ways neither party could obtain without social cooperation), but also whether other persons are *believed* by any potential contractor to contribute to as well as to benefit from the activities of others and of oneself (in ways neither party could obtain without social cooperation). Gauthier is right that, on his contractarian account,

> ... someone who did not find value in society would have no reason to agree to its conditions of interaction ... (135)

However, the crucial question is not whether someone *does* find value in society, but—given human limitations and the exigencies of the human condition—whether they *ought* to recognize the value of social cooperation. The basic question is not whether someone 'has' (*sic*) an acknowledged reason to agree to (suitably just) social conditions of interaction, in the sense of expressly acknowledging or accepting that reason, but rather, whether *there is* reason or *there are* reasons for him or her to recognize and hence to accept (suitably just) social conditions of interaction. If there are such reasons, then it is important to find ways to bring any potential contractor to recognize and to accept those reasons, presumably, to accept them for cogent and sufficient justifying reasons. By focusing solely upon express though hypothetical agreement, by regarding all fundamental social practices and institutions as matters of elective agreement, Gauthier's contractarianism omits and must omit the important prospect of correcting individuals' misunderstandings of their social interdependence and the grounds of obligation based upon our social interdependence. Alternatively, if Gauthier were to take this option seriously, he would undermine the role of contractarian agreement in the justification of social principles and practices because justificatory weight would be borne by the reasons favouring membership in society and one's recognition of these reasons, rather than by anyone's elective agreement to a merely hypothetical contract. (Yes, the Euthyphro question recurs here too.)

The problem of relevant descriptions arises here, not as a problem about how an agent describes or mis-describes one or another specific proposed or prior act, but rather how an agent describes or mis-describes the entire class of prospective social interactions, including their prospective benefits and burdens, and how an agent describes or mis-describes his or her own agency in view of those prospective social interactions. The problem with Gauthier's contractarianism is that it mis-describes the whole class of social interactions as optional, merely elective, and it mis-describes human beings as so self-sufficient that they can, at least 'in principle', opt out of society (cf. below, §33). Even Gauthier's most sophisticated version of radical contractarianism requires a radically counterfactual, profoundly mistaken, and misleading presumption of our mutual independence as human beings.

Furthermore, to maintain his claim that contractarianism provides the sole and sufficient basis of normative justification in social philosophy, Gauthier must maintain that only reasons one recognizes are reasons one *has*. This precludes in principle providing grounds to show that someone errs in dismissing (or failing to 'find' or to acknowledge), for example, the value of social interaction. (I return to this point in §34.) This is an instance of a general problem with social contract models of justification: because they can only appeal to reasons or grounds that potential contractors avow, they are incapable of addressing anyone who disregards or denies important features of their circumstances of obligation or entitlement. They are thus powerless against the socially obstinate, namely egoists, who are to social philosophy what radical sceptics are to epistemology.[13]

[13] One key reason Gauthier has to focus on reasons a contractor avows is his aim to avoid any form of objectivism about values. His main reason for rejecting objectivism about values is that only subjective values are required to explain individual action (Gauthier 1986, 56–9). This reason is ill-considered for at least two reasons. First, moral theory is concerned not simply with explaining individual actions, but also with assessing them normatively. Hence Gauthier's appeal to explanatory considerations alone misconstrues the (purported) domain of his own normative theory. Second, the explanation of individual action requires more than the individual's subjective values. Many actions are complex and extended, involving a series of steps. Despite even the best foresight such actions do not always succeed because one or another step turns out to be infeasible if not ill-conceived. In such cases the explanation of individual action requires appealing, not only to what the individual comes in these ways to believe about his or her prior plan, but also how he or she reassesses that plan and either pursues it in suitably modified form or rejects it for some other plan of action. The problem for Gauthier's subjectivism about values is that 'suitable'

As soon as the prospect of correcting someone's understanding—or rather misunderstanding—of society and of him or herself is countenanced, the radical contractarian strategy is deeply challenged, because whatever grounds there may be for correcting anyone's understanding of these crucial points may provide grounds for justifying social principles and practices, regardless of anyone's (hypothetical) contractarian agreement. More precisely, the prospect of providing sufficient reasons to justify certain principles and practices of social interaction regardless of anyone's express recognition of those reasons would render hypothetical contractarian agreement redundant, revealing it to be a dispensable epicycle on a more fundamental non-contractarian justificatory analysis. Kant's view is of this kind, and I believe he is correct about it, for reasons developed in the remainder of this study, beginning in §32.

First please note two points. The problem of relevant descriptions is a general problem for the proper use of any moral principles, criteria, guidelines, or examples. Agents properly characterizing their own actions or the actions of others, whether past, present, or proposed, requires morally sound education. This problem is neither avoided nor addressed by the philosophical fiat of aiming only to 'explain' individuals' actions by appeal to their 'motivational sets', nor by stipulating a strong form of 'reasons internalism'. Because Kant's Critical metaphysics of morals primarily aims to identify, characterize, and justify the most fundamental principles of morals, Kant says relatively little in his Critical moral philosophy—though far from nothing—about moral education (primarily in *TL*). Nevertheless, Kant's moral philosophy provides a good basis and context for developing illuminating accounts of moral 'perception' (i.e., sensitivity to morally salient features of an agent's context of action) and moral education.[14] One reason the present study aims to be clear,

here does not mean merely that the agent endorses it; 'suitability' is equally a function of what the agent's circumstances—physical, social, and normative—allow or disallow him or her to do (cf. Herman 1993, 173–7). Appeal to the belief-desire model of agency (cf. above, §17) is insufficient for *normative* moral theory and provides no adequate basis for rejecting objectivism about values. Regardless of whether they are objective or subjective, appealing to values as a basis for basic norms lands us back in the problems identified by the Euthyphro question (§5) and the Dilemma of the Criterion (§25). This is another reason why the justificatory externalism central to Natural Law Constructivism is so important.

[14] See especially Herman (1993, 2007); cf. Green (1999); Curren (2000, 2010a); Westphal (2012a).

concise, and accessible is to aid education and enlightenment in these increasingly benighted times.[15]

Those who favour contractarian strategies may rejoin to my previous objection, that it only holds against contract models which require actual agreement, but not against contract models which appeal to idealized or to hypothetical agreement. This rejoinder is insufficient for two reasons. First, to avoid my prior objection to Gauthier's view, idealized or hypothetical agreement must be highly counterfactual, with only weak links to anyone's actual 'motivational set'. This poses a severe problem, noted by Hume, of how actual obligations can be justified by merely hypothetical or idealized agreement. Second, to make any hypothetical or idealized agreement plausible requires adducing reasons in its favour. So doing, however, directly raises the prospect that those reasons carry the burden of justification, thus mooting any alleged constitutive role for agreement (and hypothetical or idealized agreement at that) in either identifying or justifying basic moral norms.

So-called 'deliberative' models of social contract theory (e.g., Goodin, 2003; Southwood 2010) aim precisely to address the problem of relevant ignorance or failure to appreciate morally or socially relevant considerations on the part of any potential party to some preferred social contract. This is an important aim, but to the extent that it is fulfilled, such social contract theories become expository or heuristic, and the purported contractual agreement plays ever less of a constitutive role in either identifying or justifying basic moral principles and the practices they structure. The explicative or heuristic value of such accounts can be significant; I focus here on Gauthier's radical contractarianism because of its clear ambitions to be the sole and sufficient form of moral constructivism for justifying basic moral principles (cf. above, §29).[16]

Contractarian strategies, too, must provide a cogent answer to the Euthyphro question, whether basic moral principles are justified because they are agreed to, or whether instead they are agreed to—or ought to be agreed to—because they are justified. Even Hume's fragment of a (Natural Law Constructivist) theory of justice suffices to auger well for the

[15] It is a paradox worth pondering that the vast majority of philosophers are, professionally, educators, only a slim minority of whom concern themselves with philosophy of education, or with pedagogy.

[16] For concise discussion of basic flaws in Southwood's (2010) account, see below, §34.3.

latter, objectivist, agreement-independent answer. Kant's Natural Law Constructivism elaborates such reasons in detail. These reasons are sketched in §32 and detailed in chapter 8.

32 Kant's Non-Contractarian Constructivism

Kant's *Rechtslehre* ('doctrine of justice'; designated '*RL*') develops a constructivist natural law theory which expressly idealizes the social contract because contractarian agreement plays no constitutive role in moral justification.[17] Agreement plays no such role because Kant's justificatory analysis addresses social arrangements which for finite rational human beings are altogether non-optional, and which we should understand and accept on the basis of Kant's justificatory analysis. In this section I consider briefly some key points of Kant's analysis of one central, non-optional social arrangement: rights to acquire and use possessions. These points are developed in greater detail in chapter 8.

Kant recognized that the principles governing rightful possession are not analytic truths, and he recognized that no norm can be justified solely on the basis of empirical evidence. Thus basic principles and practices of social interaction are a proper topic for his Critical philosophy, which aims to provide *a priori* justification for certain synthetic propositions.[18] To do this, Kant's *Metaphysics of Morals* applies a pure *a priori* universal normative principle to human nature in order to develop

[17] Using 'right' to render Kant's term '*Recht*' (as in *CEWK*)—except where Kant discusses specific rights—fails to translate Kant's term. Kant uses '*Recht*' as the German counterpart to the Latin *ius* (or *jus*), which designates justice in contrast to ethics, as one of the two coordinate species of moral philosophy.

[18] As Kant noted, the central difficulty involved in justifying rights to possess is to show, in this instance, 'how synthetic propositions regarding right are possible *a priori*, that is, without presupposing another right *i.e.* possession' (*GS* 23:302.28–30). My brief sketch here is based on previous detailed analyses (Westphal 1997), in which I explain why I focus on 'possession' rather than 'property'. Recently Byrd and Hruschka (2006) have reconstructed Kant's argument in ways designed to avoid the problems highlighted in my (1997). Their illuminating analysis, however, repeats rather than removes some of the most central of those problems. Most centrally, they—like Ludwig (2002)—disregard Kant's distinction between possession (*Besitz*) and property (*Eigenthüm*). In my (1997, esp. §1.5) I argue that the conceptual point, made in connection with Honoré (1970), sufficed to make the case, on the one hand, because so many of the incidents of property can only be specified within a legal code, and on the other, because only construing Kant's term '*Besitz*' narrowly, as 'possession' rather than 'property', affords a sound justification, on Kant's part, of rights to possess. Also see Rühl (2010) and Horn (2014, 196–220).

the basic principles of rights and duties governing human affairs (*MdS* 6:216.37–217.4). The fundamental normative principle Kant uses is the Universal Principle of Justice:

> An act is *right* if it, or if according to its maxim, one's freedom of will can coexist with everyone's freedom in accord with a universal law.
>
> (*RL Einleitung* §C, *GS* 6:230)

Above I argued (§§22, 26), as does Onora O'Neill, that this principle embodies the constructivist *conditio sine qua non* of rational justification, that any principle or course of action can be legitimate only if sufficient justifying grounds for it can be provided to all concerned (affected) parties.[19] (Recall that 'providing' sufficient reasons to others is not equivalent to their 'accepting' them.[20])

Kant's *Metaphysics of Morals* applies the Universal Principle of Justice to the human condition by appealing to the Principle of Hypothetical Imperatives and to basic facts about human nature and the circumstances of human action which belong to Kant's 'practical anthropology'.[21] To recall, the Principle of Hypothetical Imperatives states:

> Whoever wills the end, also wills (insofar as reason has decisive influence on his actions) the indispensably necessary means to it that are within his power (*Gewalt*).
>
> (*GMS* 4:417)

This Principle states a general constraint on the rational willing of ends.[22] The 'anthropological' information relevant to rights of acquisition and use is this:

[19] Westphal (1997, 2005).

[20] In my (2011a) I argue that Kant's Universal Principle of Justice is an instance of the central principle required for rational justification in non-formal domains. Cases in which sufficient justifying reasons are provided to people who do not accept them, or who perhaps refuse to accept them, obviously raise difficulties. These difficulties can be solved by a theory of constructive self- and mutual criticism of the kind Hegel developed in his *Phenomenology of Spirit* (Westphal 1989, 2003, 2013b).

[21] Though Kant relegated his 'practical anthropology' to an unwritten appendix to the *MdS* (*TL* §45, 6:469.8–12), his analyses and examples provide significant information about its contents.

[22] A possible terminological confusion may be averted here. This principle might be called 'the principle of rational willing' or 'the principle of instrumental rationality', but Kant calls it 'the Principle of Hypothetical Imperatives'. The sense and scope of this principle are clear, but his designation might mislead Anglophone readers insofar as he classifies moral imperatives generally as 'categorical' rather than 'hypothetical' imperatives

1. We human beings cannot will our ends into existence *ex nihilo*.
2. Our ends, regarding both basic needs and elective ends we choose to pursue, are complex, temporally extended and at least somewhat integrated.
3. We live on a finite surface (a globe).
4. We are sufficiently populous that we cannot, in fact, avoid each other.

(*RL* §§8, 9, 13, 42)

The first fact about our finite agency, that we cannot will our ends into existence *ex nihilo*, entails that we must make use of materials around us in order to obtain our ends. At a minimum, this includes the air, water, and food required for us to act at all, and the clothing, shelter, and tools we need to maintain ourselves.[23]

The second fact about our ends entails that no human being can simultaneously physically hold or occupy all that one's life requires, even at a subsistence level. Human life requires regular and reliable use of things, including sources of food and shelter, which cannot all be physically held or 'empirically possessed' simultaneously.[24] If we cannot count on the resources of some of our activities remaining available to us regularly and reliably, even when not presently using or holding them, we cannot engage in those activities, nor can we engage in most of our other activities.

The third and fourth facts entail that we can and do find ourselves in circumstances of relative scarcity in which our own actions affect the courses of action open to others.[25] This is the situation to which basic moral principles and practices of social interaction pertain. Hume

(*GMS* 4:414). In that context, Kant simply distinguishes between those imperatives which pertain to an agent only upon the assumption—the hypothesis—that the agent wants or desires some contingent end or other. Kant classifies moral imperatives as 'categorical' because they are obligatory regardless of our contingent wants or desires. In both cases, however, willing an end involves willing the use of sufficient means to obtain it. Willing the use of insufficient or inappropriate (ineffective) means is instrumentally irrational; not willing to use any means whatever is wishing rather than willing.

[23] I omit from this list our *de facto* interdependence (*per* Hume), not because Kant denies or neglects it, but because it is not necessary to debate substantive issues about individualism or social interdependence in order to identify and to justify basic rights to acquire, possess and use material things.

[24] Kant was clearly aware of this point (*GS* 23:230–1; translated in Kant 2016).

[25] See further Flickschuh (2000).

recognized these conditions as ones of relative scarcity and limited human generosity; Rousseau recognized that conditions of relative scarcity are a function of population density.[26] Kant's fourth point recognizes these features of the human condition.

These four facts about our agency make rights to possession necessary for human beings. In view of these facts, the Principle of Hypothetical Imperatives commits each of us to willing to possess at least some things without physically holding them (detention). It further commits each of us to willing that there be sufficient conditions for acquiring possessions and retaining them for our own use. The problem about possession and use of objects to be solved is that we must use materials in order to act at all, and yet our acquisition of any materials precludes others from acquiring those same materials, whilst unilateral imposition of obligations on others to respect one's acquisition of possessions cannot be justified. Indeed, it is ruled out by Kant's Universal Principle of Justice. Yet possessing things without physically detaining them can be effective only if one's possessions are recognized and respected by others; the very point of rights of possession is to coordinate our actions to avoid mutual interference, including interference with our possessions and the activities they enable. (This is Hobbes' 'Innocent Problem' of mutual interference.) Hence Kant's (implicit) question is, 'Under what conditions is acquiring possessions possible and legitimate?'

Kant claims that the Juridical Postulate of Practical Reason, that things can be possessed, permits us to obligate others to respect our possessions, and that their obligation stems directly from our act of taking something into possession.[27] How can this be? First acquisition appears to impose unilaterally an obligation upon others, something proscribed by everyone's innate right to freedom, which includes independence from the unilateral determining will of others.

[26] *CS* 1.6.1–2; cf. Westphal (2013d, §8).

[27] Kant states the 'Juridical Postulate of Practical Reason' twice. His first statement is: 'It is possible to have any external object of my will [*Willkür*] as mine; *i.e.*, any maxim according to which, if it were a law, an object of will must become *in itself* (objectively) *ownerless* (*res nullius*) is contrary to justice' (*RL* §2, 6:246, 5–8); Kant's second formulation is: 'It is a duty of justice, so to act toward others that what is external (usable) can also become someone's own' (*RL* §6, 6:252,13–15). On the relation between these two formulae, see §37.

Kant's analysis shows that taking things into possession involves no such unilateral imposition of obligations. Kant expressly states that the innate right to freedom only extends to freedom of action which is compatible with the freedom of others in accord with a universal law, and he expressly states that this innate right to freedom involves our innate equality, which is independence from being bound by others—so far as one cannot also mutually bind them (*RL* 6:237.29–24). One key claim in Kant's Critical metaphysics of justice is that we recognize that other human beings are finite rational agents like ourselves.[28] Consequently, we know that they too must act towards their ends by using things around them. Consequently, the same principle of permission to acquire possessions and the same correlative obligation to respect others' rights of possession govern them just as they govern us. Consequently, we are permitted to obligate others to respect our claims to acquire, retain, and use things only because we are obligated, both by our own claims and by others' claims, to respect others' claims to things, *and* because others can and must acquire similar rights to possession along with the correlative obligations to respect others' possessions, including one's own. This result can be demonstrated by using Kant's 'Contradiction in Conception Test', as shown in chapter 8.

Kant argues that our rights and obligations regarding acquisition of possessions are thus correlative and coeval, as are also the correlative rights and obligations of others. They are correlative and coeval because the entire point of rights to possession arises only in conditions of relative scarcity, in which any act of acquisition restricts the range of possible free acts of others. Gauthier's asymmetrical 'direction' of justification, that it is only others who must justify their actions to oneself, insofar as their actions impinge upon one's own freedom of action, is fundamentally mistaken.

33 Directions of Justification

How does Kant's analysis bear on Gauthier's? Gauthier might object that invoking Kant's constructivist account of justification, in which justifying one's actions to others is fundamental, commits a *petitio principii* against his own contractarian account of justification, which rejects this

[28] Cf. *RL* §42, 6:307.14–26; cp. *KdrV* A346/B404–5, A546–7/B574–5; *KdU*, 5:484.7–19. For discussion, see Westphal (2012b, 2015a); Kitcher (2013).

requirement. The first response to make is that Gauthier's contractarianism can neither evade nor forego the requirement to justify one's acts to others.

One reason for this has already been mentioned (above, §31): *pace* Gauthier, whoever achieves a maturity sufficient to consider whether membership in contractarian society is worthwhile, and yet who found 'no value in society' (135), certainly would—on grounds provided by Gauthier's analysis of the principles of social cooperation—owe it to others to justify his or her failure to reciprocate for all the benefits she or he received from society which were required for and used by him or her to reach deliberative maturity. This obligation is justified by Gauthier's own principle of reciprocity, and holds regardless of whether any egoist or fool fails to acknowledge this obligation, or fails to 'find' value in society.[29]

A second reason is that rights to acquire possessions—a very basic social principle and practice required by Gauthier's own consideration of how or whether societies offer suitable ranges of life plans and prospects for their satisfying pursuit—only become an issue in conditions of relative scarcity in which one's own acts of acquisition restrict the range of free acts of others otherwise open to them. The condition of relative scarcity has been and remains endemic to the human condition; accordingly it has been central to Modern natural law theories. The strictly asymmetrical justificatory condition central to Gauthier's analysis requires the entirely hypothetical, wildly counterfactual condition of abundance so great that one's own acts of acquisition only negligibly affect the range of free acts available to others. In this regard, the abstractness of Gauthier's analysis masks a fundamental oversimplification embedded in its basic model of justification.[30] The justificatory

[29] Note further that Gauthier's principle of reciprocity holds as a principle governing just social interactions, regardless of agents' affirming it, including those interactions concerning contributions to, and benefits derived from, social interaction, even if those benefits and burdens are considered solely in terms of (market) exchange values based upon subjective preferences. I have focused my criticism on the social requirements of one's own upbringing and education in order to forego debate about exchange values and the (allegedly) merely subjective preferences they reflect (or price).

[30] This is not the only instance of political fantasy in Gauthier's exposition. He also states: '... in a technologically advanced contractarian society persons would face impoverishment only as a consequence of their failure to take advantage of the opportunity to choose a productive and satisfying life-plan. They would not be, as many persons in our

asymmetry basic to Gauthier's hypothetical contractarian analysis requires, in effect, a Lockean proviso that, when removing anything from whatever is generally available for individuals to acquire, 'enough and as good' remains for others. Like Locke's, Gauthier's analysis requires either a fertile frontier or a garden of Eden—conditions which have long since vanished from the face of the Earth. In this crucial regard, Gauthier disregards Hobbes' 'Innocent Problem' of mutual interference (above, §8), Hume's observation that the conditions of justice are the conditions of relative scarcity (above, §11.2), and Rousseau's observation that both problems result from population growth and consequent population density (§38.2). Like Rousseau's, Kant's analysis instead maintains a strict independence requirement (that no one is to have the kind or extent of wealth, power, or privilege which enables him or her to unilaterally command the actions of others[31]): a requirement which holds within societies and without uninhabited, yet bountiful frontiers, nor mythical abundance of nature (or of technology).

For these two reasons, deliberatively mature adults are not in the asymmetrical justificatory situation claimed by Gauthier (134–5), that it is only others who must justify to oneself their restrictions upon one's actions, not *vice versa*. Thinking that contractarian deliberators are in that asymmetrical situation is a serious misunderstanding and plainly an irrelevant (mis-)description of their normative situation of a kind and severity which can only distort our understanding and appreciation of our actual social obligations and entitlements, and indeed the very character of human life, including one's own.

society are, denied such an opportunity' (146–7). Why technological advance is either required for, or would provide an advance in justice (of the kind to provide genuine, realizable access to satisfying life plans, thus eliminating their *de facto* denial to many in contemporary societies) Gauthier does not explain, but any supposed connection between them (as is clearly suggested by Gauthier's remark) regards a fundamental problem of distributive justice as a technological problem, whilst disregarding the prospect that further technological advancement would simply continue to serve those who benefit disproportionately from current social arrangements. One would have thought that Marx's untenable, messianic hope to transcend the conditions of distributive justice through massive increase in economic production would have disabused us of such utopianism.

[31] The Independence Requirement is first mentioned above, §8; Kant's justification for it is examined below, §§37.2, 38.5, 43; it is part of what Kant contends is the sole innate right to freedom.

As noted (§29), Gauthier contrasts the direction of justification involved in his own contractarian view with the direction involved in Scanlon's contractualism. According to Gauthier's contractarianism, it is others who must justify restrictions on one's activity to oneself. According to Scanlon's contractualism, one must justify one's actions to others (134–5). One merit of Kant's Natural Law Constructivism is to show that these contrasting asymmetries in the aim and direction of fundamental moral justification are both ill-conceived because both aims and directions of justification are inextricably intertwined, at least in the fundamental case of rights to acquire, retain, and use possessions. To acquire and to possess something requires more than just holding, occupying, or detaining something. It requires that others respect one's possession by regarding it as one's own and leaving it to one even when one does not physically hold it. (This is what makes rightful possession 'intelligible' or 'noumenal', in Kant's terms; *RL* §5; cf. Hume, *T* 3.2.3.7/SBN 506, quoted above, §11.1.) Justifying one's possessive claims to them likewise requires one to recognize their correlative rights with regard to their acquiring possessions. Recognizing their rights to their possessions involves recognizing one's own obligations to leave their acquisitions to them. Hence to possess something *does* require me to justify my claim to others, and *vice versa*. This case is typical in matters moral because most of morals concerns our principles and practices of interaction and because relative scarcity, population density, and basic facts about human dependency and interdependency require us to interact. The justificatory asymmetry stressed by Gauthier is thus belied; it is not Kant's, but rather Gauthier's view which suffers from hopeless abstraction.

Gauthier might rejoin that Kant's practical philosophy is based on (purported) objective values, a view rejected by his contractarianism (133). Two points should be noted briefly. First, Kant's universalization tests can be formulated and justified without appeal to Kant's views about the intrinsic, incommensurable value of free rational agency, 'dignity' (above, §§22, 26). Second, Gauthier (1986, 56–7) rejects objective accounts of value because they are not required to explain individual behaviour. Perhaps so, but normative theory is concerned with assessing, not merely explaining, individual behaviour. 'Explanation' of behaviour as such addresses no questions *de jure*; one would think the political atrocities of the twentieth century would have made this painfully obvious (see Glover 1999). Hence Gauthier's objection to objective accounts of value is misguided (above, §17), most importantly, because Hume's and Kant's Natural Law Constructivism shows that purported 'values' are not required as premises for identifying or justifying the most basic moral principles and the practices they structure and guide.[32]

34 Possible Universalisability *versus* Moral Voluntarism

34.1 The dilemmas of voluntarism

Social contract models of justification face the following dilemma: in virtue of what does contractarian agreement legitimate whatever is agreed upon? Does contractarian agreement represent anything more or other than the recognition and acceptance, by those who agree, of the merits and the justifying reasons for the proposal at hand? If it does not, if this is all that 'agreement' represents, then contractual agreement is not the fundamental basis for identifying or justifying basic norms; rather, the fundamental basis of legitimacy lies in the merits of and the justificatory reasons for the proposal in question. If, on the other hand, contractarian agreement does contribute ineliminably to the justification and thus the legitimacy of principles and practices of social interaction, in virtue of what does contractarian agreement provide this contribution which, *ex hypothesi*, cannot be accounted for in terms of the merits (justificatory grounds) of the proposal at hand?

The basic problem can be put succinctly by permuting once again the Euthyphro question: are fundamental moral principles justified because they are agreed to? Or are fundamental moral principles agreed to because they are justified? Gauthier's radical contractarianism answers affirmatively to the first question, and negatively to the second. This is why his contractarianism counts as 'radical', though in this regard, Gauthier's contractarianism is representative of any moral theory which takes consent or agreement as fundamental, because consent or agreement

[32] I reiterate 'most basic' moral principles of justice, because there is ample role for actual deliberation, legislation, and consent at the constitutional level of legislation within any just, republican, democratic society, and in its legal provisions regarding, e.g., certified titles to possessions, including their acquisition, use, and exchange.

are to play an ineliminable, constitutive role in identifying or justifying basic moral principles. I have argued, with Hume and Kant, that if agreement or consent is to play any role in identifying or justifying basic moral principles, it must be secondary to the primary reasons which show that some basic obligations or freedoms are justified independently of consent, agreement, or consensus.[33]

The problem of relevant descriptions (§§31–33) and Gauthier's own reliance upon principles and premises which must be true—both of contractors and of societies (§§29, 30)—show that Gauthier's contractarianism does not identify a distinctive, positive, ineliminable, constitutive contribution of contractarian agreement to the identification or justification of basic social norms and practices. Consequently, Gauthier cannot substantiate his central thesis, that his is the 'only' viable form of constructivism in social philosophy (132; cf. 133, 142). Instead, the failure of Gauthier's analysis in this fundamental regard suggests viable forms of constructivism are to be found in the non-contractarian branch of the Modern natural law tradition, including centrally Hume's and Kant's Natural Law Constructivism, which recognizes that social life and thus also basic principles of justice are non-optional for human beings, under broadly met conditions of moderate population density and consequent relative scarcity. Chapter 8 corroborates these findings by examining and assessing in greater detail Kant's justification of rights to acquisition, possession, and use.

34.2 Modal versus *voluntarist interpretations of Kant's universalization test*

Thomas Hill (2001, 304, 310) contends that, in Kant's statements of the Categorical Imperative, his modal locutions 'can' or 'could' can best be understood in terms of 'would', so that hypothetical consent is fundamental to Kantian constructivism.[34] However, Hill simplifies his task by restricting his considerations to his version of Kantian constructivism (301), to which hypothetical consent is basic. Initially (note 2) he claims

[33] Similar problems lodge in Höffe's attempt to identify and to justify basic human rights by appeal to a 'transcendental exchange' of freedoms to do harm for reciprocal freedoms from harm by others; see especially Höffe (1992).

[34] Further parenthetical page references in this subsection are to Hill (2001). (This subsection may be omitted by general readers.)

that his presentation includes O'Neill's interpretation, though later he acknowledges (note 70) that O'Neill's view represents a more ambitious programme than his own.

Surprisingly, Hill twice explicates hypothetical consent in *modal* terms. Hill notes the following:

> The rational standards on which the 'could will' test relies can (though they need not) be expressed in terms of what rational agents necessarily "would will if rational." Moreover, under the kingdom of ends formula, the prohibitions that hypothetical agents would will are just those that are rationally necessary for them to will, given their situation.
>
> (Hill 2001, 304)

Hill's *explanans* in this statement uses a strong modal term, 'rationally necessary', to explicate what rational agents 'would will'. Hill's *explanans* of 'would will' thus reverts to the modal formulation of Kant's 'can' or 'could', though without explicating it sufficiently. Similarly, Hill indicates that:

> considering what, as rational, persons necessarily would agree to from a certain perspective . . . is inseparable from the consideration of what we could and could not rationally will.
>
> (Hill 2001, 313)

Here again, Hill analyses 'would' in terms of 'could', rather than the reverse, as appeared to be his main claim on this issue (304, 310), in dissent from O'Neill.

Hill stresses that what agents ideally would consent to must be analysed in terms of their rational consent (or willing), so that the analytical weight is borne by the account of willing *rationally*. However, willing *rationally* must, on Kant's view, be analysed in terms of what could or can be willed, subject to the constraints of the Universal Principle of Justice, the Principle of Hypothetical Imperatives (which is central to both Hill's and to O'Neill's accounts) and to certain broad considerations about our finite form of rational agency and our worldly circumstances of action (Kant's 'practical anthropology').

Hill formulates the critical contention between his view, which rests on hypothetical consent, and the modal interpretation developed by O'Neill and favoured here, in this passage:

> What remains to be seen, however, is whether or not the suggestion that members of the kingdom [of ends] legislate by using the universal law formula

> is useful for extensions of Kantian moral theory. This depends on whether the universal law formula's possible-will standard can fulfill the hopes that Kant, and some contemporary Kantians, have for it without falling back on implicit appeals to things that would or would not be agreed to by idealized rational agents. I doubt that the standard can do this, but I will not pursue the issue here.
>
> (Hill 2001, 313)

This is an important challenge, which I contend is met by Natural Law Constructivism. Before making my final case for this claim in chapter 8, I offer four observations here.

First, this issue bears on the issue Hill raises (§D) about whether hypothetical consent is otiose because the real issue concerns antecedent substantive reasons which suffice to justify various practical principles. The strong modal interpretation purports to provide substantive reasons to identify and to justify key practical principles, so that idealized hypothetical consent would represent merely agents' *recognition* of the soundness of such (purported) proofs. This is one of my main reasons for developing the modal interpretation, to identify substantive criteria by which to assess various claims (both common-sense and philosophical) about actual, implicit, or hypothetical consent or agreement.

Second, I submit that Kant's justification of rights to possession, as reconstructed in chapter 8, meets Hill's challenge. In this central case, the modal interpretation of Kant's Universal Principle of Justice (or the *Groundwork*'s Formula of Universal Law) justifies substantive normative principles and practices without implicit appeal to hypothetical agreement. This is consistent with recognizing, as I do (and as Kant does) that consent must play a central role in determining—as matters of public policy and positive legislation—how in particular to implement the principles and practices which can be identified and justified on the modal interpretation of Kant's test central to Natural Law Constructivism. I agree with Hill's interim conclusion that 'The merits of either approach for further developments of Kantian ethics depend, in the end, on the details of how the standards of rationality are other features of the imagined choice problem are spelled out' (304). So doing is the point of Natural Law Constructivism.

Third, by developing and defending the modal interpretation of Kant's universalisation tests in this study, I defend a much more robust criterion for the identification and rational justification of basic moral principles than is provided by Scanlon's (1998, 153) contractualism, which appeals to principles which 'no one could reasonably reject'.[35] This is not to reject Scanlon's analysis, but rather to indicate that the further constraints he identifies pertain to more specific principles, reasons, and actions within the domain of those basic, core principles, reasons, and actions identified as permissible or obligatory by Natural Law Constructivism.

These points may be further illustrated, fourth, by considering Nicholas Southwood's (2010) 'deliberative' model of contractarianism.

34.3 Deliberative contractualism to the rescue?

Southwood (2010, *vii*, 4, 9) claims that his 'deliberative' model of contractualism addresses 'the central problem of moral philosophy', which is to identify 'the . . . ultimate [constitutive] grounds of morality'.[36] He advances 'the contractualist idea that the rightness and wrongness of our conduct is to be explained by reference to some . . . actual or hypothetical agreement', contending that this approach offers 'the best hope of vindicating a robust notion of moral truth while also acknowledging that morality is in some sense a human construction, that moral truths are somehow dependent on actual human capacities' (*vii*). Southwood's deliberative model of contractualism is distinct to Gauthier's 'Hobbesian' and to Scanlon's 'Kantian' contractualist models, though it claims some unspecified affinities to Habermas' discourse ethics (3, 87 n2).

The 'morality' Southwood seeks to ground is a 'complete set . . . of deontic facts . . . about what is permissible, impermissible, and obligatory', as a common code by which we are to live (102 n32), in contrast to what is 'good, worthwhile, [or] virtuous' (7) for us to do (8). Adequately grounding morality requires vindicating 'various platitudes that define morality's intensional character' and 'substantive judgments concerning morality's extensional character' (11). Morality's intensional character is specified by platitudes about its normativity and its objectivity (13). Morality's normativity consists in agents having sufficient justifying reasons to act (or to omit) as morality requires (14); 'moral requirements are necessarily *categorical* and *binding*' and 'distinctively *other-regarding*' (15). Morality's objectivity consists in its being 'non-subjective', universal,

[35] For concise discussion of some central limits of Scanlon's account of 'reasonability', see Adams (2001).

[36] All parenthetical page references in this sub-section are to Southwood (2010).

and yet knowable (16–17, 148–55). Morality's extensional character is partly specified by its permitting some forms of partiality whilst proscribing others (17, 156–71).

Southwood's model defines a standpoint betwixt Nagel's personal and impersonal points of view (17–18, 87, 161–3, 171), an interpersonal view of oneself 'as fellow participant in establishing' through collective deliberation our conjoint moral claims and entitlements (86–7, 130–3, 163); this involves neither a veil of ignorance (158), nor Scanlon's 'generic' standpoints (97 n29). It takes agents as we are, and seeks to facilitate our self-understanding and our mutual understanding of our personal points of view (87, 97, 137). Southwood claims that 'rationality is necessarily an interpersonal achievement' (90). His model idealizes our deliberative capacities to comply with the non-moral norms constitutive of good and proper deliberation (92, 158 n35, 175, 183). These include basic communicative norms, such as sincerity, effective communication, attention to relevance, receptiveness, and willingness to revise one's views on the basis of cogent deliberation (93–4); the discursive norms of persuasion, both to offer others considerations they likely regard as salient, and to modify one's own views when presented with cogent considerations (94–5). This latter involves the reflective norms of internal examination of one's own views, their coherence, and one's responsiveness to relevant considerations (95). Hence:

> The deliberative contractual situation ... is a site of relentless examination, scrutiny, and critique .... deliberative contractualism requires that we ascend to a point of view in which we are accountable to others, in which others have the authority to demand [of] us to take them seriously as fellow deliberators. (101, 129, 133, 158)

In sum, as collective deliberative contractors, we have normatively significant, though non-moral mutual relations, constitutive of 'the interpersonal point of view' (124–8).

In this situation, we are to decide upon a common code by which to live, though without supposing it is specifically a moral code (100, 126). This qualification is required, first, to allow within the scope of relevant deliberative considerations, not only our desires, aversions, aspirations, personal relations, and projects, but also specific moral judgments we may make, and more importantly, our normative judgments about 'what is important about doing things this way rather than that' (100). Second, it avoids circularity (101). Agreeing to live by a common code 'involves agreeing to accept [its] principles [. . . and its] attendant dispositions and judgments . . . ' (104). If the code chosen within the collective, deliberative contractarian situation is a moral code (185), then that collective choice ensures, via their acceptance of that moral code, that individual agents have reasons to act according to that code and to hold themselves and others accountable to it (104–5, 129–30, 133–4, 137). Deliberative contractualism would thus secure morality's normativity (144–5).

Southwood offers various considerations suggesting that the common code which would be chosen in that deliberative situation is specifically a moral code, including within its scope, not only competent decision makers, but also those incapable of making the relevant, contractual decisions (110–14, 168–71), and perhaps future generations (115–16). Southwood suggests that deliberative contractors would agree to permit individuals to pursue their life projects (159–60), but require imperfect duties of aid (165) and insure a decent standard of living (165–7).

Southwood states: 'Moral principles will be necessarily generation-relative', whilst admitting that 'generation-relative moral code' may be incoherent (116). Deliberative contractualism is 'a kind of *idealized . . . intersubjective* response-dependent theory' (150). Southwood denies that any acts are 'necessarily morally impermissible' because there may be distant possible worlds 'in which deliberatively rational individuals would fail to agree to live by a code . . . forbidding [e.g.] torturing children' (153). He rejects enlightened self-interest because it fails to account for the distinctly other-regarding character of moral reasons (36–45, 146). He rejects Kantian contractualism because it invokes the non-contractual, incommensurable value of rational agents, and because any 'kingdom of ends' suggests there is a king, whereas deliberative contractualism evokes 'an ideal participatory republic' (128 n27, 139; cf. 55).[37]

Because morality is to result from—and be explained and justified by—contract, the terms upon which its parties may agree cannot be foreordained. For deliberative contractualism to account for *morality*, a

[37] Southwood states: 'The idea of deliberative citizenship might seem to bear an important resemblance to Kant's notion of membership in a "kingdom of ends". One difference is that a kingdom suggests a king, whereas the notion of deliberative citizenship is meant to evoke something like an ideal participatory republic' (128 n27).

moral code must result from the specified kind of collective, deliberative contractual agreement. For the 'foundation' of morality to be *contractual*, that agreement must be elective. Whether both requirements can be conjointly satisfied is unclear, in part because it is unclear when or whether Southwood advances a deliberative contractualist *model* of the foundations of morality, a specifically deliberative-contractualist *foundation* of morality, or both. Often he avoids taking 'a firm stand' (116) on specific issues, to avoid prejudging contractual deliberations: 'According to the deliberative contractualist, *no* [moral] principles are valid prior to being agreed to within the deliberative contractual situation' (173), in part because 'many substantive moral questions must be decided by engaging in actual deliberation and seeing what emerges from it' (155). The qualification 'moral' is required in that prior statement because the norms of deliberative rationality are *not* elective: 'one's standing in certain relations with others means that one has certain reasons, whether one likes it or not' (137). 'Reasons of deliberative citizenship' are of this kind:

> To be a proper deliberative citizen requires honouring our shared authority and mutual accountability. The only way to do this is to live according to the common code that we would agree to live by if we were perfectly deliberatively rational, and to ensure that others do likewise ... In short, deliberative contractualist agreements give us reasons of deliberative citizenship. (129)

Southwood's 'deliberative contractualist agreements are hypothetical agreements' (124). Southwood does not explain how *hypothetical* agreements justify or generate *actual* obligations. There is no valid modal logic, nor any valid deontic logic, by which to infer validly from 'would' and 'if' agreed (whether singly or conjointly) to 'is' or 'are' obligated. Repeating the contractualist mantra that actual obligations are or can be justified by merely hypothetical agreements in counter-factual circumstances (often wildly counter-factual circumstances, such as utter mutual independence) does nothing to justify leaping across this modal, normative chasm. Nor does Southwood's account answer the standard suspicion, that social contract theories so contrive the contractual situation as to ensure their desired results. Southwood states: 'From the perspective of a contractualist, there must surely be something mysterious about the idea of an immutable moral law' (116). Whilst true, Southwood does not show why we only stand in normatively significant relations *qua* deliberatively rational agents, though not *qua* moral agents. In this connection he cannot appeal to alleged possible worlds in which rational deliberators would fail to proscribe, for example, torturing children (153), because any such world fails to vindicate the substantive moral platitudes which partly constitute Southwood's theoretical benchmark.

On behalf of Scanlon's contractualism and his own, Southwood replies to McGinn (176–9) that McGinn cannot appeal to alleged 'moral facts' unless he explains how those facts explain 'why we necessarily have reasons of the right sort not to perform acts of that [proscribed] type' (179). The link between moral facts (of whatever sort) and reasons agents *have* for acting accordingly need not be forged by philosophical legerdemain: it is forged by the moral dimensions of education.[38]

'Kantian contractualism' may be untenable, but Kant wrote of a '*Reich*' of ends, not a '*Königreich*'; his view is ardently republican. Whilst Kant affirms the incommensurable dignity of rational agency, his universalization tests are independent of that premise because at their core they embody equal respect for all persons as free rational agents who can determine what rightly to think or to do by rationally assessing relevant considerations; Kant's tests proscribe actions which cannot be justified to all affected parties by sufficient reasons. Kant's view invokes norms of rational, justificatory judgment much like Southwood's norms of deliberative rationality (O'Neill 1989, 24–7, 42–8). Southwood's 'norms of deliberative rationality' are norms of rational inquiry generally; they are not limited to governing elective decisions to institute principles by accepting the obligation to abide by them.

Southwood (21) quotes Pettit's formulation of the issue which I have emphasized here: that any substantive contractualism must show that contractual agreement plays an ineliminable, constitutive role in either identifying or justifying basic moral principles, in contrast to 'accepting' sufficient justifying reasons by acknowledging their justificatory sufficiency. Southwood's 'deliberative contractarianism' fails to show that elective, contractarian agreement is either necessary or sufficient for identifying and justifying morality (*qua* moral code). Southwood excludes 'what is important about doing things this way rather than

[38] See (as previously noted) Herman (1993, 2007); Green (1999); Curren (2000, 2010a); Westphal (2012a).

that' (100) from morality *qua* code of conduct; he does not show that such considerations are excluded from the moral domain.

Southwood's deliberative model of contractarianism is challenged by non-contractarian forms of moral constructivism; for example, Kant's (especially as developed by O'Neill or Herman), or A. Baier (1977), Becker (1986), K. Baier (1995), Pettit (2001), or Wallace (2009). These accounts provide considerable reasons to hold that any 'agreements' regarding core moral principles can only be justified by how they acknowledge agreement-independent, morally compelling features of our inherently intersubjective human lives. In the remainder, I attempt to further explicate and justify this theoretical option by further developing Hume's and Kant's Natural Law Constructivism. The persistence of the idea that social contractual models contribute constitutively and ineliminably to identifying or justifying the most fundamental moral norms indicates that an even earlier essay by Gauthier merits careful reconsideration, namely: 'The Social Contract as Ideology' (1977).[39]

[39] It is unfortunate but due to its mounting prevalence, it is necessary to observe that Southwood's study is symptomatic of how in recent decades in philosophy both graduate training and professional refereeing have become lax.

8

Kant's Justification of Rights to Usufruct

35 Introduction

The nature and justification of rights to ownership have been both central and vexed in Modern and contemporary philosophy; central, because so many of our individual and joint activities depend upon the use and distribution of goods; vexed, because there are competing definitions, justifications, and sets of rights to individual and to joint use of goods. Kant believed that his Critical philosophy could both clarify and resolve some of the most basic issues involved in this debate. However, with rare exception, Kant has not been viewed as a major theorist on these topics.[1] This is due, in part, to the difficulty of Kant's philosophy, to the relative neglect of Kant's *Rechtslehre* even amongst Kant's scholars until recently, and to the brevity and obscurity of Kant's arguments about the rights to possess found therein. I contend nevertheless that Kant establishes some very significant points about our rights of possession.[2]

Kant recognized that the most important and controversial rights of possession are not analytic truths, and he agreed with Hume that no norm can be justified solely on the basis of empirical evidence. Consequently, Kant regarded rights as a proper topic for his Critical philosophy, which aims to provide *a priori* justification for certain synthetic

[1] The exceptions are Waldron (1988); Ripstein (2008, 2009); Byrd and Hruschka (2010); Rühl (2010); and Horn (2014).

[2] Both Kant's discussion and my reconstruction of it raise many exegetical and philosophical issues, which cannot be addressed here. I examine Kant's text and analysis in detail in Westphal (1997). Would aficionados and sceptics please kindly consult that essay, which also remarks on the secondary literature.

propositions. As he noted to himself, the central difficulty involved in justifying rights to possession is to show, in this instance, 'how synthetic propositions regarding right are possible *a priori*, that is, without presupposing another right *i.e.* possession' (*GS* 23:302.28–30). With this, Kant rejects both the early Modern natural law fiction of an original common ownership of the earth and Locke's strategy of basing rights to property on ownership of one's own body. Though Kant's full account incorporates the notion of an original common ownership of the Earth,[3] this notion has its home in a theocentric view of the world, and began to wane in European political culture when Grotius realized that political philosophy must be made independent of theology, because religious schisms were too deep and too sustained to provide a univocal, uncontroversial basis for politics.[4] Locke's account directly raises two questions, *viz.*, 'How do we have an ownership right at all in our own body?', and 'Why should labouring on some unclaimed object constitute its appropriation, rather than our loss of labour power?' Locke's answers to these questions tie his theory of property directly to his specific, also sectarian (not to say idiosyncratic) theology, thus increasing rather than reducing controversy. Kant is right to seek an original, rather than a derivative, justification of rightful possession.

36 Rights to Usufruct, not Property

I have spoken deliberately of 'possession' and 'ownership', rather than 'property'. Kant rightly presents his argument in terms of 'possession' (*Besitz*), not 'property' (*Eigentum*). Individual private property is a complex package of rights containing several distinct 'incidents', that is, specific rights and liabilities (Honoré 1970, 537f). These include: (1) The right to *possess*: strictly, the exclusive right to control something physically, and freedom from unpermitted interference by others. (2) The right to *use*: the owner's personal use and enjoyment of the thing in question. (3) The right to *manage*: powers to decide how, when, and by

[3] See Edwards (1998). Kant's 'Antinomy' concerning the possibility of possession (*RL* §7, remark) also suggests that rights of possession could be generated without relying on the fiction of original common possession of the earth. I omit discussion of this 'Antinomy' because it does not advance Kant's analysis. I submit it is not coincidental that Kant states this 'Antinomy' in his indented remarks; it does not belong to his main text and analysis.

[4] See Schneewind (1998, chapters 2–4).

whom something shall be used, including licensing, contracting its use or exploitation, permitting others to enter or use it, and defining the limits of such permission. (4) The right to *income* from a thing: the right to any product of it, or a reward for exploiting it or for permitting others to use it. (5) The right to *capital* in the thing: the power to alienate something and the liberty to consume, waste, or destroy part or all of it. (6) The right to *security*: the right to remain something's owner indefinitely at will, provided one remains financially solvent. (7) *Transmissibility*: the power to transfer something to a successor indefinitely. This *absence of term* means that a thing never ceases to be one's property, unless and until one renounces that right (or becomes deceased). (8) The *prohibition of harmful use*: the owner's right to use or to manage something is restricted to activities which do not directly harm others. (9) *Liability to execution*: the liability to have property taken away for serious debt or insolvency. (10) The right of *residuary*: the thing reverts to a particular party, the owner, whenever others' subsidiary rights to it lapse.[5]

Given the complexity of private property rights, one may well doubt whether they could be justified *a priori*. One of Kant's lessons is that they cannot. Kant's *a priori* justification of ownership rights concerns only the rights to possess and to use, not to property. This crucial distinction too often has been disregarded. If ordinary usage generally fails to distinguish 'property' from 'possession[s]', even the most incidental legal usage does: the criminal charge of 'being in possession of stolen goods' would be nonsense without a distinction between possession and property. Or, to remain within the realm of legitimate norms, even the most incidental rental contract gives one party a temporary (subsidiary) right to possess and to use another's rental property. Kant appears well aware that most of the specific rights involved in individual private property can be specified, indeed constituted, only within the legal institutions of a specific society. They are thus topics of political debate and positive

[5] Some readers may wonder whether some or several of these incidents are 'necessary' to the very concept of property. Such a query presumes that conceptual analysis suffices for substantive philosophical issues. Carnap (1950, 1–8) showed otherwise when he explicated his method of conceptual explication, which he had used since at least 1928. The significance of Carnap's account of explication is underscored by fundamental problems in his empiricist semantics, highlighted by Wick (1951), though these points have been widely neglected by analytic philosophers (Westphal 2010–11). Kant recognized the insufficiency of conceptual analysis for substantive philosophy and likewise advocated explication (*KdrV* A727–30/B755–8), though by strategies different to Carnap's!

legislation. Kant's case for the legitimacy of the state, and of our obligation to be members of a state, rests on his justification of much more modest, though not at all trivial, rights to possess and use (*RL* §§1–9).[6] These I shall often designate properly as 'rights to usufruct' or 'usufructuary rights'.

More specifically, in terms of the incidents identified by Honoré listed above, Kant's analysis justifies (1), (2), and (8). Rights to possess, however, may lapse if one's (justifiable) needs to use a possession lapse. Accordingly, the other incidents would require specification and justification within legitimate positive law. For example, despite popular notions of unlimited rights to capital in one's property (incident 5), it is far from obvious that wanton destruction of one's own property can be normatively justified, if those goods could be of use to deserving others.[7] For example, it has long been recognized in the Occident that, even if one is its proprietor, no one is entitled to salt arable land. In England, private landowners still must respect the use of ancient 'rights of way' by which others may cross that land without special permission. However, it is not

[6] Even recent commentary on Kant's analysis tends unjustifiably to conflate possession and property, in part by neglecting the complexity of the very concept of property. Sometimes it is suggested that Kant's terminological association of '*Mein und Dein*' (*viz.*, mine or thine) with the Latin terms generally used for property, '*meum vel tuum*' (*RL* 6:237.24–5), or his association of '*das Seine*' with '*Eigenthum*' (property; *RL* 6:270.10–11) shows that he must be attempting an *a priori* justification of property, not merely possession. This suggestion disregards the fact that Kant's metaphysical level of analysis and argument (on which, see below) must disregard the legal specifics required to define and to institute fully fledged property rights, traditional usage to the contrary not withstanding. One clear, central example of Kant's Critical modification of legal usage concerns his use of '*res nullius*'. In law, a *res nullius* is an item which happens not to belong to anyone; in Kant's *RL* a *res nullius* is an item within our human capacities to be used, the use of which is nevertheless proscribed in principle. (Kant uses this concept in a premise of a *reductio*.) Kant's specifically Critical use of his terms must (and can!) be established by his own analysis, to which legal sources may contribute, but for which they are neither sufficient nor decisive. This holds too of Kant's use of the terms '*meum vel tuum*' ('mine or thine'), which in contemporaneous legal parlance connoted someone's property. Within Kant's Critical metaphysical analysis of private (pre-positive, non-governmental) justice these terms can only designate someone's possession. Rühl (2010, 69–71) and Horn (2014, 199) are rare exceptions in distinguishing possession from property; they kindly acknowledge my (1997, 2002) point. Horn (2014, 199–220) examines Kant's expansion from possession to property.

[7] Ripstein (2009, 88–106) contrasts Kant's account of 'property' with a 'bundle' account, but considers only a few of the incidents comprised in property rights (above, §36), and disregards how Kant's natural law analysis and justification in principle only extends to rightful possession (including acquisition and morally permissible use), not to property.

the point of this examination of fundamental principles of morals, and how these are identified and their objectivity justified by Natural Law Constructivism, to enter into specific debates about distributive justice, issues which can only be fruitfully examined once basic moral principles are established. This latter is an ample task for the present study.

I focus here on Kant's analysis of rightful possession for several reasons, worth recalling briefly. First, Kant's analysis of rightful possession most obviously parallels Hume's constructivist analysis of the basic 'rules of justice' governing possession, promise, and contract. Second, Kant's analysis of rightful possession shows how Kant's universalization tests can identify and justify fundamental moral principles without presupposing any antecedent convention or social practice. Third, Kant's analysis of rightful possession provides sufficient basis for Kant's further analysis of promising, exchange, and contract; these further rights and duties do not require fully fledged property rights, nor do they introduce any especially controversial issues. Furthermore, Kant's analysis of rightful possession matches the provisional rights to which Kant appeals in his justification of public justice (legitimate republican government).

37 Kant's Argument to Justify Rights to Usufruct

I shall reconstruct Kant's justification for rights to usufruct, and show, briefly, that Kant's justification of rights to usufruct suffice for his justification of our membership in a (legitimately constituted, republican) state. In this section I first present the key points of Kant's official justification of possession, largely following his order of discussion. This highlights some important issues, including the need to reconstruct Kant's account due to some crucial oversights in his argument. In §38, I reconstruct and defend Kant's analysis.

37.1 Kant's preparatory steps: RL §§1–5

Kant opens his discussion (*RL* §1) by noting that something distinct from oneself is rightly one's own only if another's unauthorized use of it constitutes an injury. This relation, supposedly, can hold regardless of whether one currently detains the item physically (by holding or occupying it).

The intended relation is normative and intelligible, not merely factual and physical.

Kant also asserts that '[t]he subjective condition of the possibility of use in general is *possession* [*Besitz*]' (§1 ¶1). Kant's statement is an identity. Inverting it shows (in English syntax) that his statement serves as a definition of possession, *viz.*: possession is the subjective condition of the possibility of use in general. This accords with Kant's repeated definition in his working notes of 'possession' and 'right' in terms of legitimate *use* of something.[8] As mentioned, Kant is correct to focus on possession and use, and to disregard the further incidents involved in property rights. Hence my focus upon rights to usufruct.

In *RL* §2 Kant states 'the Juridical Postulate of Practical Reason'. This postulate purports to establish that any object of will may coherently be regarded, objectively, as possibly mine or yours (6:246.33–5). This is to say, in principle any thing may be possessed by someone or other. Kant's Postulate states:

> It is possible to have any external object of my will [*Willkür*] as mine; *i.e.*, any maxim according to which, if it were a law, an object of will must become *in itself* (objectively) *ownerless* (*res nullius*) is contrary to right. (6:246.5–8)

Kant establishes this Postulate, however, only under the proviso that formally, one's will (i.e., one's chosen course of action) regarding that thing is consistent with the outer freedom of all, according to a universal law (6:246.17–19). This is a crucial assumption. Kant seeks to ensure that it is automatically fulfilled by abstracting from all characteristics of the thing in question, other than its being an object of will. This is the point of his insistence that pure practical reason can issue only formal laws governing our will (6:246.19–22). On this basis, Kant infers, there can be no absolute (i.e., unconditional) prohibition on the use of things. If there were, outer freedom, the freedom to act, the sole innate right on which all other acquired rights are based (6:237–8), would contradict itself. Presumably, this is because outer freedom would thereby block any prospect of outer action. We shall see that perhaps Kant should have taken more seriously this prospect of outer freedom being incoherent, as well as the

[8] E.g., *GS* 23:277.5–6, 278.23–5, 287.20–2, 301.11–12, 307.18–20, 309.15–18. Kant does not state the complementary 'objective' conditions of use; presumably they are two: that something can be used to some end, and especially that one's use is consistent with the free action of others in accord with a universal law.

prospect of conditional but nevertheless contingently exceptionless prohibitions on the use of things. The move from pure metaphysical principles of justice to establishing actual use rights for human beings is not so simple as Kant's official argument suggests.

The important point for now is that the 'possibility' of having objects of one's will as one's own mentioned in Kant's postulate must be understood as an extreme abstraction. This level of abstraction accords with the *metaphysical* character of Kant's analysis (6:216–17). The relevant possibility must be abstract, in part because of the two assumptions just noted, but also because nothing in Kant's postulate shows or entails that intelligible possession *is* possible. It seems fairly clear that Kant means to abstract also from the distinction between physical and intelligible possession. However, at most this abstraction specifies a general concept of ownership; ownership *per se*, with two species: physical and intelligible possession. Kant's abstraction does nothing to show that this general concept, nor one of its still mysterious species, intelligible possession, has a legitimate use; that is, that there can be such a thing as (merely) intelligible possession, possession *sans* physical detention. At the end of *RL* §1 Kant notes that the possibility of such a species of possession must be proven (6:246.1), and in *RL* §3 Kant's discussion appears to presume that he has proven that intelligible possession is possible, for there he reiterates (from *RL* §1) that someone else's unauthorized use of something could not be an injury unless one owned it. Indeed, in *RL* §4 (¶2) Kant avers that the genuine sense of 'owning' something only pertains to intelligible, not to mere physical, possession. Fortunately, the core of Kant's justification of ownership rights is where it belongs (*RL* §6), which contains Kant's express 'deduction' (i.e., legitimation, or normative justification) of the concept of intelligible or 'merely rightful' possession.

RL §2 contains two other significant points. First, Kant distinguishes between having something in one's power (*Macht*) and having it in one's control (*Gewalt*).[9] Merely to think of something as an object of will requires only being aware of having the power—the physical

[9] '*Gewalt*' can mean power to compel, control, or (political or legal) authority. It may appear that Kant intends to use the term here in a normative sense connoting 'authority'. However, his use of the term only slightly later, in a nearly parallel context (*RL* §4, 6:248.24), plainly associates *Gewalt* with direct control rather than normative authority.

capacity—to use it. To have an object in one's control requires an act of will (6:246.25–32); though Kant does not name it, it is an act of appropriation. Second, Kant claims that this Postulate constitutes a permissive law of practical reason. The postulate permits us to obligate others to refrain from using certain objects of our will, simply because we have taken them into our possession. Generating such obligations extends the scope of practical reasoning in a way which transcends mere analysis of concepts (6:247.1–8). We shall consider below whether or how this alleged 'permissive law' to obligate others is consistent with the sole innate right to freedom, freedom from the unilateral determining will of others (6:237.27–9).

RL §5 provides nominal and real definitions of outer possession. The nominal definition simply recalls the point (from *RL* §1) that one can be injured by someone else's use of something only if one possesses that thing. The real definition, which Kant claims suffices for its deduction, is this:

> Something external is mine, if and only if disturbing my use of it would constitute injury, *even if I do not possess it* (if I am not holding or occupying it). (6:249.5–7)

Only if somehow I am related to something else can its unauthorized use by another party injure me. This is not a promising basis for proving that the concept of intelligible possession has a legitimate use, because this real definition could only provide such a ground of proof if it could be shown, independently, that I could be injured by someone else's use of something. Demonstrating the possibility of such injury requires first establishing that I have such a normative relation (*viz.*, rightful possession) to the thing in question. Fortunately, Kant's official deduction (*RL* §6), though problematic, does not attempt the impossible.

37.2 Printer's errors in RL §6

There is reason to believe that the text of *RL* §6 is corrupt, because five paragraphs in it (¶¶4–8) do not contribute to Kant's analysis.[10] Kant first

[10] The response of some scholars to this corruption is excessive. Bernd Ludwig replaces §6 ¶¶4–8 with §2 in his edition of Kant's *Metaphysische Anfangsgründe der Rechtslehre* (1986), which is followed in the revised edition of Gregor's translation contained in the Cambridge Edition of the *Works of Immanuel Kant*. However, in *RL* §7 Kant clearly identifies the postulate contained in *RL* §2—*as* belonging in *RL* §2 (6:254.12). I concur with Gregor (personal discussions, August 1992, Erfurt) in rejecting such drastic re-editing

indicates (¶1) that understanding how possession is possible requires understanding how a merely rightful, non-physical or 'intelligible' possession is possible. Understanding this, in turn, requires understanding the *a priori* possibility of a synthetic principle of justice. The relevant principle must be synthetic, because the only principle of justice which can be justified analytically, Kant contends (¶2), is that interfering with someone's physical possession and use of something directly interferes with their innate right to freedom, and as such is wrong, since any maxim enjoining such interference directly contradicts 'the axiom of justice' (*Recht*; 6:250.6). This axiom appears to be his Universal Law of Justice, mentioned in the Introduction to the *Rechtslehre*:

> Act outwardly in such a way that the free use of your will can coexist with the freedom of all in accord with a universal law. (6:231.10–12)[11]

Because the innate right to freedom inherently involves the right to act outwardly, interfering with anyone's use of something he or she holds (provided that this use is itself rightful because it is compatible with the freedom of all, in accord with a universal law) directly interferes with his or her innate right to freedom and violates the Universal Law of Justice: universalizing one's maxim of interference would entail that everyone act on the maxim to interfere with others' use, and this would make some others' use impossible, and indeed preclude their acting on the maxim of interference. This implication confronts us again with Hobbes' 'Innocent Problem' of total mutual interference (above, §8).

The important case, Kant notes (¶3), concerns possession without detention. The right to possess without detention is a 'synthetic proposition' because the proscription on interfering with possession *sans* detention does not follow analytically from the innate right to freedom. Because this proposition concerns a right (which is normative, not simply factual) it must be (at least in part) *a priori* (6:249.34). Hence intelligible rights to possess are a central case in point for Kant's Critical *a priori* justification of key synthetic propositions.

of Kant's text. For detailed, conclusive critique of Ludwig's re-editing, see Friedrich (2004). Those who cannot study Kant in the original should use Gregor's first (1991) translation of *RL* §§1–6.

[11] Kant refers to this same principle also as the 'law of external freedom' (*RL* §§6, 7, *GS* 6:251.26, 253.26–7).

After contrasting his strategies for justifying theoretical and practical propositions (¶9), Kant purports to justify the possibility of rightful, intelligible possession in one short paragraph (¶10). Kant's justification is based on a second, distinct 'Juridical Postulate of Practical Reason', namely:

It is a duty of justice, so to act toward others that what is external (usable) can also become someone's own. (6:252.13–15)

Kant points out that if indeed this is a duty, then whatever conditions are required to act on this duty must be fulfilled. In this way, Kant's argument here parallels his Postulates of Practical Reason in the second *Critique*. One key condition for acting on this duty, of course, is that things *can* be rightly possessed. Kant insists that the relevant form of possession is non-physical or intelligible (6:252.15–17). If that is correct, then such non-physical possession—possession without detention—must indeed be possible, if we are obligated to respect rightful, intelligible possession; even if we cannot further understand how such possession is possible.

This does not appear to be a convincing argument, and may recall Russell's (1919, 71) ripost to Dedekind's postulates, namely, 'The method of "postulating" what we want has many advantages; they are the same as the advantages of theft over honest toil.' In the present case, Kant appears to assert that the relevant kind of possession must be intelligible, and to assert (as a 'postulate') that we have a duty to behave in ways which allow people to possess things. Surely Kant is right that, if we have this duty, then in principle things can be possessed. Yet why should we believe this is a duty? *Do* we have such a duty? Can Kant offer any insight into the grounds of such a duty?[12]

38 Reconstructing Kant's Justification of Rights to Usufruct

I shall develop affirmative answers to these questions, though deriving them requires developing Kant's Critical metaphysics, by enriching

[12] On Kant's understanding of 'postulate' in this context, see Byrd and Hruschka (2010, 135–8). The present analysis provides Kant's justification for this 'postulate', though I omit specific discussion of this point (see Westphal 1997).

somewhat the empirical concept of our finite human form of rational agency used in Kant's *a priori* analysis (i.e., his 'practical anthropology'). Deriving them also requires shifting somewhat the key question. Asking, in effect, 'How is possession *sans* detention possible?' tends to presume that such possession *is* possible, and directs attention away from the question, *whether* such possession is possible, and altogether occludes the question, 'Is such possession required, and if so, why?' The answer to this question provides grounds for Kant's 'postulate' of the duty so to act towards others that things may be possessed. Kant's Critical metaphysics provides grounds for answering this key question.

38.1 Filling in Kant's 'practical anthropology'

Even in its official version, Kant's justification of rights to possess is not purely *a priori*; it is in Kant's Critical sense 'metaphysical'. Like the *Metaphysical Foundations of Natural Science*, the *Metaphysics of Morals* takes pure *a priori* concepts in connection with an empirically given *concept* of a certain kind of being in order to explicate the basic rational principles governing that kind of being.[13] In the *Metaphysics of Morals*, Kant applies pure *a priori* universal normative principles to human nature in order to develop the basic principles of rights and duties governing human affairs (6:216.37–217.4). The whole of Kant's *Metaphysics of Morals* concerns human beings, as having *Willkür*, a mixed will which is affected but not determined by sensuous inclinations, which can decide what to do on the basis of principles and justifying reasons (6:213–14). In the *Rechtslehre*, Kant expressly appeals to another fact, not about human nature *per se*, but about the human condition, our natural environment, in order to justify our duty to be members of political states: namely the fact that we live on a finite surface (a globe, *RL* §43) and we are sufficiently populous that we cannot, in fact, avoid each other (*RL* §§9, 13, 41–3). My reconstruction shall stress two further facts about human nature, closely related to these. First, we are *finite* rational agents, because we cannot produce things *ex nihilo* by willing them into existence. The fact that we must act on things around us in order to achieve our ends (including meeting our basic needs) is a basic fact about human agency directly relevant to Kant's metaphysical

[13] *MAdN* 4:470.1–12, 473.5–10, *MdS* 6:216.28–217.8. Regarding Kant's Critical metaphysics, see Westphal (2004, §43) and Fulda (1998).

analysis of our rights and obligations. (Note that such facts are involved explicitly in Kant derivations of moral duties, e.g., relieving distress, truthfulness.) Second, I submit that it is similarly a fact—despite Marx's and Gauthier's (!) messianic hopes to the contrary—that relative scarcity is endemic to the human condition.

With this background in mind, I now offer a reconstruction of Kant's justification of rights to usufruct, based on a 'Contradiction in Conception' test using Kant's Universal Law of Justice. Because juridical rights are strict rights, the relevant test should not concern a 'Contradiction in the Will'; because the rights at issue are juridical, the test should use Kant's Universal Law of Justice. This Law tests maxims in view of their compatibility, when universalized, with like outward behaviour of all (6:230–1, 246); it abstracts from ethical considerations of motives or the moral worth of actions (i.e., whether they are to the moral credit of the agent because the agent so acts because so acting is dutiful). Introducing this test makes explicit several features of Kant's reasoning. Kant's official argument appeals to a 'maxim' which is shown to be prohibited because it directly 'contradicts' the Universal Law of Justice (*RL* §6 ¶2). Kant recognizes that his justification of possession appeals to the concept of freedom, which is only justified by the categorical imperative (*RL* §6 ¶10), and in some of his notes Kant describes the obligation to respect rightful claims to ownership as involving a 'categorical imperative' (*GS* 23:286–7).[14] An explicit Contradiction in Conception test provides a sound, distinctively Kantian argument for rightful possession, and these rights match the minimal, provisional ownership rights Kant sought to justify in his analysis of 'Private Justice' (*Privatrecht*, or pre-public justice).[15] Moreover, the main points involved in this test are clearly expressed in some of Kant's working notes.[16]

[14] Kant is entitled to mention both freedom and the categorical imperative in connection with justice, without introducing ethical considerations regarding motives, moral worth, or dignity, because freedom is required for having rights, obligations, and imputability, and because in the first instance, the categorical imperative specifies which actions are obligatory, permissible, or prohibited. All issues of motives, virtue, or moral worth are subsidiary to these primary issues.

[15] Kant's contrast between 'private' and 'public' justice expressly concerns the principles of justice so far as they are incumbent upon individuals, abstracting altogether from government, and the governmental provision of publicly acknowledged justice (*RL* §41).

[16] *GS* 23:230.26–231.5, 281.26–32, 309.29–11; included in Kant (2016) (*CEWK*).

Justifying rights to possession requires Kant's Principle of Hypothetical Imperatives, stated in the *Groundwork*:

> Whoever wills the end, also wills (necessarily in accord with reason) the sole means to it which are within his or her control (*Gewalt*).
>
> (*GMS* 4:417–8)

Though Kant discusses this principle in connection with hypothetical imperatives (i.e., imperatives directing one how to obtain something one happens to want), it holds of rational pursuit of ends generally, regardless of their source. Whether set on the basis of inclination or reason, rational pursuit of ends employs jointly sufficient means to attain them. Note, too, that Kant's *Rechtslehre* abstracts from the issues about motives which are central to his ethical contrast between hypothetical and categorical imperatives. Finally, invoking this principle does not reduce Kant's tests to prudential or consequentialist considerations.

38.2 Why rights to usufruct are a human necessity

Three basic facts about the human condition require rights to usufruct: first, we cannot will our ends into existence *ex nihilo*. Thus we must make use of materials around us in order to obtain our ends. At a minimum, this includes the air, water, and food required for us to act at all, and the clothing, shelter, and tools we need to maintain ourselves. Second, our ends, regarding both the basic needs just mentioned, and elective ends we choose to pursue, are complex, temporally extended, and more or less integrated; we cannot simultaneously physically hold or occupy all that living, even at a subsistence level, requires. Consider that we cannot simultaneously occupy shelter and obtain food. (Even a greenhouse must be built with glass and stocked with seeds, both brought from elsewhere.) Were we to produce something at home to trade with others for food, this would require intelligible rights to possess things at least on the part of those trading partners. Alternately, portable shelters which could be carried whilst obtaining food can be made only with equipment which is not simultaneously portable, at least not without using animals or machines, which would require intelligible rights to possess and to use *them*. Human life requires regular and reliable use of things, including sources of food and shelter, which cannot all be physically held, occupied, or 'empirically possessed' simultaneously. (Kant was clearly aware of this; *GS* 23:230–1.) If we cannot count on the resources of some of our activities remaining available to us regularly and reliably, even when not presently using them, we cannot engage in those activities, and we cannot engage in most of our other activities. For example, it makes no sense to leave home for the day to secure one's livelihood (however one does so) if one's home is either removed or taken over by others when one leaves. Even packs of thieves must honour their principles for distributing loot. Consider instead the simplest mode of life in the most favourable circumstances, a small nomadic group of hunter-gatherers in a temperate and abundant region. Such people need every day certain tools, clothes, and carrying devices which cannot be physically detained whilst asleep. Such groups require some form of recognized possession. This may involve collective possession of many items, but collective possession is nevertheless possession, and involves maxims—principles and practices—governing individual use of collectively possessed items. Hermits, too, cannot avoid reliance on recognized possession, for they require social upbringing before they are able to withdraw from society.[17]

The third important fact is that we are too populous to avoid one another and each other's things and projects. In conditions of superabundance, where a substitute is lying around for anything someone happens to take, there would be no need of rights of possession. Rights of possession are needed only in conditions of relative scarcity. Though Kant does not explicitly mention relative scarcity, he does mention the inevitability of living in close quarters and its attendant prospects for mutual interference (*RL* §§8, 9, 13, 42). Because mutual interference is a local phenomenon, it is tantamount to relative scarcity, and Kant's argument collapses without reference to relative scarcity. In this connection, Kant implicitly adopts Rousseau's point that our mutual interference is a function of population density, and may thus count as an historical development rather than a timeless truth about our unsociability. In this regard, Kant's justification of rights of possession is based on a logical, even an historical, contingency—though one

[17] Some philosophers may wonder here (or at other points) about what is 'conceivably possible'. Mere conceivability is a poor guide to tenability, and reflects lingering Cartesian infallibilist notions about rational justification (see Piché 1999; Boulter 2011) and adherence to conceptual analysis as a philosophically sufficient method for substantive philosophy; see Westphal (2010–11, 2016a).

which has long since been a constant and unavoidable feature of the human condition.

38.3 Using Kant's Contradiction in Conception test to justify rights to usufruct

The three facts just noted make rights to usufruct necessary. In view of these facts, the Principle of Hypothetical Imperatives commits each of us to willing to possess at least some things *sans* detention. This commitment can be formulated as a maxim, 'I will to possess some things I need, even when I do not physically hold them'. The question remains, under what conditions are such claims possible and legitimate (justifiable)? Possessing things without physically detaining them can be effective only if one's possessions are recognized and respected by others; the very point of rights of possession is to coordinate our actions to avoid mutual interference. (This was the lesson of Hobbes' 'Innocent Problem' of mutual interference; above §8.) As we saw, Kant claims that the Juridical Postulate of Practical Reason, that things can be possessed, permits us to obligate others to respect our possessions, and that their obligation stems directly from our act of taking something into possession (*RL* §§4, 8, 6:247, 255). Is this not a unilateral imposition, incompatible with the innate right to freedom? No, because others act under the same conditions we do. They, too, must will to possess things they cannot simultaneously physically hold (detain, occupy). Most importantly, a Contradiction in Conception test shows that willing to have rightful (non-physical) possession of things commits us to respecting each others' rights of possession.

The maxim to be tested is one by which an agent regards others' possessions as resources available to oneself. On this maxim, if the sole sufficient means to obtain one's end happened to include items possessed by others, one would, in accord with the Principle of Hypothetical Imperatives, will to make use of things possessed by others in order to achieve one's ends. Because the prohibition of interfering with things physically held or occupied by others follows from the innate right to freedom, the relevant sense of the phrase 'things possessed by others' concerns non-physical, 'merely rightful', or 'intelligible' possession. This kind of possession is the sole topic in the ensuing discussion.

The maxim to be tested may be called the 'Maxim of Arrogant Willing', according to which:

> Whenever the sole sufficient means to achieve my ends happen to include things possessed by others, I will nevertheless regard them as being under my control and will use them to achieve my ends.

It may be suggested that under any of three circumstances this maxim could be universalized:

1. Resources are in fact plentiful enough that amongst things *not* possessed by others there were always sufficient means for achieving one's ends.
2. One renounced an end whenever its achievement required using something held by another who denies permission to use it.
3. One allowed others freely to make use of things one possesses whenever those things were among the sole sufficient means to their ends.

The first two prospects can be directly eliminated.[18]

In the first case, one might universalize the Maxim of Arrogant Willing because one would never need to act on it. The permission it sanctions might be established, but not exercised. This strategy appears to rest on consequentialist or prudential considerations and on betting about the course of one's life in the world, all of which is foreign to Kant's central principles. As noted, Kant's justification of rights of possession is based on the historical fact that there are not now, nor have there for eons been, and there are not going to be, conditions of such abundance as to avoid issues about distributive justice. *Pace* Marx, relative scarcity is endemic to the human condition. Supposed 'prudential' reasoning or betting about

[18] A methodological note may be helpful. Only within strictly formal domains can completeness proofs be provided. Accordingly, I cannot prove that these are the only three possible scenarios on which the Maxim of Arrogant Willing might be universalizable. However, the relevant possibilities must be human possibilities; this is one key reason why (and where) Kant's pure *a priori* moral principles require 'practical anthropology' for their application to human agents and conditions of action (*per* chapter 6), including conditions of rational willing, in contrast to merely wishing, fantasizing, or irrational willing. I have devoted considerable thought to this issue since the early 1990s and have not yet identified any further prospects which are not mere variants upon the three identified here. I would be grateful, of course, for further cogent suggestions. I've sought them from colleagues for decades and have yet to receive any.

prospects of abundance sufficient to meet one's needs without ever finding that crucial means to one's ends are possessed by others is fantasy. It is tantamount to wishing, not to willing, and certainly not to rational willing. Consequently, the first circumstance for universalizing the Maxim of Arrogant Willing is empty.

In the second case, stoic self-reliance may appear to allow one to universalize the Maxim of Arrogant Willing. However, instead of universalizing that maxim, this kind of self-reliance eschews altogether the Maxim of Arrogant Willing by rescinding ends whenever they are beyond one's present, available means. Hence the second condition for universalizing that maxim is also empty.

The third case is the serious one. Can one allow others free use of one's possessions, with the proviso of making free use of theirs? This may seem to obviate the notion of rights of possession altogether. I don't believe that's quite the case, and the real problem is more revealing. On Kant's view, willing is distinguished from wishing by actual conduct using means to achieve one's end; rational is distinguished from irrational willing by employing effective and jointly sufficient means to achieve one's end. Therefore it is not rational to will to allow others freely to make use of one's possessions if they happen to be amongst the sole sufficient means to their ends. Such permission undermines one's reliable and effective use of one's own possessions. The very point of having *rights* of possession is to use things reliably and effectively. Undermining reliable and effective use of one's own possessions is instrumentally irrational because it undermines exercise of one's own rational agency. Consequently, one cannot rationally will to allow others to act on the Maxim of Arrogant Willing, that is, that others freely make use of those things one possesses whenever necessary for them to achieve their ends. Consequently, one cannot universalize the original (first-person) Maxim of Arrogant Willing, according to which one would will to make use of those things possessed by others in order to achieve one's own ends.

Because the only possible human conditions under which the Maxim of Arrogant Willing could be universalized do not obtain in human life, the Maxim of Arrogant Willing is not a permissible maxim for human agents. Consequently, given the three facts mentioned above, our commitment to willing to possess some things *sans* detention likewise commits us to respecting others' rights to possess other things. Consequently, by this Contradiction in Conception test (using the Universal Law of

Justice), we are obligated to support a system of rights to possession, in particular, by respecting others' particular rights to their possessions.

The next step in Kant's justificatory argument is to derive the right to obligate others to respect one's particular rights of possession. The Universal Law of Justice expresses a negative constraint on actions; namely, that our external actions are to be compatible with the freedom of everyone in accord with universal law. This Law thus grounds what may be called Kant's Principle of Permission, namely:

> An action is *allowed* (*licitum*) if it is not opposed to obligation; and this freedom that is not limited by any opposing imperatives is called an authorization [*Befugnis*] (*facultas moralis*).
>
> (*MdS, Einl.* §IV, 6:222.26–9)

Taking an object into possession for use is legitimate, provided that no one else already possesses it. This is the point of Kant's talk about first possession: if no one possesses an object, then no one has a right to it which would be violated if one takes it into possession; hence no one else would be injured by one's so doing. Things are 'things' insofar as they are not free agents; as such they are not morally responsible and cannot obligate us morally.[19] Because no one else would be injured by taking an unclaimed object into possession, so doing is permissible and right.[20]

One's legitimate claim to possess an object for use gives one a right to that object, a right that is not innate, but acquired. The important point here is that if someone else interferes with one's legitimate possession, this is an invasion or injury of one's freedom and rights. As an infringement of one's freedom and rights, that act is unjust. In this way, then, one's legitimate voluntary act of claiming or using an object generates obligations on the part of others to respect one's acquired right. On Kant's view we are 'authorized' to generate such obligations on the part of others by the first 'Juridical Postulate of Practical Reason' (*RL* §2),

[19] *MdS* 6:223.24–34, 418.27–419.2; cf. *GS* 23:281.17–18. On Kant's views of our obligations to non-rational (hence non-moral) nature, see O'Neill (1998) and Wood (1998).

[20] *RL* §§2, 6; 6:247.1–8, 250.18–27, 251.23–36. This draws Kant's doctrines of possession and of acquisition together. Although he devotes separate chapters to these doctrines, he in fact links them (*RL* §2, 6:247.1–8). Not harming others through first acquisition requires sufficient resources so that one person's appropriation is not directly someone else's vital loss; see below. This is, of course, one of Hume's circumstances of justice (*T* 3.2.2.15–18/SBN 493–5), which Rousseau (*CS* 1.6.1–2) recognized to be a function of population density resulting from population growth.

which states that 'it is possible to have any and every external object of my will as mine' (6:246.5–6), where an 'object of one's will' is simply anything one has the physical power to occupy or to use in some way (6:246.9–10). Kant calls this a 'permissive law of practical reason' (6:247.1–2). He states the point of this permissive law most directly a bit later:

> When I declare (by word or deed): 'I will that an external thing shall be mine', I thereby declare it obligatory for all others to refrain from the object of my will—an obligation that no one would have without this rightful act of mine.
>
> (*RL* §8, 6:255.26–9)

According to Kant, when one acquires a right to possess something, all others acquire obligations to respect one's right to that thing, and they acquire these obligations through one's very act of acquiring a right to that thing.

Furthermore, Kant argues that acquiring a right of possession also immediately generates the obligation to respect others' rights to use other things which are theirs. Included in my claim to something, Kant states,

> is an acknowledgement of being reciprocally bound to everyone else to an equivalent restraint regarding external things that are their own, since the obligation involved here derives from a universal rule of external rightful relations.
>
> (*RL* §8, 6:255.29–33).

The relevant 'universal rule', plainly, is the Universal Law of Justice. In order rationally to will that one be able to possess external objects, one must will that others not interfere with one's possessions. One cannot will that others not interfere with one's possessions consistently with one's (possible) maxim to infringe others' rights of possession. The universalized counterpart of one's maxim would be that others are to act so as to disregard one's own particular rights to possessions, and this is incompatible with one's intention to possess things for use. Kant's postulated 'duty of justice' (*RL* §6, ¶10) to respect the legitimate claims and detentions of others is thus a strict duty—a duty of *justice* rather than virtue—identified by a Contradiction in Conception test based on the Universal Law of Justice, as applied to the case of finite rational human wills and the material conditions of our agency in view of very general, morally relevant facts about our form of finite rational agency and circumstances of action (i.e., 'practical anthropology').

Kant's justification of rights to possession involves no unjust unilateral imposition of obligations upon others because, in obligating others to respect our possessions we also obligate *ourselves* to respect their possessions. This is not *unilateral* obligation because we recognize others to be like ourselves: finite rational agents living in sufficient proximity to interact with us and the things we use on a finite globe with finite resources.[21] Establishing and respecting rights to possession secures a degree and kind of freedom of action not otherwise possible, because our activities are on-going and require on-going use of various things. Under the conditions stated above, freedom from unjust interference with our use of things is necessary to act on our basic (as well as our elective) ends.

Yet one may ask whether taking an unclaimed object into possession restricts the freedom of action of others, because one's act prevents them from doing what they might otherwise have done, namely, take that very object into possession at a later date. Is this not a unilateral imposition of an obligation, such as is proscribed by their innate right to freedom, which includes independence from the determining will of others? Kant expressly denies that any of us can unilaterally obligate others (*RL* §§11, 15; 6:261.8–9, 264.20–22). Fortunately, taking things into possession involves no such unilateral obligation. Kant expressly states that the innate right to freedom only extends to freedom of action so far as it is compatible with the freedom of others in accord with a universal law,

[21] *RL*, §§9, 13, 42; *GS* 6:256.33–5, 262.22–6, 307.8–308.2. Though it may offend friends of animal rights, it is worth noting that in his 'Conjectural Beginning of Human History' (1786), Kant remarks: 'The fourth and final step that reason took in elevating the human being entirely above the society with animals was that he comprehended (however obscurely) that he was the genuine *end of nature,* and that in this nothing living on earth can offer a competitor to him. The first time he said to the sheep: *Nature has given you the pelt you wear not for you but for me,* then removed it from the sheep and put it on himself (*Genesis* 3:21), he became aware of a prerogative that he had by his nature over all animals, which now he no longer regarded as his fellow creatures, but rather as means and instruments given over to his will for the attainment of his discretionary aims. This representation includes (however obscurely) the thought of the opposite: that he may say something like this to no human being, but must regard him as an equal participant in the gifts of nature, a preparation from afar for the restrictions that in the future reason shall place upon the will in regard to his fellow human beings, and which far more than inclination and love is necessary to the establishment of society' (*GS* 8:114; A. Wood, tr.). Whilst perhaps true that rational agency, even in its imperfect human form, has a priceless, incommensurable 'dignity', I contend that Kant has sufficient justification of that modal, moral 'must' based upon his insight that universalizability is a *conditio sine qua non* of rational justification in all non-formal domains (above, §26). (Cinzia Ferrini kindly reminded me of Kant's remark.)

and he expressly states that this innate right to freedom involves our innate equality, which is independence from being bound by others—so far as one cannot also mutually bind them (6:237.29–4). One key claim in Kant's Critical metaphysics of justice is that we recognize that other human beings are finite rational agents like ourselves (cf. *RL* §42, 6:307.14–26; *KdU*, 5:484,7–19). Consequently, we know that they must act towards their ends by using things around them. Consequently, the same principle of permission to acquire possessions and the same correlative principle of obligation to respect others' rights of possession govern them just as they govern us. Consequently, we are permitted to obligate others to respect our claims to use things only because we are obligated, both by our own claims and by others' claims, to respect others' claims to use things, and because others can and must acquire similar rights to possession, and thereby also acquire the correlative obligations to respect others' possessions, including one's own.

This covers original acquisition. However, most rights to things are derivative and based upon transfer (including exchange or gift), at least of the materials used to produce things. Kant's notion of having a right to 'possess' someone else's act grounds the rights of contractual obligation generally (*RL* §§4, 7). Kant analyses transfer of title to things on the basis of contractual obligation; this justifies any second possessor's rights by fair receipt of title from previous owners of rights to those things.[22]

Each of us is thus committed to willing that rightful possession be possible, and each of us is thereby committed, via a Contradiction in Conception test, to respecting other's rights of possession. This is to say, given the three facts discussed above, we are rationally committed to establishing and honouring a joint system of rights of possession. The minimum sufficient condition of regular and reliable use of things is a system of conventions according to which things will be regularly available to individuals to possess and to use in attaining their (permissible) ends. Such a system of conventions may be considerably weaker than property rights, insofar as it need not involve sole authority over the disposition of anything, it need not involve the same object being available each time one needs an item of that kind, nor need it involve

[22] Cf. *RL* §§6, 39; 6:251.18–22, and Kant's aside, 'although according to everyone's concepts of right something external can be acquired by occupation or by contract...' (*RL* §44, 6:312.28–30).

unlimited term of use (cp. §36). These rights, of course, also do not involve the incidents of the right to the income from the thing, the right to the capital, the incident of transmissibility, the liability to execution, and the incident of residuarity, which characterize liberal private ownership of property. Because all of Kant's grounds of proof refer to use and the rightful conditions of use, he has said or shown nothing to justify stronger rights. Kant was right to formulate his argument in terms of possession (*Besitz*), not property (*Eigentum*), for he realized that most of the incidents characteristic of private property can be neither specified nor justified apart from specific legal institutions. Possession is a proper topic for what Kant calls 'private justice'; property is a creature of 'public justice', i.e., public legislation.

A system of rights to possess objects for use is obligatory for finite rational human beings living upon our Earth on the basis of a Contradiction in Conception test. The maxim that there be such a system is obviously coherent with its universalized counterpart. The maxim that there be no such system is not compatible with its universalized counterpart. This may be called the maxim of 'No Intelligible Rights to Use Things', according to which:

> I will that there be no system of conventions whereby things not physically in my grasp or occupied by me are regularly made available for my claim, detention, and use in obtaining my ends.

Under the three conditions identified above, this maxim is incompatible with anyone's willing of ends not within his or her present means! Given the fact that each of us has such ends (and the fact that we cannot count on not having such ends over the course of our lives), this maxim is in contradiction with the Principle of Hypothetical Imperatives.[23] That is a significant defect. However, to proscribe freeloading, the universalized counterpart maxim must be tested. One might will that there be no system whereby things are regularly and reliably made available for individual possession for use; provided that many others willed that

[23] Here the maxim of rescinding one's ends whenever they exceed one's own resources is relevant. However, the innate right to freedom combined with the basic needs required by our finite form of rational agency set certain limits below which the elective renunciation of ends cannot go. Cooperation with others and the agreement about principles and practices this requires is, in any event, unavoidable: Barbara Herman points out that in dire conditions one's stoic resolve may waver (and one cannot count on it not wavering), so that the self-sufficient 'stoic' may need the assistance of others to maintain his or her maxim of self-reliance! See Herman (1993, chapter 3, esp. 55–67).

there be such a system, one could benefit from that system while repudiating it 'in principle'. The prospect of freeloading is blocked by the universalization test. If the original maxim of No Intelligible Rights to Use Things is universalized, then no one would will there to be a system whereby things can be possessed for use. Given the three facts noted above, this is incompatible with rationally willing one's own ends, because it permits others to make use of one's would-be possessions, which thwarts one's own free actions by making willing unreliable and ineffective. (This approximates once again Hobbes' Innocent Problem of total mutual interference, though due to the maxim in question it is not quite so innocent.) Thus as finite rational human beings of our kind, each of us is obligated by the Universal Principle of Justice to will that there be a system of conventions governing rightful possession. In this way, individual rights to possession can be derived from the sole innate right to freedom of action, in conjunction with relevant basic facts about our finite form of rational agency and our finite circumstances of action on Earth. This derivation in the main defends Kant's justification of rights to possession *sans* detention.

Kant's justification of rights to possession and use is constructivist, and specifically of the kind I have called Natural Law Constructivism. Its affinities to Hume's construction of his three basic rules of justice should be evident, as also should be Kant's significant advance in specificity and specifically normative justification of these rights.

Reconstructing Kant's justification of possession on the basis of these facts highlights both Kant's debt to and his advance over prior natural law theories. Before Kant, natural law theories appealed to basic, salient facts about human nature and the human condition in order to determine basic principles of justice. Those facts, it was argued, so constrained our choice of principles of conduct as to make some principles 'necessary'. Prior to Hume, however, natural law theories were lax about identifying, characterizing, and justifying the relevant rights, duties, and their purported necessity. Traditional Natural Law theories exhibit the weaknesses Peirce identified in the *a priori* method of metaphysics. Such theories, he observed,

> . . . have been chiefly adopted because their fundamental propositions seemed 'agreeable to reason'. This is an apt expression; it does not mean that which agrees with experience, but that which we find ourselves inclined to believe.
>
> (Peirce 1877, 'The Fixation of Belief'; *CP* 5:382)

In inaugurating Natural Law Constructivism, Hume's analysis of the rules of justice, incomplete though it is, demonstrates that the rules he considers are necessary for human life, individually and collectively, under conditions of relative scarcity, limited benevolence, and sufficient regional population density. However, Hume did little to develop the normative justification these basic rules of justice require.

Like Hume, Kant recognized that empirical considerations alone are insufficient to generate or to justify norms (*GMS* 4:389–92). Kant contends that identifying and justifying norms requires using *a priori* principles. Occasionally Kant's rhetoric (especially in *RL* §§2–7) may suggest that *a priori* principles alone *suffice* to identify and to justify specific norms for human conduct. Hence it can appear that Kant, too, is subject to Peirce's stricture, and many of Hume's partisans have, in effect, alleged that this is so.[24]

The central point of Kant's *Kritik der reinen Vernunft* is to determine whether or to what extent pure reason can justify any synthetic propositions, and whether any form of metaphysics can be rigorously justified. Kant's Critical form of metaphysics subjects a contingent concept of a specified kind of being to *a priori* analysis. Kant's *Critique of Practical Reason* considers the contingent concept of a mixed will, a will which can determine what to do by considering either rational principles and their use, or empirical ends and desires. Kant's Critical *Metaphysics of Morals* supplements the concept of a mixed will by appeal to 'practical anthropology', that is, by appeal to some basic facts about human nature and the human condition. On the basis of the Universal Law of Justice (*Recht*), in conjunction with basic facts about human nature and the human condition, Kant argues that we are rationally committed to this obligation, regardless of and prior to any choice, convention, agreement, or calculation of utility. Consider Kant's gloss on natural justice:

> . . . by natural law (*Naturrecht*) is understood only the non-statutory, and thus simply the right that can be known *a priori* by every person's reason . . .
>
> (*RL* §36, 6:296)

In Kant's view, then, previous natural law theory provided necessary but insufficient conditions for generating and justifying norms for human

[24] Most recently, perhaps, Baier (2010, 51, 53, 94, 166, 201), whose passing remarks on Kant tend to be as dismissive as they are impatient and uninformed.

conduct.[25] In this important regard, Kant renews and extends the natural law tradition. However, Kant's approach is constructive. Nothing intrinsic to the world-order need make things liable to possession; the link between Kant's two 'Postulates' is that things can in principle be possessed (*RL* §2) only if we act towards one another in ways which allow things to be possessed (*RL* §10).

38.4 Rights to usufruct: conditional, yet non-optional

The rights to possession justified by this Kantian argument are conditional. They are conditional upon the facts mentioned above, and in two further ways. First, they are conditional upon the objects we use being in certain ways benign. In a bizarre world in which any object used by one person concurrently and ineluctably produced, say, strong toxins for others, no rights to use could be justified, and rights to possession without use would be pointless. (Then again, in such a world, our species would not long survive—certainly not long enough to develop technology for handling such toxins!) Second, they are conditional upon scarcity being relative, not abject. In a world of abject scarcity, one person's use or possession of something is directly another person's vital deprivation. In conditions of abject scarcity, one person's freedom of outer action cannot, or little of it can, coexist with the like freedom of others in accord with a universal law. In such conditions, rights to use or possess things cannot be justified; they would lapse.[26] (Kant's innate right to freedom, together with his practical anthropology, suffice to justify the prohibition on harmful use of possessions.)

It is very important to note, however, that the conditional nature of these rights and their attendant obligations does not make them elective, and does not make them heteronomous in the sense rejected by Kant.

[25] On the relations between Kant's moral philosophy and the natural law tradition, see Schneewind (1993, 1998, 518–22), and Gregor (1993, 1997). They note that natural law theorists prior to Kant appealed to some supreme authority, whether divine or monarchical, to determine the content and bindingness of obligations. Kant rejected this appeal as heteronomous.

[26] It follows, too, from Kant's analysis that we are obligated not to produce, or to enter upon, such conditions of abject scarcity, whether through war, wanton destruction, or spiralling population growth. We now live in an age and in social conditions in which population dynamics may well have succeeded economics as 'the dismal science'. Whether this is, or becomes, the case is very much up to us, and it is altogether a matter of justice: public justice, and neither charity nor individual virtue (alone).

These rights and their attendant obligations are autonomous in the sense that they are legislated by each of us for ourselves. Neither their content, their justification, nor their bindingness depends upon our contingent wants, preferences, elective ends, or choices; nor do they depend on another's will, whether human or divine. Given the basic facts about human nature and the conditions of human life discussed above, we are committed to willing there to be a system of such rights, and we are committed to accepting the attendant obligation to respect others' particular rights to possessions. The Contradiction in Conception test reconstructed here is not consequentialist in nature because it turns on confronting two intentions (one expressed in a maxim, the other expressed in its universalized counterpart), and it turns on the counterfactual case of universal behaviour in accord with the intention in question. No issues about *de facto* degrees of general compliance, or counterfactual extent of harm, or the kinds or extent of benefits, pertain to Kant's justification of rights to possession. In this regard, though the substance of Hume's account of the conventions governing property accords in many ways with Kant's, their justifications differ fundamentally. Where Hume looks to utility, Kant looks to freedom as the fundamental basis and justification of juridical norms. What justifies these conventions as legitimate is their being necessary enabling conditions for free individual action. What is wrong with non-compliance with these conventions is not disutility to some or failure to maximize overall utility, though both are true. Instead, it is that non-compliance renders impossible legitimate free acts of others. Indeed, non-compliance makes it impossible for at least some others to act on the same maxim of non-compliance. Thus they cannot act on the maxim adopted by those who disregard rights to possession; this maxim cannot be universalized because it cannot be adopted by all. Nevertheless, in the subsidiary moral-pragmatic vein of his grounds for membership within civil society (and for obedience to political authority), Kant offers such prudential considerations for compliance to those who, like the race of rational (self-disciplined) devils described in 'Perpetual Peace' (*GS* 8:366), cannot—or refuse to bring themselves to—think or act beyond their own self-interest.[27]

[27] Though it cannot be developed here, I believe this observation resolves the debate about whether Kant's principles of justice are justified (only) prudentially, on which see

38.5 Why rights to usufruct suffice to justify a republic

In conclusion, it is important to note that taking Kant at his word, that he justifies possession (*Bestitz*) not property (*Eigentum*), does not deflate Kant's argument for membership in political society. The rights and obligations justified so far are in an important sense provisional (*RL* §9). Principles specifying right action are insufficient without adequate motives to follow them. Kant insists that legislation involves two integrated aspects: a rule of action, and an incentive to act (*MdS* 6:218.11–23). Kant defines justice in terms of outward behaviour, strict compliance, and external legislation.[28] By 'external legislation', Kant means the possibility of coercive enforcement, of being compelled either to commit or omit specific outer actions (6:232.23–9). (This is distinct to punishment; punishment may be one means of coercive enforcement.) Consequently, the juridical incentive to act cannot be good intentions (of whatever kind), but can only be threat of sanctions. Kant further argues that duties of justice *per se* are coercively enforceable, because their coercive enforcement counteracts what otherwise would be the illegitimate coercive interference with rightful activity (6:230–2).

Three features of our human finitude and circumstances of action are relevant here. First, without publicly certifiable titles to possession(s), none of us can know (rather than perhaps vaguely surmise) what is rightly possessed by whom (*RL* §§15, 31, 33, 39). This Kant learned from Hobbes' innocent problem of mutual interference (above, §8). Second, we are sufficiently populous that in most regions and any region to which public justice can pertain—we cannot avoid mutual interaction and thus potential if not actual mutual interference (*RL* §§41–3). Third, it is a fact of human nature, sufficiently known to us in our own case, that people tend to impose themselves upon others (*RL* §42). Such self-interested imposition is manifest in the facts that human beings tend to infringe upon the rightful free acts of others, and that the parties to such disputes typically cannot judge such infractions impartially. No unilateral will can be entrusted, and so none can be permitted, to enforce

especially Höffe (1989); Brandt (1997); and Ludwig (1997). On the moral-pragmatic dimensions of Kant's grounds for obedience to political authority, see Westphal (1992) and Horn (2014).

[28] Setting aside, as irrelevant to these preliminary issues, the relevance of intent to distinguishing uttering falsehoods from lying, and manslaughter from murder.

principles of justice impartially; whereas 'biased enforcement of justice' is oxymoronic. Would-be unilateral enforcement of rights cannot be universalized because such a maxim, however well intentioned, is fallible and would involve unjust infringements upon legitimate free actions (*RL* §§8, 9; 6:256.5–8, 257.10), and because no unilateral will can obligate others, in this case, to comply with would-be coercive enforcement. (These points are detailed below in connection with Locke's claim to a natural right to punish violations of the law of nature within the state of nature; §45.)

Rights to possession are merely provisional if they lack legitimate means of enforcement (*RL* §§9, 44) and if they lack publicly recognized title (*RL* §15). Consequently, when social life meets the conditions outlined above, so that rights of possession are necessary, it is likewise necessary to form a civil society, that is, to establish common, official, impartial public means to secure rights to possession (*RL* §§8, 9, 15, 42; esp. 6:256.27–31). The only way to enforce rights impartially, and thus legitimately, is multi-lateral *via* public courts of distributive justice (*RL* §§41, 43–5). Hence the possibility in principle that things may be possessed, mentioned in Kant's Juridical Postulate of Practical Reason (*RL* §2 ¶1), and likewise our obligation to act towards others so that things may be possessed (*RL* §6 ¶10; which Kant also calls the 'Juridical Postulate of Practical Reason') require acting so as to establish and to follow impartial, multi-lateral, public legislation and courts of distributive justice. These are basic institutions of civil society; thus only in civil society are rights to possession peremptory, rather than provisional (6:257.4–5).

In this regard, Kant treats the social contract merely as an ideal, entirely heuristic model (*RL* §47, 6:318, 371–2).[29] Voluntary consent plays no role in Kant's idealized 'original' social contract; hence consent plays no constitutive role in identifying or justifying basic moral norms. As in the *Groundwork* (4:44) and in the *Critique of Practical Reason* (5:30–1), here in the *Rechtslehre* Kant again sides with Socrates—and Hume, and Rousseau—in answering the Euthyphro question: we are to agree to the fundamental, non-negotiable principles and practices of justice *because* these principles and the practices they structure and

[29] I discuss this point in Westphal (1992), along with Kant's republicanism. Also see O'Neill (2000b).

enable are necessary for human life and because they are rationally justifiable and so are just and legitimate—though Kant's Critical philosophy provides a far superior account of their rational justification (*per* above, chapter 6).

Kant's constructivist method for identifying and justifying these most basic moral principles does not require Hume's naturalism, which is Hume's basis for claiming that moral principles, including the principles of justice, must be artificial rather than natural. Instead, Kant's constructivist analysis identifies and justifies these basic moral principles without taking, and without needing to take, any stand on ontological issues regarding moral realism and its alternatives, or on human motivation and its relation(s) to reasons for action, or on whether there are any incommensurable values, or even on human values as substantive premises for justifying normative principles. Kant's *conditio sine qua non* for rational justification in non-formal domains, together with his universalization requirement and his judicious appeal to practical anthropology, identifies and justifies strictly objective, non-arbitrary, non-negotiable basic moral principles, whilst avoiding the subjectivism, relativism, voluntarism, or scepticism attendant upon justificatory internalism.

The principles of possession justified in 'Private Justice' are instituted, though neither constituted nor justified, by convention or social contract. The conditions which obligate us to establish rights to possession also obligate us to establish public legislation and courts. This obligation is not elective and is based neither upon desires nor upon utility. Constituted by convention or social contract—that is, by positive legislation—are only the specific methods and regulations governing possession, including certified titles, and any further rights or incidents which may define property within a particular society. In turn, public legislation and courts must themselves be legitimate, which Kant sought solely in a republican constitution, with division of legislative, executive, and judicial powers (*RL* §§45, 46, 48, 49). Within Kant's republican constitution, the sole innate right to freedom recurs as the fundamental right to civil independence or self-sufficiency, to be able to provide for 'one's own existence and maintenance' thanks to 'one's own rights and capacities (*Kräften*) as a member of the common wealth', without depending upon the elective choice (*Willkür*) of anyone else (*RL* §46). This is precisely Rousseau's *conditio sine qua non* for the legitimacy of any system of justice, not only in principle, but also in institutional practice (above, §8).[30] Kant's formulation of the 'original contract' deliberately echos Rousseau's, by rejecting the liberal individualist view (expressly stated by Hobbes) that law inherently and only restricts and sacrifices individual liberty, and affirming that consenting to republican citizenship replaces one's natural but lawless freedom with full freedom under the law, where this legal justice is legitimate because it is self-legislated (*RL* §47).[31]

[30] Note that Rousseau's and Kant's independence requirement secures substantial equality of citizenship, including (in Rousseau's terms) both moral and civil freedom, without invoking the more radically egalitarian principles of distributive justice invoked by Gauthier's contractarianism (above, §29). (According to Rousseau, moral freedom consists in obeying only self-legislated laws, whereas civil freedom is liberty of action in all private matters which do not concern general welfare.)

[31] By introducing government as a guarantor of rights of possession, I have justified neither collective nor state forms of ownership (neither possession nor property). Governmental enforcement of rights of possession does not justify a government's having any of the incidents involved either in property or in usufruct, much less having all of them. Kant's justification of civil society, which I only sketch here, deserves much closer analysis. See Herb and Ludwig (1993); Fulda (1997); Ripstein (2009, 145–266); Byrd and Hruschka (2010, 143–87); and Horn (2014).

9

Conclusion

Reintegrating Justice into Morals

39 The Aims and Scope of this Study

The primary aim of this study has been to identify a distinctive, powerful, unjustly neglected form of moral constructivism, which I have called Natural Law Constructivism, inaugurated by Hume's theory of justice in Book III of the *Treatise*, and developed much more fully by Kant in his *Doctrine of Justice* (*Rechtslehre*), which identifies and justifies strictly objective, basic moral principles and the social practices they structure, with no appeal to moral realism or to its alternatives.

I have argued that Natural Law Constructivism achieves this objectivity in part by its justificatory externalism, and that it preserves cognitivism about those basic moral principles and institutions through its account of justification, rather than by any appeal to (alleged) moral truths or truth-makers. I have further argued, if briefly, that Natural Law Constructivism affords a powerful response to the Pyrrhonian Dilemma of the Criterion, and that this is a key merit, especially in contrast to ever-controversial moral realism and to contemporary versions of moral constructivism which appeal to 'subjective' basic elements of the sorts indicated in §§5 and 6.

It has not been my aim to develop a full account of Natural Law Constructivism, nor to develop its full scope, uses, or implications, but instead to try to redirect philosophical attention away from subsidiary issues, such as moral motivation or egoism, and away from partisan distractions amongst philosophical factions, towards more important common grounds of theoretical and practical concern. Hence I conclude this essay, and leave for another occasion detailed inquiry into the relations between economics and justice.[1]

Central to this study are concerns of method as well as of substance. Much post-modern cant has it that 'the Enlightenment project' is dead, and so much the better, given its imperialist and militarist record. I am no more a friend to imperialism or militarism—or, let me add emphatically, to fanaticism, dogmatism, or sexism—than they, but their dismissal of the Enlightenment conflates an historical period with only some of its leading, and best, ideas. The problems addressed by the best minds of the Enlightenment are still very much with us today, indeed, on a far grander, truly global scale: establishing peace, justice, and welfare so far as possible and as widely as possible. Addressing these issues requires much more acute and careful attention to history, to culture, and to commonalities as well as differences, than is or can be provided by radical chic post-modern cant, which strongly tends to promote—wittingly or not—what we least can afford: relativism and cynicism. We need more, much more Enlightenment, not less.

And yes: I am convinced that, and I hope to have displayed to you convincingly why, we need more, and more careful study of Enlightenment philosophy. The issues we confront, both in theory and in practice, are far too complex to afford a dismissive attitude towards our philosophical predecessors in ways which are becoming ever more pronounced in contemporary philosophy, in Europe as well as in Anglophone circles.

40 What Today is Self-Evident?

'Self evidence' has lost much of its philosophical vogue, at least in practical philosophy, for good reasons: nothing which can equally well (purport to) justify a claim and its negation can be a method of justification. This problem of principle is exhibited by Locke's inconsistent claims about the purported right to punish in the state of nature (detailed below, §45).

Nevertheless, many of us recognize the majesty of the second sentence of the US Declaration of Independence:

[1] On these relations, see Arthur and Shaw (1991); Murphy and Nagel (2002); Waldron (2005); and Kendrick (2011).

We hold these truths to be self-evident, that all men are created equal, that they are endowed by their Creator with certain unalienable Rights, that among these are Life, Liberty and the pursuit of Happiness.

Honouring the majesty of this conviction, however, requires improving upon it in two regards. One is to include all women and *all* men, and not at all to abide the racist compromise which is Article 1, §2, ¶3 of the United States Constitution, which permitted counting three-fifths of all slaves towards district representation of white slave owners in the US House of Representatives, whilst allowing legalized slavery to stand, with its denial of legal and political representation to enslaved human beings.

The other is to justify the principle independently of even the most cautiously ecumenical reference to the Creator. Self-evidence, like various claims about a divine creator, too easily and too often serve to divide people along lines of assent to, or dissent from, whatever claim is at issue. Much of the history of such divisiveness is too sanguineous to be sanguine about self-evidence, about theological claims, or about 'the necessary course of history' taken as major premises in moral programmes—or in immoral pogroms.[2] If claims to self-evidence or to theology or to the course of history have waned in contemporary philosophy, divisions along factional lines persist in discussions which focus upon what philosophers may accept or reject, to the neglect of what philosophers may or may not be able to justify. At the outset, Logical Positivists discussed frankly 'cultural circles', and their adherence to one such. Those discussions quickly subsided, though the phenomenon of cultural circles has not only persisted within philosophy, it has grown under the cover of an ever more pervasive—because unrecognized—conventionalism.[3]

[2] NB: it is only such use that I criticize; Dawkins (2006) deluded himself about the 'God delusion'. Religious faith or theology is not a moral problem: fanaticism, dogmatism, ignorance, intolerance, and domineering violence are moral problems. On tolerance, see Williams and Waldron (2008). As for the alleged course of historical development, we simply know too little to appeal to claims about it within moral philosophy; see Iriye, Osterhammel, and Rosenberg (2012). On the left, mention is still made of 'late' capitalism; neither Marx nor anyone else has provided convincing grounds for assessing either the maturity or the morbidity of capitalism; developments, changes, yes; terminus, no; death and transfigurations, not at all. The requirements and exigencies of justice are sufficient focus for human attention and action. If we attend effectively to justice, we can let history take care of itself. Due to the sociological law of unintended consequences, we can do no better than this; as a matter of justice we are obligated to do no less.

[3] For discussion, see Westphal (2015b).

It would hardly be necessary to draw attention to these methodological matters, such as the inherent weakness of Locke's appeal to 'right reason' to know normative natural laws, but for the fact that such appeals continue to be made, despite Peirce's (1877) trenchant critique of the '*a priori* method' (above, §38.3). Consider Hume's later observation:

> Who sees not, for instance, that whatever is produced or improved by a man's art or industry ought, for ever, to be secured to him, in order to give encouragement to such useful habits and accomplishments? That the property ought also to descend to children and relations, for the same useful purpose? That it may be alienated by consent, in order to beget that commerce and intercourse, which is so beneficial to human society? And that all contracts and promises ought carefully to be fulfilled, in order to secure mutual trust and confidence, by which the general interest of mankind is so much promoted?
>
> (*ECPM* 3.2.7/SBN^{E} 195)

'Who sees not . . . ' is precisely the kind of vague appeal to 'reasonableness' of which Hume was so rightly critical in the *Treatise*, and Peirce in 'The Fixation of Belief' (1877).

Nevertheless, commenting upon a similar passage in the second Appendix to volume one of Hume's *History of England* (1:458), Annette Baier writes:

> Locke could almost have agreed with Hume in Appendix 2.
>
> (Baier 2010, 96)

This may be correct, and it may be an important feature of 'Hume's Enlargement of His Conception of Justice'—the title of Baier's chapter from which I quote—but neither their coincidence of views nor an enlargement of anyone's *concept* of justice address the key moral issues of whether those views are, or that concept is, justified or justifiable in any particular domain. About these matters, Baier (2010) is silent.

John Finnis (1980, 85–99) advanced the view that the basic aspects of one's own well-being can only be self-evident; this is entailed by his starkly individualist and foundationalist presuppositions.[4] This is not to

[4] He (1980, 85) states that 'each reader must ask himself, What *are* the basic aspects of my well-being? Here each one of us, however extensive our knowledge of the interests of other people and other cultures, is alone [*sic*] with his own intelligent grasp of the indemonstrable (because self-evident) first principles of his own practical reasoning.' Whilst 'values clarification' and the like can be useful and instructive, these sorts of individual meditation and any of their practical results presuppose the basic kinds of rights

disagree with his list of seven basic forms of good, but rather to note that they focus upon 'human self-determination and self-realization' in ways which are not universally recognized or shared, and that mere agreement even amongst those who agree with his list of seven basic forms of good—life, knowledge, play, aesthetic experience, friendship, practical reasonableness, and religion—is too meagre a premise by which to identify or upon which to justify fundamental moral principles, especially since beneath those apparently splendid headings can be arrayed a host of socially vicious attitudes and practices. This is to recall the point made previously about Hume's estimate of the value of friendship and the vagaries of usage (§§15, 16), and its bearing upon the choice of 'basic elements' in constructing a moral theory (§§5.2, 9). Finnis (1980, 92) claims his seven basic goods are 'self-evident'. This history of claims to 'self-evidence' belies its claim to provide adequate justification.

Despite the fact that property rights are complex products of positive legislation, and so can be neither defined nor justified on any sound natural law (constructivist) basis (above, §36), Lockean property rights are widely espoused still today, especially in the USA, and even Kant's recent commentators typically fail to distinguish between possession and property. Such neglect thwarts sound justification. Baier claims to:

> find the Humean account the best account we have of these rights and obligations [*viz.*, Hume's three rules of justice] and their relation to the wider field of morality when that is seen as cultivation of virtues . . .
>
> (Baier 2010, 123)

Baier thus disregards the further issues involved in justifying rights to acquisition Kant identified and addressed, along with the distinction between those rights to possession and use which can be justified by Natural Law Constructivism (whether Hume's or Kant's) and the further rights (incidents) constitutive of property (whether private or public). Baier's claims on behalf of Hume's account—this and the one quoted just above—reflect, it must be said, the bias of those moral philosophers who treat ethics as primary, and dismiss justice as secondary, and of those who settle for consensus, when what is required is clear and cogent

and responsibilities identified by Natural Law Constructivism, which are indispensable preconditions for the individual pursuits central to Finnis' (paradigmatic) teleological ethics.

justification. Hume's account of the three basic rules of justice is only a fragment of a theory of rightful possession, though it is an important fragment further developed by Kant. Their common form of Natural Law Constructivism merits careful attention; it should not have been neglected for so long.

41 Does Ethical Theory Rest on a Mistake?

In January, 1912, *Mind* published H. A. Prichard's provocative article, 'Does Moral Philosophy Rest on a Mistake?' Like Moore (1903) before him and Ross (1930, 1939) after, and with express parallels to epistemology (1912, 21, 34–6) and indeed to Cartesian geometry (1912, 28), Prichard contends that moral reasoning consists in recognizing various specific actions as obligatory (presumably, including both omissions and commissions), without inferring their obligatory status from any principles or criteria. Whilst non-moral reasoning may help lead us to recognize our obligations, he contends that the presumption that obligations are not self-evident but require proof stems merely from incomplete statement of any obligation (1912, 28). Specifically, Prichard maintained:

> The sense of obligation to do, or of the rightness of, an action of a particular kind is absolutely underivative or immediate. The rightness of an action consists in its being the origination of something of a certain kind A in a situation of a certain kind, a situation consisting in a certain relation B of the agent to others or to his own nature. To appreciate its rightness two preliminaries may be necessary. We may have to follow out the consequences of the proposed action more fully than we have hitherto done, in order to realise that in the action we should originate A . . .
>
> (Prichard 1912, 27–8)

> This apprehension is immediate, in precisely the sense in which a mathematical apprehension is immediate, *e.g.*, the apprehension that this three-sided figure, in virtue of its being three-sided, must have three angles. Both apprehensions are immediate in the sense that in both insight into the nature of the subject directly leads us to recognise its possession of the predicate; and it is only stating this fact from the other side to say that in both cases the fact apprehended is self-evident.
>
> (Prichard 1912, 28)

'Moral Philosophy', understood as the inquiry into, and the assessment and justification of moral principles which can demonstrate that various actions are morally obligatory to do or omit, is fundamentally misguided, he argued, because:

> . . . there is no such knowledge, and all attempts to attain it are doomed to failure because they rest on a mistake, the mistake of supposing the possibility of proving what can only be apprehended directly by an act of moral thinking.
>
> (Prichard 1912, 36)

In moral philosophy, Moore, Pritchard, and Ross all adopted and advocated the method Chisholm later designated 'Particularism' (above, §28.2), that we must begin with evident examples, and can do no more than construct a theory which might account for those particular claims systematically, and show why they count as the kinds of justified claims we initially and originally take them to be.

Nothing in this methodological form of moral particularism excludes juridical duties; neither does the particularlist method require their inclusion—indeed, the silence of moral intuitionists about justice is striking.

Theoretically and historically, it appears, this is where and how 'moral philosophy' became refashioned into Anglophone analytic ethics, dropping its traditional taxonomy as a genus with two proper, coordinate species: ethics and justice, adopting instead the notion that ethics is primary, whilst social and political philosophy are no more than secondary. This same conception is apparent when consideration of moral reasoning and 'the moral point of view' were re-injected mid-twentieth century into Anglophone ethics, in revolt against excessively narrow meta-ethical focus upon the conceptual analysis of ethical language or concepts and emotivist accounts of ethical discourse. The primacy of individual(ist) ethics and consequent neglect of moral issues of justice is clearly evident in two leading works on the moral point of view, Kurt Baier's (1958) book bearing that banner as its title, and Marcus Singer's *Generalisation in Ethics* (1961).

Credit to re-launching discussion of the moral point of view is often given to Stephen Toulmin's *An Examination of the Place of Reason in Ethics* (1953).[5] It is worthwhile to re-examine some significant passages from Toulmin's *Examination* here. Granting primacy to ethics does not neglect social aspects of ethics, insofar as individual ethics considers

[5] E.g., Nielsen (1999); Becker and Becker (2001, entry on 'The Moral Point of View').

other-regarding duties. 'Other-regarding duties', however, is a very broad classification, which strictly speaking includes duties of justice, though these were only put back onto the moral agenda of Anglophone philosophy by Rawls' *Theory of Justice* (1971). Nevertheless, Toulmin's *Examination* shows much greater appreciation of law, justice, and social institutions than is found in other works in this period, especially in works on the moral point of view. For example, only much later did Baier (1995) recognize the social roots of ethics, but still did not consider them as comprehensively as Toulmin.

Having examined the character of moral reasoning in some detail, Toulmin brings his discussion of ethics to bear upon social institutions in this way:

> The remaining topics will form something in the nature of a coda: I shall just rough them in, . . . leaving the detailed work . . . for another . . . place. All have to do with the social character of ethics; and the first is the relation between ethics and social institutions.
>
> Since the function of ethics is to reconcile the independent aims and wills of a community of people, the account which I have given could provide the skeleton for an essay in social history. All the principles, which together make up a moral code, can be related to some institution within the society, the code as a whole to the complete social organisation.
>
> (Toulmin 1953, 170)

Amongst the institutions organizing any society are those pertaining to law. In this connection, Toulmin (1953, 196–8) discusses Bentham's campaign for legal reform sympathetically. More generally, Toulmin highlights the centrality to ethics of social harmony:

> Ethics is concerned with the harmonious satisfaction of desires and interests. On most occasions it is a good reason for choosing or approving of an action that it is in accordance with an established maxim of conduct, for the existing moral code, and the current institutions and laws, provide the most reliable guide as to which decisions will be happy—in the kind of way as codes of standard practice in engineering.
>
> At the same time, it is not right to accept the present institutions uncritically—they must evolve, along with the situations to which they apply. There is, therefore, always room in a society for the 'moralist', the man who criticises the morality and institutions, and advocates practices nearer to an ideal. And the ideal he must keep before him is that of a society in which no misery or frustration is tolerated within the resources and state of knowledge. It is for those who are in the natural sciences to discover the means of reducing the amount of misery in the world, and so to provide fresh channels for satisfaction

and fulfilment: but the evidence of science remains evidence about what is practicable, and so about facts—what *is* or *could be*, not what *ought to be*. It is in the hands of the moralist that possibility becomes policy, what *can* be done becomes what *ought* to be done. All his experience and wisdom are needed to bridge the gap between facts and values. But the gap can be bridged.

(Toulmin 1953, 223)

Toulmin's emphasis on moral judgment is salutary; using our best information and our best understanding of relevant moral principles does not enable us to calculate results to moral questions.[6] Toulmin relinquishes any quest for a general answer specifying good ethical reasoning or valid ethical argumentation:

I myself do not feel the need for any *general* answer to the question, 'What makes some ethical reasoning "good" and some ethical arguments "valid"?': answers applicable to particular types of argument are enough .... In fact, it seems to me that the demand for any such general answer (however it is to be obtained) must lead one to paradox .... For ... such a general answer will, in particular cases, be equivalent to the rules which we have found .... In [that] case ... it can point out, in a more or less roundabout way, the advantages—indeed, 'the absolute necessity to the existence of society'*—of harmonious co-operation.

(Toulmin 1953, 161)

Toulmin clearly recognizes that the broader is the scope of the principles and practices in question, the more difficult is informed, cogent, constructive moral judgment. This problem underlies Toulmin's *Examination*:

Here is the problem that I had at the back of my mind. It is one thing to recognise the logical criteria appropriate to moral decisions, and another to apply them. In our day-to-day *judgements*, we can all rely on the existing code as a guide; but to criticise the code, and to recognise in which directions it needs changing, are jobs in which we cannot all be equally expert, for which very marked qualifications are needed. As a matter of logic, it is easy enough to define the criteria to be used: as a matter of practice, their application becomes increasingly difficult, the more we leave behind the elementary daily decisions, and try instead to judge the worth of existing institutions, the desirability of particular reforms. We must, therefore, not only answer the question, 'What kinds of reasoning is it proper to accept in support of an ethical judgement?'; we must also answer the question, 'What kinds of qualification should be required of a man, if his judgement about the reform of the moral code and institutions is to be trusted?'

(Toulmin 1953, 177)

6 Toulmin (1953, 177–87) cautions against misunderstanding the term 'moralist' and his use of it.

This issue about who is properly qualified and able to assess and advise on broad matters of the adequacy of a society's—of our own—moral code in principle and in practice is urgently important. In this regard, so too is Toulmin's (1953, 161) remark, quoted just above, about the paramount importance of harmonious cooperation. Toulmin quotes the phrase from Hume's *Natural History of Religion* (§13), where Hume states:

> Nothing can preserve untainted the genuine principles of morals in our judgment of human conduct, but the absolute necessity of these principles to the existence of society.
>
> (*NHR* 13.7)

Precisely which 'genuine principles of morals' these are, Hume does not here state, yet Toulmin's remark reaches only half-way: that our cooperation is necessary to society may be sufficiently clear and evident; why is social cooperation necessary for any of us as individuals?

Precisely here Toulmin's account of reasoning in ethics falls far short of that provided by Natural Law Constructivism, which rightly addresses Hobbes' founding insight into the Innocent Problem of mutual interference, that without coordinating our behaviour publically and reciprocally, our individual lives are not merely 'poor, nasty, brutish and short', but vanishingly brief due to total, fatal mutual interference (above, §8). Although Toulmin paid much more attention than his contemporaries and most of his successors in ethical theory to the social and legal aspects of ethical reasoning, in this decisive regard, Toulmin too failed to grasp how fundamental social coordination problems lodge at the heart of moral philosophy because they lodge at the heart of the possibility of free individual human action, including those actions involved in assessing and justifying our actions. Accordingly justice is at least as fundamental to moral philosophy as is ethics. Thinking otherwise is morally deficient, and diminishes the qualifications of its proponents to advise us on the adequacy of our most important social principles and practices: the basic principles of justice, by which alone any of us can be alive, active, engaged, responsible, and able so much as to consider whether, in what regards, or in what conditions our actions can or cannot be rationally justified.[7]

[7] This is to corroborate Paton's (1952) assessment, that Toulmin (1953) makes an excellent step in the right direction, though does not pursue the character and justification of basic moral principles far enough.

Moral particularlism, whether methodological or substantive, cannot address these issues credibly. Pritchard's famous article appeared not two years before the outbreak of yet another thirty years of even more terrible war in Europe, sweeping into its maelstrom both Asia and the Americas. However confident Prichard and others may be of their particular moral judgments, often those who disagree are equally confident, and too often they are also bellicose to boot. Unlike Pritchard's Cartesian analogy of a triangle necessarily having three sides and three angles, no denial of a statement of any of our moral obligations is self-contradictory. Pritchard repeats Descartes' most fundamental self-deception about the apparent self-transparency and infallibility of his clear and distinct conceptions, which can nevertheless be either false or inadequate.[8] Pritchard and the other ethical intuitionists also show that, no matter how self-evident some duties may appear, moral particularlism can err by neglecting other basic moral duties, such as those of justice.

This neglect was not due to lack of an indigenous Anglophone tradition of moral philosophy encompassing both ethics and justice. Bentham and Mill regarded both ethics and justice as continuous. Hume's writings on economics launched Scottish political economy, stimulating not only the moral, political, and economic works of such authors as John Millar and Adam Ferguson, but also Adam Smith, whose *Theory of the Moral Sentiments* (1759) is as significant as *An Inquiry into the Nature and Causes of the Wealth of Nations* (1776), and the latter is much more responsive to the moral ravages of industrial production than are his present-day *laissez faire* fans. Not coincidentally, Smith also lectured on jurisprudence. This integrated approach to ethics, justice, and political economy is, perhaps, epitomized by Smith's friend, Dugald Stewart, filling as it does four continuous volumes of his *Collected Works* (1859, vols 6–9). Stewart was the first to lecture on political economy as a regular course offering. That economics is a social science, properly designated 'political economy', is made plain by an author not intent on making this point: David Landes, in *On the Wealth and Poverty of Nations* (1999). Coming to grips with the exigencies, both advantages and disadvantages, of social cooperation requires moral philosophers—and economists (see Buchanan 2011; Hodgeson 2011)—to expand their artificially restricted

[8] I re-examine Descartes *Meditations* in this specific regard in Westphal (2014b); on Locke's related mistake, see below, §45.

perspectives. Specialists may protest that such scope produces superficiality. However, so too does excessive specialization.[9] More importantly, as our societies become more complex and more integrated, the prospects of the powerful taking advantage of others—whether wittingly or unwittingly, whether directly or indirectly, whether overtly or covertly—expand proportionally. It is morally imperative to keep abreast of these developments and monitor their advantages and disadvantages for justice, freedom, and legitimate social cooperation (see Ghaus-Pasha and Rowen 2007). Doing less will only hasten the collapse of our all-too complex societies (see Tainter 1988). Neither justice nor accountancy are mere luxuries we can afford to neglect, whether financially or morally.

In contrast even to Toulmin's much more broadly social view of moral reasoning, Modern natural lawyers rightly sought principles and justificatory strategies for resolving those fundamental disagreements about rights, duties, obligations, and just principles and practices of social cooperation, which involve, are tantamount to, or escalate into the Pyrrhonian Dilemma of the Criterion (above, §25). None of us who are reasonable or responsible will ever convince dogmatists that they are mistaken, but especially in connection with the obstinate, the wicked, or the incompetent we must be as clear and cogent as possible about what justice permits, what it requires, and what it forbids, so that we can determine whether, when, or how egregiously the bellicose or other sociopaths violate basic requirements of justice, and to determine what are the morally permissible measures to restrain, redress, or when necessary combat their injustices. Hume's and Kant's Natural Law Constructivism justifies the objectivity of these most fundamental moral principles, the principles of justice, and does so without embroiling us in subsidiary meta-ethical disputes about moral realism and its alternatives, including moral relativism. Decision procedures it does not provide; but it provides core principles for sound moral reflection, judgment, and action.[10]

[9] I examine some relevant methodological issues in Westphal (2010–11, 2013b).

[10] Toulmin's salutary points about moral judgment about fundamental social principles and practices are developed much more thoroughly by Will (1988, 1997), in part through sustained reflection upon and analysis of constitutional law and legal reasoning. The present analysis of Natural Law Constructivism complements Will's pragmatic realist analysis of philosophical reflection and justification. (Will 1997, which collects his preceding articles and provides a comprehensive, critical introduction, should be read before his 1988; for critical discussion of Will's views, see Westphal 1998b.)

42 Republicanism and Independence

Some readers may wonder whether their political differences may make Hume and Kant peculiar theoretical bedfellows: Hume is widely viewed as conservative, whilst Kant is famously republican, though also notorious for absolutely denying any right of resistance against despots. Hume's conservatism is easy to over-estimate. The closing paragraphs of 'Of the Liberty of the Press' make plain he regarded the British government as a mixed form, combining monarchical and republican elements (*EMPL* 1.2.4–6). He concludes 'Of the First Principles of Government' by clearly approving of republicanism in principle, though advising reform rather than experimentation (*EMPL* 1.4.8), as he does again—as a matter of political realism—when concluding 'Whether the British Government inclines more to Absolute Monarchy, or to a Republic' (*EMPL* 1.7.7–8): freedom was more fundamental to Hume than the form of government (*EMPL* 1.14.24–7). Rather than sifting further through Hume's cautious hints of his own political sympathies, note that subsequent to his break with him, no less an authority on the topic than Rousseau testified to Hume's 'great love of republicanism'.[11] More directly, Hume's justification of government is thoroughly functional: government exists to fulfil certain functions—legislative, juridical, administrative, military, and municipal—so that failing to fulfil these functions renders a government illegitimate. In this regard, Hume argues that social contract theorists drew the correct conclusion, though from specious premises (*T* 3.2.9.1–2/SBN 549–50). Hume instead looks first to the interest which undergirds government and our obedience to it:

> I seek, therefore, some such interest more immediately connected with government, and which may be at once the original motive to its institution, and the source of our obedience to it. This interest I find to consist in the security and protection which we enjoy in political society, and which we can never attain when perfectly free and independent. As interest, therefore, is the immediate sanction of government, the one can have no longer being than the other; and whenever the civil magistrate carries his oppression so far as to render his authority perfectly intolerable, we are no longer bound to submit to it. The cause ceases; the effect must cease also.
>
> (*T* 3.2.9.2/SBN 550–1)

[11] *Confessions*, 2.12; *Oeuvres* (1817, 16:248).

That settles the natural basis of obligation to political authority, and the moral obligation closely follows suit, according to Hume, because it rests entirely upon the principle of public interest:

> There evidently is no other principle than public interest; and if interest first produces obedience to government the obligation to obedience must cease whenever the interest ceases in any great degree, and in a considerable number of instances.
>
> (*T* 3.2.9.4/SBN 553)

Indeed, Hume contends:

> It is certain, therefore, that in all our notions of morals, we never entertain such an absurdity as that of passive obedience, but make allowances for resistance in the more flagrant instances of tyranny and oppression. The general opinion of mankind has some authority in all cases; but in this of morals it is perfectly infallible.
>
> (*T* 3.2.9.4/SBN 553)

Passages such as these amply corroborate Rousseau's report: so much so, that it may appear that Hume was the courageous author, rather than Kant.

Kant was a staunch republican, both in principle and in public. He was well known to speak out in favour of republican principles, even after the French Revolution descended into the Reign of Terror.[12] There are two important philosophical points regarding Kant's views to note briefly. One is that Kant's unconditional duty to obey political authority is formulated within, and so only holds within, his *a priori* 'metaphysical' principles of justice, so that unconditional obedience is only required by—and *to*—fully just, and hence fully legitimate republics. Kant's infamous denunciations of resistance and revolt are consistently carefully qualified in advance in ways which make this clear, if readers will but attend carefully to his views and statements. And readers unable to do so ought not, in Kant's view, to pass judgment about whether resistance or revolt may in some cases be justified. Parallel to these unconditional matters of *a priori* principle Kant provides very strong pragmatic, hence conditional grounds supporting obedience to actual

[12] See Kuehn (2001, 116, 343, 383–4).

governments, though here too, Kant agrees in principle, even if he was cautious in print, with Hume, that those governments—or rather, more properly speaking, those governors—who are 'the more flagrant instances of tyranny and oppression' have no legitimate claim to obedience, in which case, resistance to them violates no duty.[13]

The other point about Kant's republicanism, as he noted in print, is that he had not fully formed his views on government in the published *Rechtslehre*. One important issue with which he had not yet grappled is the distinction between a strict separation of governmental powers and a system of checks and balances. A strict separation of governmental powers results *de facto* in tyranny, because the executive branch alone commands the police and military. Some passages in Kant's *Rechtslehre* reflect this implication, despite Kant's equally clear rejection of tyranny. Fortunately, other passages in the *Rechtslehre* state and recommend a republican tripartite division of powers without requiring their strict separation. Though Kant's published statements are not entirely consistent, it is clear that his principles are unequivocally republican.[14]

43 Justice, Economics, and Accountancy

Earlier we noted that Hume justifies returning a lost sum of money to a seditious bigot or a miser for these reasons:

> Property must be stable, and must be fixed by general rules. Though in one instance the public be a sufferer, this momentary ill is amply compensated by the steady prosecution of the rule, and by the peace and order which it establishes in society. And even every individual person must find himself a gainer on balancing the account; since, without justice, society must immediately dissolve, and

[13] The principles involved in this aspect of Kant's analysis are as straightforward as their textual documentation is convoluted. For concise discussion, see Westphal (1991b), for full details, see Westphal (1992).

[14] The avowed reform conservative, Klaus Epstein (1966, 366), notes that Kant's response to the Prussian censor, which Kant published together with the censures in the Preface to *Struggle of the Faculties* (1798; *GS* 7:5–10), makes a 'rather painful impression'. Epstein is right that the censor had to respond to Kant's patent stratagems; Kuehn (2001, 365, 371–2, 380–1) is right that Kant provoked the confrontation as a political act. I submit that Kant's response was composed to exhibit in exquisite, painful detail exactly the damages to be expected of censorship in matters of intellectual and religious orthodoxy; cp. the closing pages of Kant's essay, 'What does it Mean to Orient oneself in Thinking? (1786), discussed above, §26.

every one must fall into that savage and solitary condition, which is infinitely worse than the worst situation that can possibly be supposed in society.

(*T* 3.2.2.22/SBN 497)

Plainly, the twentieth century of this Common Era produced far greater human injustice and artificial evil than Hume found possible to suppose within society (Glover 1999). Let us hope—and strive, and *act*—so that the twenty-first century improves on the side of justice rather than expands the scope of injustice. True, within recent memory one of the great dictatorships died of bankruptcy. One key problem with the Soviet command economy is that for most of its history it disregarded basic microeconomic analysis and the accountancy it involves. Only in the mid-1970s did the Soviet planners begin to introduce such bookkeeping.[15] (That alone discredits the USSR's claims to have been 'Marxist'; Marx understood accountancy and its crucial financial and economic roles perfectly well.[16])

The Soviet route into bankruptcy may not be the only one. In 2001, headlines were made by the collapse and (at that time) largest ever bankruptcy case of Enron Corporation. Double-bookkeeping was a core strategy of Enron's financial shell game. Sixteen people involved pleaded guilty; five more were found guilty at trial, most prominently, Kenneth Lay and Jeffrey Skilling. They were the poster-boys; media focus on them and upon Enron diverted scrutiny from other corporations engaged in similar kinds of fraud. Arbogast (2008) uses the Enron case for series of case studies in business ethics; may it be intensively studied and its admonitions widely followed! Significantly, Arbogast highlights cases of ethically responsible decisions made—and made effective—by various persons involved in Enron's operations; Arbogast studies salutary, instructive cases of integrity and adroit tact, not only cases of irresponsibility become habitual.

In the USA (and similarly elsewhere) accountants are designated 'public accountants' for a very good reason: ultimately they are responsible to the public to certify a company's compliance with, or its failure(s) to comply with, proper, legally binding accountancy procedures, which themselves are required for proper functioning, not only of the company in question, but of the larger economy and of society as a whole.

[15] I have this directly from an economist who consulted to the Soviets about these matters.

[16] Cf. 'Critique of the Gotha Programme' (Marx 1962, 19:18–20, 1996, 212–13).

Credible, reliable, effective public accounting is a basic point of justice, required for companies to conduct business in public, especially if they are bidding for public investments (by public offerings of stock), and if they are corporations—moral persons which exist only due to legal provisions. Bookkeeping is a matter of justice, and justice requires proper bookkeeping: all the more so when bookkeeping takes the form of official auditing. The sheer scope of operations of large-scale US corporations, however, makes their accounting and auditing nightmarishly complex. Since the 2008 market collapse we know that major banks have hidden both foolish and also illegal dealings behind those nightmarish complexities. Arbogast makes plain that the integrity of a company's operations is in the first instance a function of its financial control principles, procedures, and practices, and the extent to which these comply in theory and in practice with applicable laws and regulations. This integrity is at once economic, financial, operational, ethical, and a cardinal instance of justice. Arbogast notes:

> Business ethics and financial control are thus deeply intertwined.... an individual's ability to act ethically is gravely hampered when a firm's financial controls are weak.... The integrity of a firm's control system is demonstrated by when controls are given priority over the pressures of the day; this integrity is preserved when the essence of an ethics issue remains the focal point for consideration despite all tactics of disinformation and deception that perpetrators may use.
>
> (Arbogast 2008, 2–3)

Arbogast rightly emphasizes the complexity of moral issues arising within corporate business life, detailing them with great skill and illumination. I hope the present study may complement his by unequivocally identifying and justifying the most fundamental moral principles, which are principles of justice required by, and required for, individual, social, and also corporate integrity. Our clear and cogent understanding, justification, and enactment of these principles is possible and can be actual in our behaviour, judgments, and attitudes without debating our fundamental 'values', commitments, motivational psychology, tradition, scripture, or theology. May I mention: Arbogast writes after serving more than thirty years as a financial officer for Exxon Chemical and Exxon-Mobile Chemical.[17] We are entirely agreed that 'accurate accounting is a

[17] Arbogast retired from that employ and began teaching business several years before BP's disaster in the Gulf of Mexico—the burning and sinking of their drilling platform, Deepwater Horizon, in 2010 and the massive leak it caused (see Tainter and Patzek 2012).

prerequisite to following the law' (Arbogast 2008, 251); his detailed description of firms with strong traditions of sound financial practices and controls—and their distinctions from less credible firms—is excellent, and should be read in the original, not excerpted here.

Arbogast notes that the financial scandals at Enron, WorldCom, Adelphia, and others occurred within fifteen years of the previous major financial scandal concerning Wall Street brokerage firms. Going to press prior to 2008, Arbogast concludes by highlighting the temporal propinquity of these financial disasters (1993–2008):

> America's financial markets absorbed two of their worst scandals within a period of only fifteen years. Existing law and regulatory oversight failed to preempt either. This history should sober anyone tempted to think that business has learned the lessons of Enron.
>
> Although some businesses learn to value ethical cultures and good controls, others will always find the pressures or temptations to cheat irresistible. What has allowed our financial markets to develop and deepen has not been some self-governing improvement throughout the corporate world but rather the development of strong law and regulation backed by effective enforcement....
>
> The core reforms enacted in Enron's wake must thus be protected and preserved. They address real problems that will emerge again if the law is weakened or enforcement slackens. And, should the ever-inventive business world find new routes around these latest boundaries, further steps to ensure the independence of corporate gatekeepers and the accuracy of the reports they bless will be warranted.
>
> Only by preserving this legacy will the destruction wrought at Enron be partially redeemed by an enduring improvement in the ethical climates of our corporations and our capital markets.
>
> (Arbogast 2008, 256–7)

The financial crisis which broke in 2008 was centrally the collapse of a vast, unregulated shadow banking industry.[18] Those in the US corporate community and their Congressional Representatives who complain most loudly about 'unnecessary government regulation'—as if matters of justice can be denigrated as regulatory interference; as if those same corporate advocates and their ilk have not over decades urged and

That disaster resulted directly from many of the short-cuts in financial and control operations against which Arbogast warns.

[18] See (in chronological order) White (2004); Rowe and Day (2007); Tett and Davies (2007); Johnson and Neave (2008); Cairns and Roberts (2009); Ferguson and Johnson (2009a, 2009b); and Nersisyan and Wray (2010).

obtained the ever larger scales and complexities of corporate activities which require correspondingly complex systems of oversight!—are precisely the same people who have once again brought us confirmation that the next depression only requires enough time to lapse for people to forget how the last one came about.

In response to the 2008 market collapse, major banks and corporations were declared 'too big to fail'. In effect this really means 'too big to be allowed by the government to fail'. The problem with corporations 'too big to fail' is that they are also too big to be held to book: whether to the book of law, or to the accountants' books. By bailing out such corporations, the US public has been made guarantor of those companies' debts, whilst leaving in private hands their profits upon recovery. The working class in the USA has known for decades what this is: 'corporate welfare'. They were already calling it that during Reagan's administration (no later than 1982). Let us hope we neither require nor receive further proof of the merits of the long-standing policy of *The Economist*, that corporations should not be allowed to become the financial behemoths they are in the USA, which are able—in effect—to strong-arm the US government and the US public. Unfortunately, the last US President who thought, talked, or did anything serious about trust-busting was Theodore Roosevelt. That was half a century before Dwight Eisenhower warned the US about the development of its military-industrial complex.

These recent financial upheavals were preceded in the 1980s and 1990s by a crisis with small-scale financial institutions, called 'Savings and Loan' ('S&L') companies, which were allowed to enter into banking services previously barred to them. Inexperience, greed, and foolishness took their toll then. At that time, the president of a small bank, interviewed about the S&L crisis, observed that, in contrast to earlier methods, in the 1990s in the USA 'the best way to rob a bank is to own it'.[19] Let us consider: might something like this also be done to a country? Has it already been done? The answers will require just accounting, as well as accounting to justice. The basic structural problems of undue commercial influence upon the political process even at

[19] 'The best way to rob a bank is to own one'—William Crawford, Commissioner of the California Department of Savings and Loans, introducing his congressional testimony before the U.S. House Committee on Government Operations (1988); see Black (2005).

the highest levels is not new; it has only become more in-grown, extensive, and intensive since Truman (1951) and Mills (1956) wrote.[20]

Reducing and confining the size and complexity of major public corporations—moral persons which are entirely creatures of public law—need not reduce or confine the size or productivity of a national economy. Indeed, to the contrary: one central reason for the resilience of the German economy is that its banking sector is far more diversified than any other in Western Europe or the Americas. In matters of banking reform and regulation, the Occident could benefit from the model of Islamic banking principles and procedures; that would be a very constructive exercise in inter-cultural dialogue.[21] Doubtless many capitalists and conservatives would protest that adopting such banking principles would unduly restrict investment and economic growth. There is room to debate whether such restriction would be 'undue'—that is, unjust—but more importantly, let those who wish to defend business prerogatives demonstrate they are not merely self-interested ideologues by proposing effective, feasible measures for instituting and preserving responsible, legal, just business practices, and for restricting, reducing, and redressing their violations, not only in theory, but in practice, domestically and internationally. That would be a very welcome, potentially constructive contribution to solving rather than perpetuating these problems. Such recommendations have now been made by the 'Group of Thirty' (G30, 2015), and they are salutary and sound. It is an urgent matter of basic justice that their recommendations be made policy and effective practice domestically and internationally. It must be remarked, that it should not have required the 2008 financial crisis to demonstrate the elementary truth that, if they are at all self-regulating, financial markets are self-regulating only under extremely idealized, other-worldly counter-factual circumstances (cf. Schultz 2001; van der Does de Willebois, et al. 2011).

The fundamental principles of justice, and their fundamental links to economics and to accountancy, are neither mysterious nor arcane, nor can they be dismissed as mere ideology or fantasy. Those principles have been examined and defended in this study. The present study may not be

[20] See, e.g., Waxman et al. (2008); Hensarling (2015).

[21] There is now much discussion of this topic; one good recent contribution is Abdul-Rahman (2010).

a complete accounting of the principles of justice, but they form a crucial core of justice, and suffice to identify a wide range of forms of injustice. I am under no illusions about the power and wiles of vested interests, but to distinguish legitimate from illegitimate vested interests requires clear and cogent principles of justice. Those presented here form a solid core of such principles.

Gauthier's (1997, 140) contractarian principles require providing benefits to others proportional and indeed at least roughly equal to the benefits one receives from them; he acknowledges that this requirement is 'revolutionary' (148). Rawls's (1999, 65–70) 'Difference Principle' requires systemic social inequalities be made to work also to improve the position of those least well off. Rather than examine the merits of these and other principles of distributive justice, I close by underscoring the baseline of distributive justice established by Natural Law Constructivism. We noted earlier (§§8, 16) that in the *Treatise* Hume provides only a fragment of a theory of justice, in part because his three rules of justice are consistent with obviously unjust social conditions. Hume's theory of justice is based squarely upon conventions, though he later observed that conventions of justice can only develop amongst those roughly equal in power, and roughly equally able to make palpable to those who perpetrate injustice their resentment at being treated unjustly (*EPM* 3.1.18/ SBN^{E} 190). Hume's reliance upon sentiments and upon susceptibility to sentiments such as resentment in this connection should recall Kant's concern about moral empiricism (§19). Hume's recognition of the role of rough equality of power in developing conventions of justice highlights again the presumed boundary conditions which must hold for interactions to produce roughly just results: rough equalities in power, but also in resources and resourcefulness, including information and its uses. Conversely, Hume's observation signals how easily significant differences in power, resources, or resourcefulness enable those who have to treat those who lack less than fully justly. This is why Rousseau made independence a *sine qua non* of social and institutional justice,[22] and why Kant adopted this independence condition: that no one is to have the kind or extent of wealth, power, or privilege which enables him or her to

[22] *CS* 1.6.4, 1.7.8, 2.11.1; cf. Westphal (2013d).

command the will of anyone else (provided those others do not themselves infringe upon justice and so merit restraint or punishment).

Kant states:

> There is only one innate right.
> *Freedom* (independence from being constrained by another's choice), insofar as it can coexist with the freedom of every other in accordance with a universal law, is the sole original right belonging to everyone by virtue of being human. —This principle of innate freedom already involves the following authorizations, which are not really distinct from it (as if they were members of the division of some higher concept of a right): innate *equality, i.e.*, independence from being bound by others to more than one can in turn bind them; hence a human being's quality of being *one's own master* (*sui iuris*), as well as being someone *beyond reproach* (*iusti*), since before he performs any act concerning rights he has wronged no one; and finally, his authorization to do to others whatever does not as such diminish what is theirs, if they do not want to accept it—such things as merely communicating his thoughts to them, telling or promising them something, whether what he says is true and sincere or untrue and insincere (*veriloquium aut falsiloquium*); for it is entirely up to them whether they want to believe him or not.
>
> (*RL*, Einl., 6:237–8)

The sole innate right Kant identifies is not merely asserted: it is required by, and required for, the autonomy of rational judgment, which is required for omnilateral giving, taking, assessing, perhaps revising, and when warranted adopting justifying reasons, which itself is required for justifying one's principles and one's actions by being able to provide all concerned (affected) others sufficient reasons for so acting, reasons which they too can adopt in thought or in action, including on the occasion of one's own act. This *conditio sine qua non* of rational justification in non-formal, substantive domains, together with elementary, pervasive facts about our finite form of rational agency and our circumstances of action (Kant's 'practical anthropology'), suffice to identify and to justify significant rights and obligations regarding possessions, including their acquisition, use, and exchange, coordinating our actions *via* promise or contract, and for identifying basic rights and obligations of republican citizenship and government—though these latter have only been mentioned here *en passant*.

Earlier we noted Gauthier's (1997, 146) recognition that human beings can become rational deliberators only through and on the basis of an economically and emotionally secure and stable upbringing, and that this basic demand imposes important constraints upon both parents and society (above, §30).[23] I also argued that Gauthier's error about this requirement lay in having to regard this non-optional requirement as optional to fit it into the proper scope of elective, contractarian agreement (§31). To the contrary, this demand is not optional for our form of finite rational agency, and meeting this demand remains an urgent desideratum of justice, which is becoming more, not less, urgent as societies continue to become more complex, and as educational institutions succumb to financial contraction caused by executive mismanagement, largely in some major corporations in the USA, though also in governments, especially those who have adopted the same mismanagement methods which fostered the current financial crisis.[24] Yes, both governments and educational institutions must pay their way, but we must never forget that economies exist for the sake of their societies; societies do not exist solely for the sake of their economies, and certainly not solely for the sake of those who profit most from their economies. Accountancy, financial accounting, and internal as well as external audits are fundamental matters of justice insofar as they are crucial for determining whether financial agents act within the limits of the law and the provisions of justice, and for exposing their excesses if, when, and to the extent that they occur.

One can acknowledge the importance of Hayek's (1960, 1983) two cardinal theses, that centralized planned economies cannot possibly have the information required to set proper prices or production targets, and that markets are effective distributed information channels for producers and consumers, and yet recognize with Keynes that a good deal more legal structure and hence government activity are required to ensure economies function properly rather than dysfunction massively. The kinds of spontaneous order Hayek advocated can only develop and function within proper legal and governmental frameworks (Schultz 2001; Muller 2007). More significantly, the 'spontaneity' of social order Hayek prized distinguishes not at all between swarm intelligence (which may be valuable) and mere herd behaviour, such as a herd of greedy bulls stampeding over a financial cliff (as in 2002–2008; see below, §46).

[23] For details of what must be provided, see Westen (1985); Turiel (2004); Deneulin and Shahani (2009); Garber (2010).

[24] See Head (2011); Thomas (2011); Watson (2012); Curren (2008).

The information transmitted via markets—even of the sorts advocated by Hayek—only concerns select features of economic production, consumption, and distribution. Both production and consumption produce non-market benefits and burdens, including employment patterns, household weal or woe for employees and employers—and for managers at all levels in between—as well as waste, pollution, and human dislocation as labour distributions change. Hayek over-simplifies the economic, political, and social alternatives by pitting (nearly) *laissez-faire* capitalism against centralized planned economies, by pitting individualist liberalism against monolithic collectivism, to the persistent neglect of liberal forms of moderate collectivism which recognize the vital roles of proper government, law, and non-governmental agencies within civil society to monitor, facilitate, ameliorate, or correct good or ill effects of economic activities—the kinds of views represented by, for example, Hegel (1821), T. H. Green (1883, 1886a–c), John Dewey (1930), and in practice by Johan Vilhelm Snellman (1806–1881), an Hegelian who contributed centrally to founding and developing modern Finland, whose liberal, moderately collective republicanism is fundamental to Finnish politics, society, and culture, and typifies the political and social policies and practices of Nordic and Scandinavian polities. Snellman's statue sits before the entrance to the National Bank of Finland; his portrait adorned the 100 (and the 5000!) Markkaa banknote until Finland adopted the Euro in 1999. The Scandinavian and Nordic countries are splendid examples of justice—including far higher levels of social justice—being achieved, consistently with an excellent standard of living and ample rewards for enterprising, responsible entrepreneurs.[25]

These policies and practices have never been allowed to make public, political sense in the USA or England. Consider some landmark dates: Upton Sinclair's *The Jungle* appeared in 1906; *Black Elk Speaks* in 1932; John Steinbeck's *The Grapes of Wrath* in 1939; Richard Wright's *Black Boy* in 1945; Simone de Beauvoir's *Le deuxième sexe* in 1949, translated into English in 1952; Rachel Carson's *Silent Spring* and Michael Harrington's *The Other America* both in 1962; Paul Ehrlich's *The Population Bomb* in 1968. These works spurred much important reform, but the issues they spearheaded remain all too current, and indeed are becoming

[25] They are also splendid empirical examples of Schultz's (2001) theoretical demonstration that economic efficiency can only be achieved within moral constraints.

Figure 2 J. V. Snellman.

more rather than less urgent, indeed acute (cf. Tainter, Allen, and Hoekstra, 2012; Curren 2010b, 2015).

Granting that effective, constructive political, legal, and social reform requires considerable time and effort, as Kant knew,[26] there are three philosophical points about justice to be made here. First, the kinds of officially 'non-economic' products or forms of discrimination indicated by the works just mentioned are exactly the kinds of factors which

[26] E.g., *GS* 8:146–7n; quoted above, §26.

producers and marketers strongly tend to exploit, if and as they can. Second, Rousseau was profoundly insightful when he insisted that the theory of justice requires taking 'men as they are and laws as they might be' (*CS* Proem). One characteristic trait of 'men as they are', is that those who benefit—or those who believe they benefit—from neglecting or disregarding material damages or social discrimination strongly tend to such neglect or disregard, whereas those who suffer from them strongly tend to recognize such malefactions or injustices. Such differential responses are also typical of philosophers, many of whom, if they have read this far, may be expected to protest at my having mixed politics into philosophy. Justice and the theory of justice are not idle intellectual pursuits. So regarding them contributes to the problems highlighted here rather than to their solutions. Even more so does regarding ethics as primary and justice as no more than secondary—or regarding meta-ethics as the 'serious' discipline to the denigration of normative ethics—contribute to neglect and disregard of fundamental moral issues of justice, both in theory and in practice. All such efforts made in the twentieth century—whether unwitting, intentional, or strenuous—are themselves political efforts with real political consequences, both tangible and intangible. We can be morally and politically responsible without fallaciously affirming the (political) consequent or *petitio principii*; indeed, we can *only* be morally, politically, and intellectually responsible by avoiding such fallacies.

Tyranny of the majority—or of the vocal minority—is a constant threat within democracies and to democracy, unless democracy is rooted fundamentally and actively in (small 'r') republicanism: only thus can government of the people also be government by the people and for the people—*all* the people! Anything less fails to be republican and fails to be democratic. If indeed 'democracy is the worst form of government, except for all those other forms which have been tried', as Churchill (1947, 206–7) observed, it is morally imperative as a matter of justice, not merely of virtue, that we keep it from being worse than it is, and worse than it need be. Recent proposals for 'deliberative' forms of democracy belatedly acknowledge that 'democratic' legitimacy requires comprehensive, active, robustly *republican* citizenship—and citizens!

We saw above that Toulmin identified two important questions:

What kinds of reasoning is it proper to accept in support of an ethical judgement?

What kinds of qualification should be required of a man, if judgement about the reform of the moral code and institutions is to be trusted?

(Toulmin 1953, 177)

To these I add a third question:

How can we ordinary members of the public identify proper moral reasoning and sound moral judgments offered by others, whether lay, expert, or wise?

Answering these three questions, both in theory and in practice in any particular case, requires developing and exercising what may be called 'mature judgment'. Mature judgment involves the abilities to discern and define the basic parameters of a problem; to distinguish relevant from irrelevant and more relevant from less relevant considerations bearing on a problem; to recognize and to formulate important questions and sub-questions which must be answered in order to resolve a problem; to determine proper lines of inquiry to answer those questions; to identify historical or social factors which lead people—including ourselves!—to formulate questions or answers in particular ways; to think critically about the formulation or reformulation of the issues; to consider carefully the evidence or arguments for and against proposed solutions; to accommodate as well as possible the competing considerations bearing on the issue; through these reflections and inquiries to resolve a problem so far as possible and ultimately to organize and to present these considerations clearly and comprehensively to all interested parties.

These qualities of judgment are cardinal intellectual virtues. They are central to a liberal education, and they are crucial to constructive, intelligent inquiry in any of life's many activities, whether professional, commercial, political, academic, scientific, or personal. However, these qualities of judgment cannot be learned 'by taking a course' in them. Instead they are the indirect result of training, education, and experience in more specific subjects and activities. They are correlated with a subtle understanding of a topic, but they are not reducible to mastery of the factual component of the topic understood.[27] Mature judgment is required for recognizing and benefiting from others' critical assessment of one's judgments or surmises, in the ways Kant identified as necessary for our thinking cogently and correctly, so far as we very

[27] I detail these issues in Westphal (2012a), from which this explication of mature judgment is drawn.

finite, semi-rational beings are able (above, §26); it is required for sorting sense from non-sense, especially in the moral domain—whether in ethics, politics, justice, or law; it is required for responsible exercise of that supremely important public office: the office of citizen (Green 1999).

It has been observed that simply studying 'the humanities' has no known effects upon making students more humane. Of course not; it is not merely the subject matter but the *way* these subjects are taught which is paramount. Education at all levels must be re-oriented towards the development of mature judgment. Unfortunately, mature judgment is the first casualty of the manifold economic imperatives now foisted upon educational institutions. Mature judgment is also far too often a casualty of academic professionalism, in which too many of us pretend to be experts but guard our modest achievements all too jealously against critical examination, even by the loyal opposition.[28]

Mainstream Anglophone philosophy is only beginning to come to terms with the ill effects of the ideologically inflamed twentieth century, including its toll upon philosophy (see Reisch 2005, 2007; Erickson et al. 2013), which included the simplistic if expedient polarization of a starkly individualistic centre against the monolithic totalitarianisms of right- and left-wing extremists. I shall not repeat what I have said previously about these matters (Westphal 2013e), except to note that it behoves philosophers—and especially those philosophers who attempt to insulate their philosophizing from philosophical, intellectual, and cultural history—to reflect more conscientiously upon their own historical, social, and intellectual contexts, the contexts they ineluctably presuppose when framing their philosophical inquiries (cf. Scharff 2014). The 'divide-and-conquer' approach to solving philosophical problems piecemeal, one at a time in splendid isolation, died in principle when Carnap explicated his account of philosophical explication and his view of linguistic frameworks. Both developments brought with them a moderate though ineluctable (if 'molecular') semantic holism. Both developments were announced in 1950; their undermining of the semantic atomism required for the alleged mutual independence of philosophical

[28] I discuss these issues about education more fully in Westphal (2012a); also see Buchanan (2004); Curren (2010b, 2015).

problems or 'puzzles' was announced by Wick (1951). Too much of present-day philosophical method and practice still lags behind, still wedded to strong semantic internalism, access internalism, and conceptual 'analysis' (Westphal 2010–11). These presumptions are not merely Cartesian, they are directly indebted to Descartes' mediaeval source, authorized by none less than the Roman Pope: the Bishop of Paris, Étienne Tempier's, condemnation in 1277 of 220 neo-Aristotelian theses (Piché 1999). The direct and express implications of Tempier's condemnations are that natural philosophers are limited to proposing merely possible explanations, and that only strict logical necessity demonstrated by deduction suffices to justify any claim to 'scientific' knowledge (*scientia*) (Boulter 2011; Westphal 2016a). These methodological presumptions ineluctably reduce philosophy to an idle, conventional, orthodox talking shop. Such practitioners of the trade will have no legitimate grounds for complaint if and when others economize by closing such shops.

Consider this unjustly neglected observation:

> My limits do not allow me to discuss in detail the various forms of strife carried on within an orderly modern community, from which destructive physical violence is approximately excluded. But, if space permitted, I think it might be similarly shown that, in the graver disputes between classes with in a state, we cannot rely on the external method alone for realizing the social peace and concord which only justice—I do not mean ideal justice, but a fair human approximation to justice—can give. For the most skilfully adjusted representative system will not really protect us against a majority, formed by a combination of selfish interests, becoming practically judge in its own cause; and the belief in the natural right of the majority of any community to do what it likes is a political superstition which is rapidly passing to the limbo of such superstitions. The only hope of preventing strife within modern states from growing continually more bitter and dangerous lies in persuading the citizens, of all classes and sections, that it is not enough to desire justice sincerely; it is needful that they fit themselves, by labourious and sustained efforts to understand the truths mingled with opposing errors, for the high and deeply responsible function, which democracy throws on them, of deciding and declaring social justice. Otherwise, I see no reason why the strife of sections within a community should not lead to war in the future, as it has done in the past.

With this admonishment Henry Sidgwick concluded the lead article of the premier issue of *The International Journal of Ethics*—forerunner of the journal now known simply as *Ethics*, already published (as it still is) by the University of Chicago Press—titled 'The Morality of Strife' (1890,

15). It was no merely occasional piece; Sidgwick included it as the fourth chapter of his *Practical Ethics* (1898).[29]

In his review of Sidwick's *Practical Ethics*, Bernard Bosanquet made special mention of that article in particular. His review opens with this assessment:

> Professor Sidgwick would, perhaps, not object to be described as a teacher of ethics according to general principles. Neither those who heard some of the addresses contained in the present volume, nor those who will read it, can fail to be impressed by the courage and loftiness of mind with which the claims of rational principle and the need for justification by reasonable argument are maintained by the author in every sphere which he touches. The address, for example, on the Morality of Strife will convey to the reader, as it did to those who heard it, a just conception of what is too commonly disregarded, the ethical value of sheer intelligence, of the mere understanding by the parties to any dispute of the true point and bearing of the controversy, and of the real nature of the claims put forward on either side. We hear so much of the duty of sympathy and kindliness that it is both pleasant and wholesome to be reminded that especially under the conditions of modern democracy perhaps the first duty of all is to make the effort to understand. The reader will learn from this volume how to uphold the supremacy of reason, and to argue upon problems of practical ethics acutely, fully, and dispassionately, according to general ideas and principles. The spirit is the spirit of Mill and Bentham, as Professor Sidgwick would probably admit; but it is transformed by a range of philosophical knowledge very different from theirs and by an experience of criticism which transcends their horizon.
>
> (Bosanquet 1889, 390)

Bosanquet's suggestion that in modern democracies our foremost duty is to strive to understand recalls Kant's answer to the question, 'What is Enlightenment?' (*GS* 8:35);[30] his noting that this duty requires us to strive to understand one another, despite whatever differences or disagreements we may confront, recalls Kant's stress upon the crucial role of thinking publicly in actual communication with one another for thinking accurately and cogently oneself (above §26).

The range of Sidgwick's knowledge, which so facilitates his understanding, to which Bosanquet refers, includes his concerns with social justice, deeply informed by his studies of political economy and political history. If Sidgwick's concern with social justice may now be unexpected,

[29] The quotation is from Sidgwick (1890, 15, 1898, 111–12).

[30] '*Sapere aude!* Dare to know! is . . . the motto of enlightenment.'

this has much to do with selective focus upon his justly famous *Methods of Ethics* (1874), to the neglect of his extensive and substantial contributions to *The Principles of Political Economy* (1883), *The Elements of Politics* (1891), *The Development of European Polity* (1903), and his several essays on political economy in his *Miscellaneous Essays and Addresses* (1904), including his 1885 Presidential Address to the Royal Statistical Society (Section F of the British Association), 'The Scope and Method of Economic Science'.[31] No other twentieth-century Anglophone moral philosopher devoted such attention to political history and political economy; today only James Buchanan and Amartya Sen have approached his example.[32]

Understanding, fulfilling, and working effectively to improve the requirements and provisions of justice is a fundamental moral duty. Discounting or disregarding justice by asserting the primacy of ethics—or still more so of meta-ethics—over justice is a philosophical dereliction of duty. 'Formal' though the principles and methods of Natural Law Constructivism may be, they are neither empty nor trivial, and they are identified and justified without having to take any stand on issues about moral realism or its alternatives, or about moral motivation, or about egoism, or about 'values'. This is the central lesson of Hume's and Kant's Natural Law Constructivism. If this study has made this much clear and convincing, the further scope and implications of Natural Law Constructivism may be considered separately.

Having argued for the moral duty of each and all to uphold justice conscientiously, publicly, effectively, in theory and in practice, allow me to conclude by noting that this is no time for despair, resignation, cynicism, or *Weltschmerz*: these are precisely the attitudes and inactions which allow crime, corruption, and sociopathy to flourish and abound. Fortunately, excellent resources now available introduce much of the required multi-disciplinary information.[33] There are practical, effective

[31] Singer's collection of Sidgwick's essays (Sidgwick 2000) includes only one chapter on juridical topics, 'Law and Morality', from Sidgwick's *Elements of Politics* (1891), and only one on social science, 'The Relation of Ethics to Sociology' (1899). Sidgwick's role in the development of economics as a discipline is discussed in Collini, Winch, and Burrow (1983, 277–307).

[32] Parfit (2011, 460 n133) criticizes Sidgwick's scant attention to justice, but appears to have given only scant attention to Sidgwick's *oeuvre*.

[33] Two such are O'Neill (1998) and Peil and van Staveren (2009).

forms of analysis, detection, exposure, and redress, if we but consider these matters seriously.[34] As for neglect of such issues of justice, it makes good moral sense to ask: 'Who benefits from such neglect, and exactly how so?'

[34] Cf. Roberts *et al* (2006); Fisman and Miguel (2008); Meyer (2009); Prammer (2010).

Appendix

44 Hobbes in *Leviathan* does not Espouse Egoism

44.1 A fatal equivocation in Hobbes' Thesis about Ends

Anglophone moral philosophy—both ethics and theory of justice—have been more markedly empiricist, and more marred by empiricism, than is generally recognized. One important such characteristic is persistent presumption that agents' motives are centrally required to justify moral principles, where 'justification' is understood as justifying principles *to* agents by appeal to their motives. Accordingly, egoists are to this broad swath of moral theory what sceptics are to epistemology. One key to effective reply to both kinds of view is to reject justificatory internalism, and to recognize that—and how—basic moral principles can be identified and justified without appeal to agents' motives or other subjective states. This is one cardinal advantage and advance of Natural Law Constructivism. Preoccupation with egoism has distorted Anglophone discussion of Hobbes. Recognizing that Hobbes does not espouse egoism in *Leviathan* underscores the deleterious effects of preoccupation with justificatory internalism and hence with agents' motives in moral theory. It may also serve to remind philosophers that philosophical means and methods are not particularly apt for psychological speculation, not to say psychological investigation (cf. above, §17.5).

Hobbes innovates significantly in *Leviathan*, in particular, by distinguishing categorically between natural right and natural law: natural right permits actions—any actions—whereas law—any law—restricts action by proscribing some actions whilst prescribing others (*L* 1.14.3; Ludwig 1998, 271–91). As counsels of prudence, Hobbes' three 'laws' of nature, though correct and crucial, are not properly laws; they are only laws as divine (*L* 1.15.41) or as sovereign commands (*L* 2.26.8). As Ludwig (1998, 283) rightly stresses, a crucial feature of Hobbes' 'civil philosophy' is to analyse and to justify political right and obligation without appeal to divine revelation, but solely by appeal to reason and reasoning; these are categorically distinct sources of knowledge (*L* 4.46.4). Nevertheless, it is important to modern natural law, and to

Hobbes's analysis in *Leviathan*, that the dictates of unaided reason converge with divine law. Important here is that, even as counsels of prudence, Hobbes' three dictates are not merely descriptive; it is not redundant to say that they forbid imprudent, and enjoin prudent behaviour (*L* 1.14.3).[1] Rephrased for brevity, Hobbes' three 'laws' of nature are:

Seek the peace, but if it is unattainable, use every advantage of war. (*L* 1.14.4)[2]

To obtain peace, be willing to revoke as much liberty as are others. (*L* 1.14.5)[3]

Perform covenants made. (*L* 1.15.2)

Hobbes' three 'laws' of nature are *prescriptive*, even if they accord with our own self-interest. This is because it is possible to act otherwise than they enjoin; hence they are normatives, regardless of the extent of compliance with them.

Psychological egoism is a thesis about human motivation, that self-interest is the *only* human motive. It is a factual claim, distinct from the normative claim of ethical egoism, according to which self-interest *ought* to be our only motive (even if in fact it is not). Hobbes appears to state psychological egoism in what we may call his Thesis about Ends, namely this crucial premise:

. . . of the voluntary acts of all men, the object is some good to himself. (*L* 1.14.8)

This statement merits closer consideration than it has received. Psychological egoism is a very strong claim about the content of human desires and ends, which maintains that they are solely self-regarding and always aim at one's own individual good. Though this may appear to be Hobbes' claim, does Hobbes believe that we each always so infallibly aim at our own individual good? No. To the contrary, it is central to Hobbes'

[1] On this point I differ with Ludwig (1998, 278).

[2] '. . . it is a precept, or general rule of reason, that every man, ought to endeavour peace, as far as he has hope of obtaining it; and when he cannot obtain it, that he may seek, and use, all helps, and advantages of war. The first branch of which rule, containeth the first, and fundamental law of nature; which is, to seek peace, and follow it. The second, the sum of the right of nature; which is, by all means we can, to defend ourselves.'

[3] '. . . be willing, when others are so too, as far-forth, as for peace, and defence of himself he shall think it necessary, to lay down this right to all things; and be contented with so much liberty against other men, as he would allow other men against himself'.

political analysis that we easily become quarrelsome, a kind of behaviour which is plainly *not* for our own individual good, because such behaviour violates the first Law of Nature, 'Seek the peace!', by causing its opposite, strife, which is not in our self-interest (disregarding for now the sub-population of inveterate trouble-makers, bullies, fiends, power-mongers, sadists, or sociopaths who foment discord for its own sake).

Consider Hobbes' remarks on the causes of quarrel:

> ... in the nature of man, we find three principal causes of quarrel. First, competition; secondly, diffidence; thirdly, glory.
>
> (*L* 1.13.6, cf. 1.13.4–7)

Competitiveness, diffidence, and vainglory all pertain to human motivation. Clearly such quarrels aim at some *presumed* good for the agent him- or herself; do they also aim at an *actual* good for the agent, all things considered? To the extent that our competitiveness, diffidence, and vainglory (together with limited resources and lack of government) generate the solitary, nasty, brutish, and life-shortening conditions of the state of nature, such motives do *not* aim at any actual good for individual human agents, all things considered. There are two distinct aspects of Hobbes' Thesis about Ends, a motivational aspect and a cognitive aspect, to this effect: we aim at what *is* good for ourselves. Not only are these two aspects distinct, they can easily diverge to the point of disconnection, as even these brief remarks about quarrelsomeness show.

More important, however, is that Hobbes' claim about human motivation is not a statement of psychological egoism. Reading Hobbes' Thesis about Ends as a statement of psychological egoism *presupposes* that one's own good is *solely* one's own good, and never also a good for others. Consider Hobbes' statement again, together with a small revision, which results in an unambiguous statement of psychological egoism. Hobbes' Thesis about Ends states:

> Of the voluntary acts of all men, the object is some good for himself.
>
> (*L* 1.14.8)

A Hobbesque statement of psychological egoism would instead be:

> 'Of the voluntary acts of all men, the object is some good *solely* for himself.'

Taken strictly and literally, *Hobbes*' own stated Thesis about Ends allows that individuals may perhaps act to obtain a good for themselves which is also a good for some others and which the agent may knowingly seek as a good also for some others—e.g., for one's family, clan, tribe, faction, or collaborators. Hobbes' Thesis about Ends, taken strictly and literally, is *not* egoistic because it is *not* restricted solely to self-regarding individual goods. Indeed, granting the possibility of some shared goods is central to Hobbes' positive political proposal, as also to his political concerns about clans and factions. More generally, the possibility of shared goods is required for any political theory to avoid being, or entailing, a zero sum game.

Hobbes' analysis in *Leviathan* of sovereignty and sovereigns highlights both the central role of shared goods, and of acting in view of shared goods, within his analysis, and the untenability of the cognitive claim embedded in his Thesis about Ends. If human psychology is as wretched as Hobbes often avers, then there would be a serious problem about absolute sovereigns, who share in this same purported human psychology: what, if anything, precludes absolute sovereigns from being or becoming absolute despots?

44.2 Why expect moderate rule from absolute sovereigns?

Very briefly, Hobbes advanced four kinds of reasons to show that absolute sovereigns rule moderately rather than despotically:

1. Establishing a Hobbesian sovereign terminates the prior state of war of all on all. Hence the sovereign, who wields state power, need not worry about domestic threats.
2. The Hobbesian sovereign, too, aims at 'some good for himself'. The good of any sovereign—namely state power—derives directly and indirectly from the industriousness, prosperity, wealth, and domestic peace of the country, and the loyalty of subjects if and when external threats arise. Conversely, poor, disorderly countries cannot mount effective militaries.
3. The Hobbesian sovereign remains in a state of nature regarding all other sovereigns. To maintain one's sovereignty requires preserving one's territory against external threats. So doing includes making evident to foreign powers that one's country is equipped, able, and willing to defend itself. This requires both a vital economy and genuine loyalty on the part of one's subjects, either to go to war or to support war efforts (*per* 2).

4. The loyalty of subjects all depends upon *their* having a sufficient stake in the welfare of their country to defend it. The wealth of the sovereign depends upon the wealth and productivity of subjects. None of this can be achieved by despotic rule; it can only be achieved by moderate rule, which allows and enables subjects to be industrious and to become and to remain loyal.

Hobbes elaborates these reasons with great care. So doing makes a very significant case for both peace and the common weal being shared goods; they are not solely good for each individual person, and they are shared by both subjects and sovereign. This holds even if individuals are ignorant of, or neglect the fact that, these goods are shared amongst individual subjects and also their sovereign.

44.3 Human fallibility and Hobbes' Thesis about Ends

A serious problem lurks here. What if an absolute Hobbesian sovereign isn't intelligent enough to understand those four reasons for moderate rule, and all the policies and practices they entail? Or what if an absolute sovereign isn't sufficiently self-disciplined to act in accord with those four reasons and all the policies and practices they entail? Both prospects are consistent with psychological egoism, which as a motivational thesis cannot involve any significant cognitive claim, much less any fail-safe psychological capacity for acting solely upon and achieving enlightened self-interest.

The central problem here is that Hobbes' positive political proposal requires that absolute sovereigns act on their genuine good(s), rather than act badly if not despotically upon their (merely) apparent good(s). This observation prompts a further re-consideration of Hobbes' Thesis about Ends:

> Of the voluntary acts of all men, the object is some good for himself.
>
> (*L* 1.14.8)

In this statement Hobbes' use of 'is' is equivocal. Clearly, Hobbes makes a factual claim about human motivation. However, Hobbes also makes a claim which cannot be about human motivation, namely,

> . . . the object of any voluntary action is some good for the agent.

Hobbes' unqualified final clause expressly states that we each aim at what *is* (in fact) good for ourselves, as if each of us infallibly knows our own actual individual good! This is both empirically false and, much more importantly, it can*not* be a thesis about human *motivation* or desires; it is a claim about human cognition, specifically, about our broad and reliable—literally our comprehensive and infallible!—understanding of our own good. If as a basic matter of human psychology we had such understanding, *and* we always acted on that basis—as is stated in Hobbes' final clause—then we would not be so damnably quarrelsome and diffident to begin with. To the contrary, Hobbes' use of 'is' in this sentence is fatally flawed, because it conflates issues of motivation with issues about cognition, and makes an absurd claim about each individual's cognition of his or her actual individual good.

To state an unequivocal thesis about human motivation, and to be precise about our chosen ends of our actions, Hobbes' Thesis about Ends requires this pair of revisions:

'Of the voluntary acts of all men, the object is some *presumed* good for himself.'

'... and their object ought to be some (actual) good for himself.'

This pair of theses solely concerns our human ends of action and our human motives to act towards those ends. It omits any motivationally irrelevant claim about human cognition of actual goods or the good. Hobbes' Thesis about Ends literally though illicitly ascribes thoroughly enlightened self-interest to all human beings. Hobbes' political analysis, to the contrary, denies that ordinary people are sufficiently enlightened about their self-interest—witness their unpeaceable quarrelsomeness—whilst nevertheless presuming that absolute sovereigns *are* sufficiently enlightened about their self-interest to be rightly expected to rule moderately. This is a fatal equivocation in Hobbes' positive political analysis, which exposes that it matters materially who is to become an absolute sovereign (cf. Locke, *ST* §93), a sure occasion for precisely the kind and extent of quarrelling Hobbes sought above all to avoid.

Disambiguating Hobbes' equivocal Thesis about Ends confirms that, as a thesis about *motivation*, psychological egoism must be formulated in terms of aiming at some object which *is believed to be* good for the agent. Claims about motivation cannot justify or support claims about our knowledge of our own good, much less infallible cognition of one's own actual good. Historically, of course, absolute sovereigns—much like the rest of humanity—have exhibited considerable variation in the extent to which their actions aim at something genuinely good for themselves, or instead they governed according merely to something they believed to be good for themselves, though they were mistaken, indeed rather too often monstrously so.

Now Hobbes' reasons why absolute sovereigns rule moderately do not require them to have infallible knowledge of their own good, they only require sufficiently enlightened sovereign self-interest to rule, on the whole, moderately. This is a far weaker claim. It too, however, cannot be supported or justified by Hobbes' Thesis about Ends, which fails to note that any general statement about the ends of all human actions being some good or other must include the qualifier that these are presumptive goods, and allow that it is possible, and indeed common, that only some of our presumptive goods are in fact human goods, or one's own good.

Disambiguating Hobbes' equivocal Thesis about Ends undermines entirely his four reasons why absolute sovereigns rule moderately. Hobbes' political analysis and positive political proposal—his covenant of society (*L* 2.17.13)—are irremediably flawed on grounds internal and central to his own analysis. Hobbes' positive political proposals have, of course, been widely rejected from his own day to ours, and rightly so. I do not believe, however, that this fundamental internal flaw in his analysis has been noted previously.[4]

It is very much to Hobbes' credit that the failure of his positive political proposal does not leave us theoretically empty-handed. This pair of equivocations in Hobbes' Thesis about Ends show that Hobbes' appeals to individual self-interest are at best a secondary issue: his Thesis about Ends is confused, equivocal, tendentious, and easily replaced by more moderate and realistic psychological claims, about our ends, motivation, and cognition of (or beliefs about) goods or the good. Replacing Hobbes' confused Thesis about Ends enables us to focus on much more fundamental issues about the principles and institutions of social coordination and the common—and the individual—weal they alone made possible. These issues are posed incisively by Hobbes' two main social coordination problems identified by his analysis of the state of nature (above, §8). Hobbes lacks an adequate solution to these

[4] Ludwig (1998, 276–7) neglects Hobbes' equivocation.

coordination problems, but his recognition and formulation of them remain profound contributions to moral philosophy, as vital today as in 1651.

45 Natural Law, Self-Evidence, and Locke's Laws of Nature

45.1 Locke, reason, and natural law

Locke uses alleged natural laws as premises to justify further claims; he doesn't seek to justify them, because he thinks they are obviously true and can be known simply by reasoning about them:

> The *state of nature* has a law of nature to govern it, which obliges everyone: and reason, which is that law, teaches all mankind, who will but consult it, that being all *equal and independent*, no one ought to harm another in his life, health, liberty, or possessions.
>
> (*ST* §6)

However obvious these alleged laws of nature were to Locke, and however popular appeals to natural law have been in the history of political philosophy, there has been understandable controversy about whether there are such natural laws. Bentham remarked in connection with the French Declaration of Rights that natural rights are non-sense and imprescriptible natural rights are non-sense upon stilts.[5] Rather than rejecting Natural Law outright, which would be as much a *petitio principii* as Locke's claims to know various Natural Laws, the moral epistemology implicit in Locke's natural law theory can be assessed by querying whether the natural laws Locke claims to know can be known in the way he claims.

45.2 Locke's inconsistent views about punishment in the state of nature

Punishment is distinct from revenge. Revenge involves inflicting harm on someone whom one regards as having wronged or harmed oneself, to the extent necessary to 'get satisfaction' or to dissuade that person from repeating such perceived aggression. In cases of revenge, only the

[5] Bentham (1795, 330): 'Natural rights is simple nonsense: natural and imprescriptible rights, rhetorical nonsense, nonsense upon stilts.'

victim's sense of injury specifies the initial harm, only the victim's imagination specifies suitable forms of retaliation, and only the victim's sense of satisfaction specifies the extent of such retaliation. In contrast, punishment is meted out only for specifiable infractions of specifiable rules, where further rules specify appropriate kinds of punishment and set limits on fitting punishments; within those limits it is the task of an impartial, authorized judge to apportion the punishment to suit the infraction (*ST* §8).

Locke expressly holds that in the non-governmental 'state of nature' each person has the right to punish transgressions of the law of nature:

> . . . the *execution* of the law of nature is, in that state [of nature], put into every man's hands, whereby everyone has a right to punish the transgressors of that law to such a degree, as may hinder its violation . . .
>
> (*ST* §7)

Locke further recognizes that punishment requires careful consideration of the appropriate harm to be inflicted on a transgressor. By the right of punishment in the state of nature:

> . . . *one man comes by a power over another*; but yet no absolute or arbitrary power, to use a criminal, when he has got him in his hands, according to the passionate heats, or boundless extravagancy of his own will; but only to retribute to him, so far as calm reason and conscience dictate, what is proportionate to his transgression, which is so much as may serve for *reparation* and *restraint*: for these two are the only reasons, why one man may lawfully do harm to another, which is that we call *punishment*.
>
> (*ST* §8)

As Locke here notes, distinguishing properly between punishment and revenge requires 'calm reason and conscience'. About this he is surely correct. The problem here, once again, is that our common-sense rational knowledge of the principles of punishment does not suffice in practice properly to judge, identify, or act upon the relevant instances to which these principles pertain.

According to Locke, punishment can be legitimate in the state of nature when those who are supposed to mete it out are not partial, self-interested, or naturally vicious. In the state of nature, those who are supposed to mete out 'punishment' are victims (or perhaps their associates too), not neutral bystanders. Locke himself identifies the key problem: he expressly recognizes that due to our self-interest, partiality, and varying strength and wits, we cannot be entrusted to mete out appropriate punishments (*ST* §§13, 124, 128). This is central to the 'inconveniences' of the state of nature which require and justify a legitimate (executive) government (*ST* §§124–6). Specifically, Locke acknowledges the following:

> . . . though the law of nature be plain and intelligible to all rational creatures; yet men being biassed by their interest, as well as ignorant for want of study of it, are not apt to allow of it as a law binding to them in the application of it to their particular cases.
>
> (*ST* §124)

> . . . every one in that state [of nature] being both judge and executioner of the law of nature, men being partial to themselves, passion and revenge is very apt to carry them too far, and with too much heat, in their own cases; as well as negligence, and unconcernedness, to make them too remiss in other men's.
>
> (*ST* §125)

In sum, Locke here testifies that, in particular cases of putative punishment, the 'calm reason and conscience' required to distinguish punishment from revenge is not what human beings can generally be expected to exercise. Instead, in practice, judgments about alleged violations of the law of nature and about putative punishments thereof typically are swayed by common (if not 'common-sense') ignorance of natural law, conflicts of interest (as both party to a dispute and its would-be judge and executioner), bias, passion, negligence, and lack of concern. Accordingly, we are commonly apt to mete out not punishment, but rather 'force without right, upon' the alleged transgressor's 'person'. Such exercise of 'force without right', Locke himself states, 'makes a state of war, both where there is, and is not, a common judge' (*ST* §19). Our common human frailties, in particular our readiness to dispense with 'calm reason and conscience' whenever these most matter, entail that—in his own terms and for his own reasons—Locke's state of nature is ultimately also a state of war. So far Locke corroborates rather than supercedes Hobbes' analysis of the state of nature. Locke himself concedes that,

> . . . were it not for the corruption and vitiousness of degenerate men, there would be no need of any [law] other [than the law of nature] . . .
>
> (*ST* §128)

This significant concession pertains to moral epistemology, not merely to human psychology or anthropology, due to the context of Locke's concession, namely: the problems of determining, in any case and in practice, exactly what counts as an instance of rightful ownership, an instance of a violation of natural law, or an instance of punishment. For these reasons, there can be no Lockean *right* to *punish* in the state of nature. Punishment requires the remedies of civil society: promulgated legislation backed by impartial judges and authoritative execution. On Locke's own account, there can be no Lockean right to punish in the state of nature. Locke's fundamental error about this alleged natural right undermines the credibility of his own use of 'reason' to know any alleged (normative) Natural Laws. (Some contemporary echos of Locke's epistemic naiveté are noted above, §§40–1.)

46 The 2008 Financial Crisis: Negligence In/Action

In semi-annual testimony as Chairman of the US Federal Reserve Board, Alan Greenspan (2002) stated the following as a matter of public, government record:

> Why did corporate governance checks and balances that served us reasonably well in the past break down? At root was the rapid enlargement of stock market capitalizations in the latter part of the 1990s that arguably engendered an outsized increase in opportunities for avarice. An infectious greed seemed to grip much of our business community. Our historical guardians of financial information were overwhelmed. Too many corporate executives sought ways to 'harvest' some of those stock market gains. As a result, the highly desirable spread of shareholding and options among business managers perversely created incentives to artificially inflate reported earnings in order to keep stock prices high and rising. This outcome suggests that the options were poorly structured, and, consequently, they failed to properly align the long-term interests of shareholders and managers, the paradigm so essential for effective corporate governance. The incentives they created overcame the good judgment of too many corporate managers. It is not that humans have become any more greedy than in generations past. It is that the avenues to express greed had grown so enormously.
>
> Perhaps the recent breakdown of protective barriers resulted from a once-in-a-generation frenzy of speculation that is now over. With profitable opportunities for malfeasance markedly diminished, far fewer questionable practices are likely to be initiated in the immediate future. To be sure, previously undiscovered misdeeds will no doubt continue to surface in the weeks ahead as

chastened CEOs restate earnings. But even if the worst is over, history cautions us that memories fade. Thus, it is incumbent upon us to apply the lessons of this recent period to inhibit any recurrence in the future.

(Greenspan 2002, excerpt)

Despite its being 'incumbent upon us to apply the lessons of this recent period to inhibit any recurrence in the future', a few short years thereafter, in the Hearing before the Committee on Oversight and Government Reform, Greenspan (2008) testified in part as follows:

Well, if I may, Congressman, the markets have already punished the people whom you are referring to. A lot of these products have disappeared and they probably will never return. Some of the fees that were charged and paid when euphoria and essentially which led to significant greed showed up, they're gone. And I suspect that we are going to find that this is a very chastened market and that many of the problems that we've observed during the euphoria stage of the expansion will not be back if—at any time if ever.

(Greenspan 2008, excerpt)

Both of Greenspan's testimonies (2002, 2008) and their published discussion deserve careful study: as fundamental moral issues of justice. That Greenspan's own observations in 2002 failed to prompt the kinds of legal reforms of justice which would have restrained or diminished the financial disaster of 2008 amounts to culpable negligence of the highest order.

This point is made directly by questions put to Greenspan by the chairman of that committee, Hon. Henry A. Waxman (2008). Their discussion includes the following exchange:

CHAIRMAN WAXMAN: Dr. Greenspan, I am going to interrupt you. The question I had for you is you had an ideology. You had a belief that free, competitive—and this is shown—your statement, I do have an ideology. My judgment is that free, competitive markets are by far the unrivaled way to organize economies. We have tried regulation, none meaningfully worked.

That was your quote. You have the authority to prevent irresponsible lending practices that led to the subprime mortgage crisis. You were advised to do so by many others.

Now, our whole economy is paying its price. You feel that your ideology pushed you to make decisions that you wish you had not made?

MR. GREENSPAN: Well, remember, though, whether or not ideology is, is a conceptual framework with the way people deal with reality. Everyone has one. You have to. To exist, you need an ideology. The question is, whether it exists is accurate or not. What I am saying to you is, yes, I found a flaw, I don't know how significant or permanent it is, but I have been very distressed by that fact. But if I may, may I just finish an answer to the question . . .

CHAIRMAN WAXMAN: You found a flaw?

MR. GREENSPAN: I found a flaw in the model that I perceived is the critical functioning structure that defines how the world works, so to speak.

CHAIRMAN WAXMAN: In other words, you found that your view of the world, your ideology, was not right, it was not working.

MR. GREENSPAN: Precisely. That's precisely the reason I was shocked, because I had been going for 40 years or more with very considerable evidence that it was working exceptionally well. But let me just, if I may . . .

CHAIRMAN WAXMAN: Well, the problem is that the time has expired.

MR. DAVIS OF VIRGINIA: He wishes to answer. Can you just let him answer.

CHAIRMAN WAXMAN: We have many Members.

MR. GREENSPAN: If I could have just a minute. The reason, basically, is this—Governor Gramlich said to me, that he had problems. Indeed, I agreed that I had heard very much the same thing. I frankly thought that when our meeting ended, that a subcommittee of the board which supervises all of the various aspects of consumer and community affairs within the Board of Governors and the Federal Reserve system, would move forward and present to the board as a whole, recommendations to be made. That was not made, and I presumed, at the time, that essentially the subcommittee didn't think it rose to the higher level.

But, just quickly, to say that the overall view that I take of regulation is that I took a pledge, when—I took an oath of office when I became Federal Reserve chairman, and I recognized that you do with that, what I did is I said that I am here to uphold the laws of the land passed by the Congress, not my own predilections.

I think you will find that my history is that I voted for virtually every regulatory action that the Federal Reserve board moved forward on. Indeed, I voted with the majority at all times, and I was doing so because I perceived that was the will of the Congress. In fact, you go back and you look at the record, I felt required by my oath of office to adhere to what I am supposed to do, not what I would like to do. And that is my history, and I think the evidence very strongly supports that.

CHAIRMAN WAXMAN: Well, I appreciate that. On the other hand, you didn't get to vote on regulations that didn't put before the Federal Reserve Board, even though you have the legal authority for those regulations. That's more—not a question but a comment.

(Waxman *et al*, 2008, excerpt)

Greenspan's failure to distinguish between empirical economic theory and 'ideology' is striking testimony to the ideological character of his socio-economic assumptions and predilections, which has typified 'supply side' economics and the persistent deregulationist efforts so prominent in Anglophone economic theory and policy over the past 50 years.

That Greenspan's own observations in 2002 failed to prompt the kinds of legal reforms of justice which would have restrained or diminished the financial disaster of 2008 amounts to negligence of the highest order: not only regarding Greenspan's own responsibilities—both actions and omissions—and not only regarding the responsibilities of government officials and offices, but also regarding the responsibilities of all those holding the fundamental office of citizen. That office is occupied *inter alia* by ethicists, meta-ethicists, and economists, however reluctant they may be to think about justice, social philosophy, institutional economics or the implications and effects of their selective professional preferences.[6] Regarding—or rather: disregarding—these issues as 'someone else's problem' contributes substantially and materially to these issues becoming everyone's problems, domestically and internationally. That, too, constitutes professional and personal negligence, which affords, if not condones, the violation of everyone's sole innate right to freedom (above, §43).

[6] Economics as a discipline has been distorted by comparable selectivities; see Phelps (2015); Ord et al. (2015).

Bibliography

Abdul-Rahman, Yahia, 2010. *The Art of Islamic Banking and Finance*. Hoboken, NJ: John Wiley & Sons.

Adams, Robert, 2001. 'Scanlon's Contractualism', *The Philosophical Review* 110.4: 563–84.

Adkins, W. H., 1963. '"Friendship" and "Self-Sufficiency" in Homer and Aristotle', *The Classical Quarterly*, New Series 13.1: 30–45.

Allison, Henry, 1990. *Kant's Theory of Freedom*. Cambridge: Cambridge University Press.

Allison, Henry, 1997. 'We Can Act Only Under the Idea of Freedom', *Proceedings and Addresses of the American Philosophical Association* 71.2: 39–50.

Annas, Julia, 1977. 'Plato and Aristotle on Friendship and Altruism', *Mind*, New Series 86.344: 532–54.

Arbogast, Stephen, 2008. *Resisting Corporate Corruption: Lessons in Practical Ethics from the Enron Wreckage*. Salem, Mass.: M & M Scrivener.

Arthur, John and William Shaw, eds, 1991. *Justice and Economic Distribution*, 2nd rev. edn, Englewood Cliffs, NJ: Prentice-Hall.

Axelrod, Robert, 1984. *The Evolution of Cooperation*. New York: Basic Books.

Baier, Annette, 1977. *The Commons of the Mind*. LaSalle, Ill.: Open Court.

Baier, Annette, 1991. *A Progress of Sentiments*. Cambridge, Mass.: Harvard University Press.

Baier, Annette, 2010. *The Cautious, Jealous Virtue. Hume on Justice*. Cambridge, Mass.: Harvard University Press.

Baier, Kurt, 1958. *The Moral Point of View: A Rational Basis of Ethics*. Ithaca, NY: Cornell University Press.

Baier, Kurt, 1995. *The Rational and the Moral Order*. LaSalle, Ill.: Open Court.

Baron, Marcia, 2013. 'Moral Worth and Moral Rightness, Maxims and Actions', in D. Archard, M. Deveaux, N. Manson, and D. Weinstock, eds, *Reading Onora O'Neill*. London: Routledge, 11–16.

Baron-Cohen, Simon, 2013. *The Science of Evil: On Empathy and the Origins of Cruelty*. New York: Basic Books.

Barry, Brian, 2010. 'David Hume as a Social Theorist', *Utilitas* 22.4: 369–92.

Barry, Melissa, 2013. 'Constructivist Practical Reasoning and Objectivity', in D. Archard, M. Deveaux, N. Manson, and D. Weinstock, eds, *Reading Onora O'Neill*. London: Routledge, 17–36.

Beauvoir, Simone de, 1949. *Le deuxième sexe*. Paris: Gallimard.

Beauvoir, Simone de, 1952. H. M. Parshley, ed. and tr., *The Second Sex*. New York: Knopf.

Becker, Laurence, 1986. *Reciprocity*. Chicago: University of Chicago Press.

Becker, Laurence and Charlotte Becker, eds, 2001. *The Encyclopedia of Ethics*, 3 vols, 2nd edn. London: Routledge.

Beiser, F. C., 1987. *The Fate of Reason*. Cambridge: Harvard University Press.

Bentham, Jeremy, 1795. 'Nonsense upon Stilts, or Pandora's Box Opened, or the French Declaration of Rights prefixed to the Constitution of 1791 laid open and exposed—with a comparative sketch of what has been done on the same subject in the Constitution of 1795, and a sample of Citizen Sieyès', in P. Schofield, C. Pease-Watkin, and C. Blamires, eds, *Rights, Representation, and Reform: 'Nonsense Upon Stilts' and Other Writings for the French Revolution. The Collected Works of Jeremy Bentham*. Oxford: The Clarendon Press, 2002, 2: 317–434.

Berlin, I., 1980. 'Hume and the Sources of German Anti-Rationalism', rpt. in I. Berlin, *Against the Current*. New York: Viking, 162–87.

Besch, Thomas, 2008. 'Constructing Practical Reason: O'Neill on the Grounds of Kantian Constructivism', *The Journal of Value Inquiry* 42: 55–76; DOI: 10.107/s10790-008-9097-9.

Besch, Thomas, 2009. 'Kantian Constructivism, the Issue of Scope, and Perfectionism: O'Neill on Ethical Standing', *European Journal of Philosophy* 19.1: 1–20; DOI: 10.1111/j.1468-0378.2009.00376.x.

Beyleveld, Deryck, 1991. *The Dialectical Necessity of Morality: An Analysis and Defense of Alan Gewirth's Argument to the Principle of Generic Consistency*. Chicago: University of Chicago Press.

Bird, Graham, 2006. *The Revolutionary Kant*. LaSalle, Ill.: Open Court.

Bittner, Rüdiger, 2010. *What Reason Demands*. Cambridge: Cambridge University Press.

Black Elk, 1932. *Black Elk Speaks; Being the Life Story of a Holy Man of the Ogalala Sioux*, as told to John G. Neihardt (Flaming Rainbow), illustrated by Standing Bear. New York: W. Morrow & Co.

Black, Kurt W., 2005. *The Best Way to Rob a Bank is to Own One: How Corporate Executives and Politicians Looted the S&L Industry*. Austin: University of Texas Press.

Blackburn, Simon, 1993. *Essays in Quasi-Realism*. New York: Oxford University Press.

Blackburn, Simon, 1998. *Ruling Passions: A Theory of Practical Reasoning*. Oxford: Oxford University Press.

Blackburn, Simon, 2002. 'Précis of *Ruling Passions*', *Philosophy and Phenomenological Research* 55.1: 122–35.

Bohmann, James, 2009. 'Living without Freedom: Cosmopolitanism at Home and the Rule of Law', *Political Theory* 37.4: 539–61.

Bonjour, Laurence, 1997. 'Haack on Justification and Experience', *Synthese* 112: 13–23.

Bosanquet, Bernard, 1889. 'Review of Sidgwick, *Practical Ethics*', *International Journal of Ethics* 8.3: 390–4.

Boulter, Stephen, 2011. 'The Mediaeval Origins of Conceivability Arguments', *Metaphilosophy* 42.5: 617–41.

Bowles, Samuel and Herbert Gintis, 2011. *A Cooperative Species: Human Reciprocity and its Evolution*. Princeton, NJ: Princeton University Press.

Brand, Walter, 1992. *Hume's Theory of Moral Judgment: A Study in the Unity of A Treatise of Human Nature*. Dordrecht: Kluwer.

Brandt, Reinhard, 1997. 'Antwort auf Bernd Ludwig: Will die Natur unwiederstehlich die Republik?', *Kant-Studien* 88: 229–37.

Broad, C. D., 1930. *Five Types of Ethical Theory*. London, Routledge & Kegan Paul.

Buchanan, James, 1975. *The Limits of Liberty*. Chicago: University of Chicago Press; rpt. in *The Collected Works of James M. Buchanan*, vol. 7. Indianapolis: The Liberty Fund, 2000.

Buchanan, James, 2004. 'Political Liberalism and Social Epistemology', *Philosophy and Public Affairs* 32.2: 95–131.

Buchanan, James, 2011. 'The Limits of Market Efficiency', *Rationality, Markets and Morals* 2: 1–7; <http://www.rmm-journal.de/>, accessed October 2015.

Buckle, Stephen, 1991. *Natural Law and the Theory of Property: Grotius to Hume*. Oxford: The Clarendon Press.

Budde, Kerstin, 2009. 'Constructivism all the Way Down—Can O'Neill Succeed Where Rawls Failed?', *Contemporary Political Theory* 8.2: 199–223; DOI: 10.1057/cpt.2008.41.

Byrd, B. Sharon and Joachim Hrushka, 2006. 'The Natural Law Duty to Recognize Private Property Ownership: Kant's Theory of Property in his *Doctrine of Right*', *University of Toronto Law Journal* 56: 217–82.

Byrd, B. Sharon and Joachim Hrushka, 2010. *Kant's Doctrine of Right: A Commentary*. Cambridge: Cambridge University Press.

Byrd, B. Sharon, Joachim Hruschka, and Jan C. Joerden, eds, 2008. 'Kants Metaphysik der Sitten im Kontext der Naturrechtslehre des 18. Jahrhunderts', in *Jahrbuch für Recht und Ethik/Annual Review of Law and Ethics* 16. Berlin: Duncker & Humblot.

Caird, Edward, 1889. *The Critical Philosophy of Immanuel Kant*, 2 vols. Glasgow: Maclehose & Sons.

Cairns, George and Joanne Roberts, guest eds, 2009. Special issue on the 2008 financial crisis, *Critical Perspectives on International Business* 5.1/2: 1–164.

Canada, Judgments of the Supreme Court of, 1959. *Roncarelli v Duplessis*; <http://scc.lexum.org/decisia-scc-csc/scc-csc/scc-csc/en/2751/1/document.do>, accessed October 2015.

Canada, Judgments of the Supreme Court of, 1984. *Perka v The Queen* (File Nr 17217); <http://scc.lexum.org/decisia-scc-csc/scc-csc/scc-csc/en/5277/1/document.do>, accessed October 2015.

Canada, Judgments of the Supreme Court of, 1992. *Hofer v Hofer* (File Nr 22382); <http://scc.lexum.org/decisia-scc-csc/scc-csc/scc-csc/en/923/1/document.do>, accessed October 2015.

Canadian Charter of Rights and Freedoms, Part I of the Constitution Act, 1982; Canadian Department of Justice; <http://laws-lois.justice.gc.ca/eng/Const/page-15.html>, accessed October 2015.

Carnap, Rudolf, 1950. *Logical Foundations of Probability*. Chicago: University of Chicago Press.

Carroll, Lewis, 1939. *Complete Works*. London: The Nonesuch Press; New York: Random House.

Carson, Rachel, 1962. *Silent Spring*. Boston: Houghton Mifflin; Cambridge, Mass.: Riverside Press.

Chakraverti, Suranjan, 1967. *Natural Justice, or Fundamental Principles of Judicial Procedure*. Lucknow and Delhi: Eastern Book Co.

Chwaszcza, Christine, 2013. 'Hume and the Social Contract: A Systematic Evaluation', *Rationality, Markets and Morals: Studies at the Intersection of Philosophy and Economics* 4: 108–30.

Chisholm, Roderick, 1973. *The Problem of the Criterion*. Marquette University Aquinas Lecture, Milwaukee: Marquette University Press.

Chisholm, Roderick, 1982. *The Foundations of Knowing*. Minneapolis: University of Minnesota Press.

Churchill, Winston, 1947. Speaking in Commons, 11 Nov. 1947, 3:33p.m.; HC Deb 11 November 1947, vol. 444, cc.203–321; <http://hansard.millbanksystems.com/commons/1947/nov/11/parliament-bill#column_206>, accessed October 2015.

Cohon, Rachel, ed., 2001. *Hume: Moral and Political Philosophy*. Aldershot: Ashgate.

Collini, Stefan, Donald Winch, and John Burrow, 1983. *That Noble Science of Politics. A Study in Nineteenth-century Intellectual History*. Cambridge: Cambridge University Press.

Cooper, John M., 1980. 'Aristotle on Friendship', in A. Rorty, ed., *Essays on Aristotle's Ethics*. Berkeley: University of California Press, 301–40.

Crisp, Roger, 1998. 'Moral particularism', in E. Craig, ed., *Routledge Encyclopedia of Philosophy*. London: Routledge; <http://www.rep.routledge.com/article/L131>, accessed October 2015.

Curren, Randall, 2000. *Aristotle on the Necessity of Public Education*. Lanham, MD: Rowman & Littlefield.

Curren, Randall, 2008. 'Cardinal Virtues of Academic Administration', *Theory and Research in Education* 6.3: 337–63.

Curren, Randall, 2010a. 'Aristotle's Educational Politics and the Aristotelian Renaissance in Philosophy of Education', *Oxford Review of Education* 36.5: 543–59; DOI: 10.1080/03054985.2010.514434.

Curren, Randall, 2010b. 'Education for Global Citizenship and Survival', in Y. Raley and G. Preyer, eds, *Philosophy of Education in the Era of Globalization*. London: Routledge, 67–87.

Curren, Randall, 2013. 'Aristotelian Necessities', *The Good Society* 22.2: 247–63; URL: http://www.jstor.org/stable/10.5325/goodsociety.22.2.0247.

Curren, Randall, 2014. 'Motivational Aspects of Moral Learning and Progress', *Journal of Moral Education* (online: 29.08.14); DOI: 10.1080/03057240.2014.935306.

Curren, Randall, 2015, forthcoming. 'Global Civic Education', in M. Spieker and K. Stojanov, eds, *Philosophy of Education—Main Topics, Disciplinary Identity, Political Significance*. Tutzig: Nomos.

Dawkins, Richard, 2006. *The God Delusion*. New York: Houghton-Mifflin.

de Jasay, Anthony, 2013. 'Conduct and Contract', *Rationality, Markets and Morals: Studies at the Intersection of Philosophy and Economics* 4: 53–60.

Deneulin, Séerine, with Lila Shahani, eds, 2009. *An Introduction to the Human Development and Capability Approach: Freedom and Agency*. London: Earthscan.

Dewey, John, 1930. *Individualism, Old and New*. New York: Minton, Balch & Co.

Diggs, B. J., 1974. *The State, Justice, and the Common Good: An Introduction to Social and Political Philosophy*. Glencoe, Ill.: Scott-Foresman.

Draper, Theodore, 1991. *A Very Thin Line: The Iran-contra Affairs*. New York: Hill and Wang.

Edwards, Jeffrey, 1998. 'Disjunktiv- und kollektiv-allegemeiner Besitz: Überlegungen zu Kants Theorie der ursprünglichen Erwerbung', in D. Hünning and B. Tuschling, eds, *Recht, Staat und Völkerrecht bei Immanuel Kant*. Berlin: Duncker & Humblot, 121–39.

Ehrlich, Paul, 1968. *The Population Bomb*, 2nd rev. edn, 1971, New York: Ballantine.

Elgin, Katherine Z., 1999. *Considered Judgment*. Princeton, NJ: Princeton University Press.

Epstein, Klaus, 1966. *The Genesis of German Conservatism*. Princeton, NJ: Princeton University Press.

Erickson, Paul, Judy Klein, Lorraine Daston, Rebecca Lemov, Thomas Sturm, and Michael Gordin, 2013. *How Reason Almost Lost Its Mind: The Strange Career of Cold War Rationality*. Chicago: University of Chicago Press.

Falkenburg, Brigitte, 2012. *Mythos Determinsmus. Wie viel erklärt uns die Hirnforschung?* Berlin: Springer.

Ferguson, Thomas and Robert Johnson, 2009a. 'Too Big to Bail: The "Paulson Put," Presidential Politics, and the Global Financial Meltdown, Part 1: From Shadow Financial System to Shadow Bailout', *International Journal of Political Economy* 38.2: 3–34.

Ferguson, Thomas and Robert Johnson, 2009b. 'Too Big to Bail: The "Paulson Put," Presidential Politics, and the Global Financial Meltdown, Part 2: Fatal Reversal—Single Payer and Back', *International Journal of Political Economy* 38.2: 5–45.

Finnis, John, 1980. *Natural Law and Natural Rights*. Oxford: The Clarendon Press.

Fisman, Raymond and Edward Miguel, 2008. *Economic Gangsters: Corruption, Violence, and the Poverty of Nations*. Princeton, NJ: Princeton University Press.

Flickschuh, Katrin, 2000. *Kant and Modern Political Philosophy*. Cambridge: Cambridge University Press.

Foot, Philippa, 1972. 'Morality as a System of Hypothetical Imperatives', *Philosophical Review*. 81.3: 305–16.

Forbes, Duncan, 1977. 'Hume's Science of Politics', in G. P. Morice, ed., *David Hume: Bicentenary Papers*. Edinburgh: Edinburgh University Press, 39–50.

Fraiberg, Selma Horwitz, 1959. *The Magic Years. Understanding and Handling the Problems of Early Childhood*. New York: Charles Scribner's Sons.

Frederick, Danny, 2013. 'Social Contract Theory Should Be Abandoned', *Rationality, Markets and Morals: Studies at the Intersection of Philosophy and Economics* 4: 178–90.

Friedrich, Reiner, 2004. *Eigentum und Staatsbegründung in Kants Metaphysik der Sitten*. Berlin: deGruyter.

Fulda, Hans-Friedrich, 1997. 'Kants Postulat des öffentlichen Rechts (*RL* §42)', *Jahrbuch für Recht und Ethik/Annual Review of Law and Ethics* 5: 267–90.

Fulda, Hans-Friedrich, 1998. 'Zur Systematik des Privatrechts in Kants *Metaphysik der Sitten*', in D. Hünning and B. Tuschling, eds, *Recht, Staat und Völkerrecht bei Immanuel Kant*. Berlin: Duncker & Humblot, 141–56.

G30/Group of Thirty, 2015. 'Banking Conduct and Culture: A Call for Sustained and Comprehensive Reform'. Special report issued July 2015; Washington,

D.C., Group of Thirty (1726 M Street, N.W., Suite 200; 20036 USA); <http://group30.org/rpt_67.shtml>, accessed October 2015.

Garber, Benjamin D., 2010. *Developmental Psychology for Family Law Professionals: Theory, Application, and the Best Interests of the Child.* New York: Springer.

Garner, Richard, 1993. *Beyond Morality.* Philadelphia: Temple University Press.

Gaus, Gerald, 2013. 'Why the Conventionalist Needs the Social Contract (and *Vice Versa*)', *Rationality, Markets and Morals: Studies at the Intersection of Philosophy and Economics* 4: 71–87.

Gauthier, David, 1977. 'The Social Contract as Ideology', *Philosophy and Public Affairs* 6.2: 130–64.

Gauthier, David, 1979. 'David Hume, Contractarian', *The Philosophical Review* 88: 3–38.

Gauthier, David, 1986. *Morals by Agreement.* Oxford: The Clarendon Press.

Gauthier, David, 1997. 'Political Contractarianism', *Journal of Political Philosophy* 5.2: 132–48.

Gauthier, David, 2013. 'Achieving Pareto-Optimality: Invisible Hands, Social Contracts, and Rational Deliberation', *Rationality, Markets and Morals: Studies at the Intersection of Philosophy and Economics* 4: 191–204.

George, Rolf, 2007. 'Kantian Constructions: On Westphal's *Kant's Transcendental Proof of Realism*', *Dialogue: Canadian Journal of Philosophy/Revue canadienne de philosophie* 46.4: 717–28.

Geuss, Raymond, 2011. *Kritik der politischen Philosophie.* Hamburg: Hamburger Editionen.

Ghaus-Pasha, Aisha and Meredith Rowen, 2007. *Towards Participatory and Transparent Governance: Reinventing Government.* Report on the Sixth Global Forum on Reinventing Government: Towards Participatory and Transparent Governance, 26–27 May, 2005, Seoul; sponsored by the UN Department of Economics and Social Affairs (DESA). United Nations: Sales No. E.07.II.H.6; ISBN 978-92-1-123165-6. (Websearching these two numbers leads directly to the document download.)

Gintis, Herbert, Samuel Bowles, Robert Boyd, and Ernst Fehr, eds, 2005. *Moral Sentiments and Material Interests: The Foundations of Cooperation in Economic Life.* Cambridge, Mass.: MIT Press.

Glover, Jonathan, 1999. *Humanity: A Moral History of the Twentieth Century.* New Haven: CT, Yale University Press.

Goodin, Robert, 2003. *Reflective Democracy.* Oxford: Oxford University Press.

Goodman, Nelson, 1965. *Fact, Fiction, and Forecast.* Indianapolis: Bobbs-Merril.

Gouges, Marie Olymp de, 1791. 'Décleartion des droits de la femme et de la citoyen', Paris: n.p.

Green, Thomas F., 1999. *Voices: The Educational Formation of Conscience*. Notre Dame, Indiana: University of Notre Dame Press.

Green, Thomas Hill, 1883. *Prolegomena to Ethics*, 5th edn, 1906, London: Longmans, Green & Co.

Green, Thomas Hill, 1886a. 'Lectures on the Philosophy of Kant II. The Metaphysic of Ethics', in R. L. Nettelship, ed., *Works of Thomas Hill Green*, 3 vols. London: Longmans, Green & Co., 2: 83–155.

Green, Thomas Hill, 1886b. 'On the Different Senses of "Freedom" as Applied to the Will and to the Moral Progress of Man', in R. L. Nettelship, ed., *Works of Thomas Hill Green*, 3 vols. London: Longmans, Green & Co., 2: 307–33.

Green, Thomas Hill, 1886c. 'Lectures on the Principles of Political Obligation', in R. L. Nettelship, ed., *Works of Thomas Hill Green*, 3 vols. London: Longmans, Green & Co., 2:334–553.

Green, Thomas Hill, 1911. R. L. Nettelship, ed., *Works of Thomas Hill Green*, 3 vols. Sixth printing; first published 1886, London: Longmans, Green & Co.

Greenspan, Alan, 2002. 'Testimony of Chairman Alan Greenspan', delivered to the US Federal Reserve Board's semi-annual monetary policy report to the Congress, before the Committee on Banking, Housing, and Urban Affairs, U.S. Senate, 16 July 2002; <http://www.federalreserve.gov/boarddocs/hh/2002/july/testimony.htm>, accessed October 2015.

Greenspan, Alan, 2008. 'Statement of Mr. Greenspan'. Made to the Hearing before the Committee on Oversight and Government Reform: 'The Financial Crisis and the Role of Federal Regulators', Second Session, 23 October 2008; US House of Representatives, 110th Congress. US Government Printing Office, Serial No. 110-209; <http://www.gpoaccess.gov/congress/index.html; http://www.house.gov/reform>; <http://www.gpo.gov/fdsys/pkg/CHRG-110hhrg55764/html/CHRG-110hhrg55764.htm>, accessed October 2015.

Gregor, Mary, 1993. 'Kant on Obligation, Rights and Virtue', *Jahrbuch für Recht & Ethik/Annual Review of Law & Ethics* 1: 69–102.

Gregor, Mary, 1997. 'Natural Right or Natural Law?', *Jahrbuch für Recht & Ethik/Annual Review of Law & Ethics* 3: 11–35.

Griffin, James, 1996. *Value Judgment: Improving our Ethical Beliefs*. Oxford: Clarendon Press.

Guyer, Paul, 2002. 'Kant's Deductions of the Principles of Right', in Mark Timmons, ed., *Kant's Metaphysics of Morals: Interpretive Essays*. New York: Oxford University Press, 24–64.

Haack, Susan, 1993. *Evidence and Inquiry: Towards Reconstruction in Epistemology*. Oxford: Blackwell.

Haakonssen, Knud, 1981. *The Science of a Legislator: The Natural Jurisprudence of David Hume and Adam Smith*. Cambridge: Cambridge University Press.

Haakonssen, Knud, 1993. 'The Structure of Hume's Political Theory', in D. F. Norton, ed., *The Cambridge Companion to Hume*. Cambridge: Cambridge University Press, 182–221.

Haakonssen, Knud, 1996. *Natural Law and Moral Philosophy. From Grotius to the Scottish Enlightenment*. Cambridge: Cambridge University Press.

Haines, Charles G., 1965. *The Revival of Natural Law Concepts. A Study of the Establishment and of the Interpretation of Limits on Legislatures with special reference to the Development of certain phases of American Constitutional Law*. New York: Russell & Russell.

Hale, Bob, 1993a. 'Can There Be a Logic of Attitudes?', in J. Haldane and C. Wright, eds, *Reality, Representation, and Projection*. New York: Oxford University Press, 337–63.

Hale, Bob, 1993b. 'Postscript', in J. Haldane and C. Wright, eds, *Reality, Representation, and Projection*. New York: Oxford University Press, 385–8.

Hale, Bob, 2002. 'Can Arboreal Knotwork Help Blackburn out of Frege's Abyss?', *Philosophy and Phenomenological Research* 55.1: 144–9.

Hamann, Johann Georg, 1784–8. *Metakritik über den Purismum der reinen Vernunft*. Golgatha and Scheblimini; rpt. in Hamann, *Sämtliche Werke*, vol. 3.

Hamman, Johann Goerg, 1952. J. Nadler, ed., *Sämtliche Werke*, 6 vols. Wien: Herder.

Harcourt, Edward, 2005. 'Quasi-Realism and Ethical Appearances', *Mind* 114: 249–75.

Hardin, Russell, 2007. *David Hume: Moral and Political Theorist*. Oxford: Oxford University Press.

Hargreaves-Heap, Shaun and Yanis Varoufakis, 2004. *Game Theory: A Critical Text*. London: Routledge.

Harper, William, 2007. 'Comments on Westphal', *Dialogue: Canadian Journal of Philosophy/Revue canadienne de philosophie* 46.4: 729–36.

Harrington, Michael, 1962. *The Other America: Poverty in the United States*. New York: Macmillan.

Harrison, Jonathan, 1976. *Hume's Moral Epistemology*. Oxford: Oxford University Press.

Harrison, Jonathan, 1981. *Hume's Theory of Justice*. Oxford: The Clarendon Press.

Hayek, Friedrich August, 1960. *The Constitution of Liberty*, Definitive edn by R. Hamowy, ed., 2011. *The Collected Works of F. A. Hayek*, vol. 17. Chicago: University of Chicago Press.

Hayek, Friedrich August, 1983. *Law, Legislation and Liberty*, 3 vols. London: Routledge.

Head, Simon, 2011. 'The Grim Threat to British Universities', *The New York Review of Books*, 13 Jan. 2011; <https://www.readability.com/articles/n9pjbxmz>, accessed October 2015.

Hegel, G. W. F., 1821. *Grundlinien der Philosophie des Rechts oder Naturrecht und Staatswissenschaft im Grundrisse*. Berlin: Nicolai.

Hensarling, Jeb, 2015. 'An Open Letter on the U.S. Export–Import Bank', *The Wall Street Journal* 3 June, 2015 19:08 p.m. GMT–1; print edition: Friday–Sunday, 5–7 June 2015, 13; <http://www.wsj.com/articles/an-open-letter-to-republicans-on-the-ex-im-bank-1433372926>, accessed October 2015.

Herb, Karlfried, 1989. *Rousseaus Theorie ligitimer Herrschaft: voranssetzungen und Begründungen*. Würtzburg: Königshausen und Neumann.

Herb, Karlfried, and Bernd Ludwig, 1993. 'Naturzustand, Eigentum und Staat', *Kant-Studien* 83: 283–316.

Herder, Johann Gottfried, 1799. *Eine Metakritik zur Kritik der reinen Vernunft*. Leipzig: Hartknoch.

Herman, Barbara, 1993. *The Practice of Moral Judgment*. Cambridge, Mass.: Harvard University Press.

Herman, Barbara, 2006. 'Reasoning to Obligation', *Inquiry* 49.1: 44–61.

Herman, Barbara, 2007. *Moral Literacy*. Cambridge, Mass.: Harvard University Press.

Herman, Barbara, 2010. 'The Differences that Ends Make', in L. Jost and J. Wuerth, eds, *Perfecting Virtue: New Essays on Kantian Ethics and Virtue Ethics*. Cambridge: Cambridge University Press, 92–115.

Herman, Barbara, 2011a. 'A Mismatch of Methods', in S. Scheffler, ed., *On What Matters*, vol. 2. Oxford: Oxford University Press, 83–115.

Herman, Barbara, 2011b. 'Embracing Kant's Formalism', *Kantian Review* 16.1: 49–66.

Herman, Edward S. and Noam Chomsky, 1988. *Manufacturing Consent: The Political Economy of the Mass Media*. New York: Pantheon; reissued with a new Introduction, 2002.

Hill, Thomas E., Jr, 2001. 'Hypothetical Consent in Kantian Constructivism', *Social Philosophy and Policy* 18.2: 300–29; rpt. in Thomas E. Hill, Jr, 2002. *Human Welfare and Moral Worth: Kantian Perspectives*. Oxford: Oxford University Press, 61–95.

Hobbes, Thomas, 1651. *Leviathan, or the Matter, Forme, & Power of a Common-Wealth Ecclesiasticall and Civill*. London, Crooke.

Hobbes, Thomas, 1996. R. Tuck, ed., *Leviathan*, 2nd rev. ed. Cambridge, Cambridge University Press.

Hodgeson, Geoffrey M., 2001. *How Economics Forgot History: The Problem of Historical Specificity in Social Science*. London and New York: Routledge.

Höffe, Otfried, 1987. *Politische Gerechtigkeit. Grundlegung einer kritischen Philosophie von Recht und Staat*. Frankfurt am Main: Suhrkamp. (Translation: Höffe 1995.)

Höffe, Otfried, 1989. 'Kant's Principle of Justice as Categorical Imperative of Law', in Y. Yovel, ed., *Kant's Practical Philosophy Reconsidered*. Dordrecht: Kluwer, 149–67.

Höffe, Otfried, 1990. *Kategorische Rechtsprinzipien. Ein Kontrapunkt der Moderne*. Frankfurt am Main: Suhrkamp. (Translation: Höffe 2002.)

Höffe, Otfried, 1991. *Gerechtigkeit als Tausch? Zum politischen Projekt der Moderne*. Baden-Baden: Nomos Verlagsgesellschaft.

Höffe, Otfried, 1992. 'Ein transzendentaler Tausch. Zur Anthropologie der Menschenrechte', *Philosophisches Jahrbuch* 99.1: 1–28.

Höffe, Otfried, 1995. J. Cohen, tr., *Political Justice: Foundations for a Critical Philosophy of Law and the State*. Cambridge, Mass.: Polity (Wiley).

Höffe, Otfried, 1996. *Vernunft und Recht. Bausteine zu einem interkulturellen Rechtsdiskurs*. Frankfurt am Main: Suhrkamp.

Höffe, Otfried, 2002. M. Migotti, tr., *Categorical Principles of Law. A Counterpoint to Modernity*. State College, PA: Pennsylvania State University Press.

Honoré, A. M., 1970. 'Ownership'; rpt. in E. A. Kent, ed., *Law and Philosophy: Readings in Legal Philosophy*. New York: Appleton-Century-Crofts, 533–48.

Horn, Christoph, 2014. *Nichtideale Normativität. Ein neuer Blick auf Kants politische Philosophie*. Frankfurt am Main: Suhrkamp.

Hruschka, Joachim, 1987. 'Die Konkurrenz von Goldener Regel und Prinzip der Verallgemeinerung in der juristischen Diskussion des 17./18. Jahrhunderts als geschichliche Wurzel von Kants kategorischm Imperativ', *Juristen Zeitung* 42.20: 941–52.

Iriye, Akira, Jürgen Osterhammel, and Emilz Rosenberg, eds, 2012a. *A World Connecting*. Cambridge, Mass.: Harvard University Press. (English version of Irive, Osterhammel, and Rosenberg 2012b.)

Irive, Akira, Jürgen Osterhammel, and Emilz Rosenberg, eds, 2012b. *Geschichte der Welt. Weltmärkte und Weltkriege 1870–1945*. München: C. H. Beck. (German version of Irvine, Osterhammel, and Rosenberg 2012a.)

Jacobi, Friedrich Heinrich, 1785. *Briefe über die Lehre des Spinoza*, 2nd rev. edn, 1789, 3rd rev. edn, 1819, Breslau: Löwe; rpt. in Jacobi, *Gesammelte Werke*, vol. 2.

Jacobi, Friedrich Heinrich, 1786. *Jacobi wider Mendelssohns Beschuldigung betreffend die Briefe über die Lehre des Spinoza*. Leipzig: Goeschen; rpt. in Jacobi, *Gesammelte Werke*, vol. 4, 2: 169–276.

Jacobi, Friedrich Heinrich, 1812–25. F. Köppen and F. Roth eds, *Gesammelte Werke*, 6 vols. Leipzig, Fleischer.

Jacobi, Friedrich Heinrich, 1994. G. di Giovanni, ed. and tr., *The Main Philosophical Writings and the Novel Allwill*. Montreal: McGill Queen's University Press.

Johansson, Ingvar, 2002. 'Hume's Scottish Kantianism', *Ruch Filozoficzny* 59.3: 421–53; English version available from author's website; http://hem.passagen.se/ijohansson/, accessed October 2015.

Johnson, L. D. and E. H. Neave, 2008. 'The Subprime Mortgage Market: Familiar Lessons in a New Context', *Management Research News* 31.3: 12–26.

Kendrick, Leslie, 2011. 'The Lockean Rights of Bequest and Inheritance', *Legal Theory* 17.2: 145–69.

Kersting, Wolfgang, ed., 1997. *Gerechtigkeit als Tausch? Auseinandersetzungen mit der politischen Philosophie Otfried Höffes*. Frankfurt am Main: Suhrkamp.

Kettner, Matthias, 1997. 'Otfried Höffes transzendental-kontraktualistische Begründung der Menschenrechte', in Wolfgang Kersting, ed., 1997. *Gerechtigkeit als Tausch? Auseinandersetzungen mit der politischen Philosophie Otfried Höffes*. Frankfurt am Main: Suhrkamp, 243–83.

Kitcher, Patricia, 2013. 'Kant *versus* the Asymmetry Dogma', *Kant Yearbook* 5: 51–77.

Klemperer, Victor, 1947. *LTI: Notizbuch eines Philologen*. Berlin: Aufbau-Verlag.

Korsgaard, Christine, 1996. *The Sources of Normativity*. Cambridge: Cambridge University Press.

Kuehn, Manfred, 2001. *Kant: A Biography*. Cambridge: Cambridge University Press.

Kummiskey, David, 1996. *Kantian Consequentialism*. Oxford: Oxford University Press.

Lahno, Bernd, 2013. '"Can the Social Contract Be Signed by an Invisible Hand?": A New Debate on an Old Question', Introductory note, *Rationality, Markets and Morals: Studies at the Intersection of Philosophy and Economics* 4: 39–43.

Landes, David, 1999. *On the Wealth and Poverty of Nations*. New York: Norton; first published 1998; epilogue added in 1999.

Levitt, Steven D. and Stephen J. Dubner, 2006. *Freakonomics: A Rogue Economist Explores the Hidden Side of Everything*. New York: Harper Torchbooks.

Lloyd, Sharon (S. A.), 2007. *Morality in the Philosophy of Thomas Hobbes: Cases in the Law of Nature*. Cambridge: Cambridge University Press.

Lloyd, Sharon (S. A.) and Susanne Sreedhar, 2008. 'Hobbes's Moral and Political Philosophy', in E. Zalta, ed., *Stanford Encyclopedia of Philosophy*; (12.02.2002), rev. 23.08.2008; <http://plato.stanford.edu/entries/hobbes-moral/#StaNat>, accessed October 2015.

Locke, John, 1967. P. Laslett, ed., *Two Treatises on Government*. Cambridge: Cambridge University Press.

Louden, Robert B., 2002. *Kant's Impure Ethics: From Rational Beings to Human Beings*. Oxford: Oxford University Press.

Ludwig, Bernd, 1997. 'Will die Natur unwiderstehlich die Republik?', *Kant-Studien* 88: 218–28.

Ludwig, Berndt, 1998. *Die Wiederentdeckung des Epikurischen Naturrects: Zu Thomas Hobbes' philosophischer Entwicklung von* De Cive *zum* Leviathan *im Pariser Exil 1640–1651*. Frankfurt am Main: Klosterman.

Ludwig, Bernd, 2002. 'Whence Public Right? The Role of Theoretical and Practical Reasoning in Kant's *Doctrine of Right*', in M. Timmons, ed., *Kant's Metaphysics of Morals: Interpretive Essays*. Oxford: Oxford University Press, 159–83.

Ludwig, Bernd, 2010. 'Die ‚consequente Denkungsart der speculativen Kritik'. Kants radikale Umgestaltung seiner Freiheitslehre im Jahre 1786 und die Folgen für die Kritische Philosophy als Ganze'. *Deutsche Zeitschirft für Philosophie* 58.4: 501–72.

Maihofer, Werner, ed., 1962. *Naturrecht oder Rechtspositivismus?* Darmstadt: Wissenschaftliche Buchgesellschaft.

Manson, Neil and Onora O'Neill, 2007. *Rethinking Informed Consent in Bioethics*. Cambridge: Cambridge University Press.

Marx, Karl, 1996. T. Carver, ed., *Later Political Writings*. Cambridge: Cambridge University Press.

Marx, Karl and Friedrich Engels, 1961–. *Werke*, 43 vols. Berlin: Dietz.

McCarty, Richard, 2009. *Kant's Theory of Action*. Oxford: Oxford University Press.

McDowell, John, 1994. *Mind and World*. Cambridge, Mass.: Harvard University Press.

Meyer, Bernd, 2009. *Wie muss die Wirtschaft umgebaut werden?* Frankfurt am Main: Fischer.

Mill, John Stuart, 1861. *Utilitarianism*; rpt. in J. M. Robson, gen. ed., 1963–91. *The Collected Works of John Stuart Mill*, vol. 4. Toronto: University of Toronto Press (cited as '*CW*'), 205–29. OnLine edition: The Liberty Fund; <http://oll.libertyfund.org/index>, accessed October 2015.

Miller, Alice, 1980. *Am Anfang war Erziehung*. Frankfurt am Main: Suhrkamp. (English translation: Miller, 1983.)

Miller, Alice, 1981. *Du sollst nicht merken. Variationen über das Paradies-Thema*. Frankfurt am Main: Suhrkamp. (English translation: Miller, 1990.)

Miller, Alice, 1983. *For Your Own Good: Hidden Cruelty in Child-rearing and the Roots of Violence*. London: Faber. (Translation of Miller, 1980.)

Miller, Alice, 1990. *Thou Shalt Not be Aware: Society's Betrayal of the Child*. London, Pluto. (Translation of Miller, 1981.)

Miller, David, 1981, *Philosophy and Ideology in Hume's Political Thought*, Oxford: The Clarendon Press.

Mills, C. Wright, 1956. *The Power Elite*. New York: Oxford University Press.

Moore, George Edward, 1903. *Principia Ethica*. Cambridge: Cambridge University Press.

Moore, George Edward, 1912. *Ethics*. Oxford: Oxford University Press.

Morris, Charles R., 2008. *The Trillion Dollar Meltdown: Easy Money, High Rollers, and the Great Credit Crash*. New York: Public Affairs (Perseus Books).

Morris, Christopher W., 1996. 'A Contractarian Account of Moral Justification', in W. Sinnott-Armstrong and M. Timmons, eds, *Moral Knowledge? New Readings in Moral Epistemology*. New York: Oxford University Press, 215–42.

Morris, Christopher W. and Arthur Ripstein, eds, 2001. *Practical Rationality and Preference. Essays for David Gauthier*. Cambridge: Cambridge University Press.

Mossner, Ernest Campbell, 1980. *The Life of David Hume*. Oxford: The Clarendon Press.

Muller, Jerry Z., 2007. 'The Limits of Spontaneous Order: Skeptical Reflections on a Hayekian Theme', in L. Hunt and P. McNamara, eds, *Liberalism, Conservatism, and Hayek's Idea of Spontaneous Order*. New York: Palgrave Macmillan, 197–209.

Murphy, Liam and Thomas Nagel, 2002. *The Myth of Ownership: Taxes and Justice*. New York: Oxford University Press.

Nagel, Thomas, 1959. 'Hobbes's Concept of Obligation', *The Philosophical Review* 68.1: 68–83.

Narveson, Jan, 2013. 'Social Contract: The Last Word in Moral Theories', *Rationality, Markets and Morals: Studies at the Intersection of Philosophy and Economics* 4: 88–107.

Nersisyan, Yeva and L. Randall Wray, 2010. 'The Global Financial Crisis and the Shift to Shadow Banking', Levy Economics Institute Working Paper No. 587; <http://hdl.handle.net/10419/56997>, accessed October 2015.

Nielsen, Kai, 1989. *Why be Moral?* Buffalo, NY: Prometheus.

Nielsen, Kai, 1999. 'Moral Point of View Theories', *Crítica, Revista Hispanoamericana de Filosofía* 31.93: 105–16.

Norton, David F., ed., 1993. *The Cambridge Companion to Hume*. Cambridge: Cambridge University Press.

O'Neill, John, 1998. *The Market: Ethics, Knowledge and Politics*. London: Routledge.

O'Neill [then Nell], Onora, 1975. *Acting on Principle*. New York: Columbia University Press; 2nd rev. edn, Cambridge: Cambridge University Press, 2013.

O'Neill, Onora, 1989. *Constructions of Reason*. Cambridge: Cambridge University Press.

O'Neill, Onora, 1992. 'Vindicating Reason', in P. Guyer, ed., *The Cambridge Companion to Kant*. Cambridge: Cambridge University Press, 280–308.

O'Neill, Onora, 1996. *Towards Justice and Virtue*. Cambridge: Cambridge University Press.

O'Neill, Onora, 1998. 'Necessary Anthropocentrism and Contingent Speciesism', *Proceedings of the Aristotelian Society*, Supplement 72.1: 211–28.

O'Neill, Onora, 2000a. *Bounds of Justice*. Cambridge: Cambridge University Press.

O'Neill, Onora, 2000b. 'Kant and the Social Contract Tradition', in F. Duchesneau, G. Lafrance, and C. Piché, eds, *Kant Actuel: Hommage à Pierre Laberge*. Montréal: Bellarmin, 185–200.

O'Neill, Onora, 2002a. 'Autonomy and the Fact of Reason in the *Kritik der praktischen Vernunft* (§§7–8, 30–41)', in O. Höffe, ed., *Kritik der praktischen Vernunft*. Berlin: Akademie Verlag, 81–97.

O'Neill, Onora, 2002b. 'Instituting Principles: Between Duty and Action', in M. Timmons, ed., *Kant's Metaphysics of Morals: Interpretive Essays*. Oxford: Oxford University Press, 331–47.

O'Neill, Onora, 2003a. 'Constructivism in Rawls and Kant', in S. Freeman, ed., *The Cambridge Companion to Rawls*. Cambridge: Cambridge University Press, 347–67.

O'Neill, Onora, 2003b. 'Autonomy: The Emperor's New Clothes', *Proceedings and Addresses of the Aristotelian Society* 77.1: 1–21.

O'Neill, Onora, 2004a. 'Autonomy, Plurality and Public Reason', in N. Brender and L. Krasnoff, eds, *New Essays in the History of Autonomy*. Cambridge: Cambridge University Press, 181–94.

O'Neill, Onora, 2004b. 'Self-Legislation, Autonomy and the Form of Law', in H. Nagl-Docekal and R. Langthaler, eds, *Recht, Geschichte, Religion: Die Bedeutung Kants für die Gegenwart, Deutschen Zeitschrift für Philosophie*, Supplement. Berlin: Akademie Verlag, 13–26.

O'Neill, Onora, 2004c. 'Kant: Rationality as Practical Reason', in A. R. Mele and P. Rawling, eds, *The Oxford Handbook of Rationality*. Oxford: Oxford University Press, 93–109.

O'Neill, Onora, 2013. 'Responses', in D. Archard, M. Deveaux, N. Manson, and D. Weinstock, eds, *Reading Onora O'Neill*. London: Routledge, 219–43.

O'Neill, Onora, 2016 (forthcoming). 'Enactable and Enforceable: Kant's Criteria for Right and Virtue'. *Kant Studien* 107.1.

Ord, Frit, et al., 2015. 'What's Wrong with the Economy—and with Economics?', International conference sponsored by The New York Review of Books Foundation and the Dan David Prize, 14–15 March, 2015; Scandinavia House, New York. Proceedings posted online; <http://www.nybooks.com/blogs/gallery/2015/mar/29/whats-wrong-with-the-economy/>, accessed October 2015.

Parfit, Derek, 2011. *On What Matters*, 2 vols. Oxford: Oxford University Press.

Paton, Herbert J., 1947. *The Categorical Imperative*. New York: Harper.

Paton, Herbert J., 1952. 'Review of Stephen Toulmin, *The Place of Reason in Ethics*', *Philosophy* 27: 81–4.

Peil, Jan, and Irene van Staveren, eds, 2009. *Handbook of Economics and Ethics*. Cheltenham (UK) and Northampton, Mass.: Elger.

Peirce, Charles Sanders, 1868. 'Some Consequences of Four Incapacities', *Journal of Speculative Philosophy* 2: 140–57; *CP* 5: 264–317.

Peirce, Charles Saunders, 1877. 'The Fixation of Belief', *Popular Science Monthly* 12: 1–15; rpt. in *CP* 5: 358–87.

Peirce, Charles Saunders, 1931–35, 1958. C. Hartshorne, P. Weiss, and A. W. Burks, eds, *The Collected Papers of Charles Sanders Peirce*, 8 vols. Cambridge, Mass.: Harvard University Press; electronic edition: 'Past Masters' series, Charlotte, NC: The Intelex Corp., n.d.; designated '*CP*', cited by volume:¶ numbers.

Perlmutter, Martin, 1998. 'Moral Intuitions and Philosophical Method', in K. R. Westphal, ed., *Pragmatism, Reason, and Norms*. New York: Fordham University Press, 203–18.

Pettit, Philip, 2001. *A Theory of Freedom*. Oxford: Oxford University Press.

Phelps, Edmund S., 2015. 'What Is Wrong with the West's Economies?', *New York Review of Books* 62.13 (13 Aug. 2015): 54–6; <http://www.nybooks.com/articles/archives/2015/aug/13/what-wrong-wests-economies/>, accessed October 2015.

Piché, David, 1999. *La condamnation parisienne de 1277*. Paris: Vrin.

Prammer, Heinz Karl, ed., 2010. *Corporate Sustainabililty. Der Beitrag von Unternehmen zu einer nachhaltigen Entwicklung in Wirtschaft und Gesellschaft*. Festschrift für em. o. Univ.-Prof. Ing. Dr. Adolf Heinz Malinsky. Wiesbaden: Gabler.

Prichard, H. A., 1912. 'Does Moral Philosophy Rest on a Mistake?', *Mind* NS 21.81: 21–37.

Prost, Winfried, 2009. *Vom Umgang mit schwierigen Menschen*. Wiesbaden: Gabler.

Radcliffe, Elizabeth S., ed., 2008. *A Companion to Hume*, Malden, Mass.: Blackwell Publishing.

Rawls, John, 1971. *A Theory of Justice*, 2nd rev. edn, 1999. Cambridge: Harvard University Press.

Rawls, John, 1985. 'Justice as Fairness: Political, not Metaphysical', *Philosophy and Public Affairs* 14: 223–52; rpt. in John Rawls, 1999. S Freedman, ed., *Collected Papers*. Cambridge: Harvard University Press, 388–414.

Rawls, John, 1999. S. Freeman, ed., *Collected Papers*. Cambridge: Harvard University Press.

Rawls, John, 2005. *Political Liberalism*, rev. edn; 1st edn, 1993. New York: Columbia University Press.

Redding, Paul, 1989. 'Habermas' Theory of Argumentation', *The Journal of Value Inquiry* 23: 15–32.

Reidy, David, 1999. 'Rawls's Idea(l) of Public Reason', *Polis* 6: 93–113.

Reidy, David, 2000. 'Rawls's Wide View of Public Reason: Not Wide Enough', *Res Publica* 6: 49–72.

Reisch, George, 2005. *How the Cold War Transformed the Philosophy of Science*. Cambridge: Cambridge University Press.

Reisch, George, 2007. 'From "the Life of the Present" to the "Icy Slopes of Logic": Logical Empiricism, the Unity of Science Movement, and the Cold War', in A. Richardson and T. Uebel, eds, *The Cambridge Companion to Logical Empiricism*. Cambridge: Cambridge University Press, 58–87.

Riley, Patrick, 1986. *The General Will Before Rousseau: The Transformation of the Divine into the Civic*. Princeton: Princeton University Press.

Ripstein, Arthur, ed., 2008. *Immanuel Kant*, International Library of Essays in the History of Social and Political Thought. Aldershot: Ashgate.

Ripstein, Arthur, 2009. *Force and Freedom: Kant's Legal and Political Philosophy*. Cambridge, Mass.: Harvard University Press.

Roberts, Alan, et. al., 2006. *Ethical Trading Initiative Workbook*, 2nd edn. London: Ethical Trading Initiative; <http://www.ethicaltrade.org>, accessed October 2015.

Ross, W. David, 1930. *The Right and the Good*. Oxford: The Clarendon Press.

Ross, W. David, 1939. *Foundations of Ethics*, The Gifford Lectures delivered in the University of Aberdeen, 1935–36. Oxford: The Clarendon Press.

Rouse, Joseph, 2002. *How Scientific Practices Matter*. Chicago: University of Chicago Press.

Rousseau, Jean-Jacques, 1762. *Du Contrat Social*. Amsterdam: Marc Michel Rey; cited as '*CS*', by Bk.Ch.¶ numbers.

Rousseau, Jean-Jacques, 1817. *Oeuvres de J. J. Rousseau, Citoyen de Genève*. Paris: Belin.

Rousseau, Jean-Jacques, 1976. *Du contract social*, in B. Gagnebin and M. Raymond, eds, with F. Bouchardy, et al., *Oeuvres complètes*, vol. 3. Paris: Gallimard (Pléiade), 3: 347–470.

Rousseau, Jean-Jacques, 1994. *The Social Contract*, in *Social Contract, Discourse on the Virtue Most Necessary for a Hero, Political Fragments, and Geneva Manuscript*, J. R. Bush, R. D. Masters, and C. Kelly, tr., in R. D. Masters, ed., *Collected Writings of Rousseau*. Hannover, NH: Dartmouth College Press, 1994, 4: 129–224.

Rowe, David M. and Thomas Day, 2007. 'Credit Risk Management's 25-Year Transformation', *The RMA Journal* 90.2: 40–6.

Rühl, Ulli F. H., 2010. *Kants Deduktion des Rechts als intelligibler Besitz. Kants ›Privatrecht‹ zwischen vernunftrechtlicher Notwendigkeit und juristischer Kontingenz.* Paderborn: Mentis.

Russell, Bertrand, 1919. *Introduction to Mathematical Philosophy.* London: George Allen & Unwin; New York, Macmillan.

Rutschky, Katharina, ed., 1977. *Schwarze Pädagogik. Quellen zur Naturgeschichte der bürgerlichen Erziehung.* Frankfurt am Main: Ullstein.

Savigny, Ike von, 1991. 'Self-conscious Individual *versus* Social Self: The Rationale of Wittgenstein's Discussion of Rule Following', *Philosophy and Phenomenological Research* 51: 67–84.

Sayer-McCord, Geoffrey, ed., 1988. *Essays on Moral Realism.* Ithaca, NY: Cornell University Press.

Scanlon, Thomas, 1998. *What We Owe to Each Other.* Cambridge, Mass.: Harvard University Press.

Scharff, Robert C., 2014. *How does History Matter to Philosophy?* New York: Routledge.

Schmölz, Franz-Martin, ed., 1963. *Das Naturrecht in der politischen Theorie.* Vienna: Springer.

Schneewind, J. B., 1991. 'Natural Law, Skepticism, and Methods of Ethics', *Journal of the History of Ideas* 52.2: 289–308.

Schneewind, J. B., 1993. 'Kant and Natural Law Ethics', *Ethics* 104: 53–74.

Schneewind, J. B., 1998. *The Invention of Autonomy.* Cambridge: Cambridge University Press.

Schneewind, J. B., 2001. 'History of Western Ethics 8. Seventeenth and Eighteenth Centuries', in L. C. Becker and C. B. Becker, eds, *The Encyclopedia of Ethics*, 2nd edn. London: Routledge, 2: 730–9.

Schnoor, Christian, 1989. *Kants Kategorischer Imperativ als Kriterium der Richtigkeit des Handelns.* Tübingen: J. C. B. Mohr (Paul Siebeck).

Schultz, Walter, 2001. *The Moral Conditions of Economic Efficiency.* Cambridge: Cambridge University Press.

Sellars, Wilfrid, 1963. *Science, Perception and Reality.* London: Routledge & Kegan Paul.

Sellars, Wilfrid, 1968. *Science and Metaphyiscs: Variations on Kantian Themes.* London: Routledge & Kegan Paul.

Seneca, L. Annaeus, 1900. *Minor Dialogues Together with the Dialogue 'On Clemency'*, A. Stewart, tr. London: George Bell and Sons.

Sensen, Oliver, 2009. 'Kant's Conception of Human Dignity', *Kant-Studien* 100: 309–31.

Sextus Empiricus, 1933. *Outlines of Pyrrhonism*, in Rev. R. G. Bury, ed. and tr., *Works*, 4 vols., Greek with English translation. Cambridge, Mass.: Harvard

University Press; Loeb Library, vol. 1; cited as '*PH*' by Bk.Ch.¶ numbers thus: *PH* 2.4.20.

Sidgwick, Henry, 1874. *The Methods of Ethics*. London: Macmillan.

Sidgwick, Henry, 1883. *The Principles of Political Economy*. London: Macmillan; rpt. in 1887, 1901.

Sidgwick, Henry, 1885. 'The Scope and Method of Economic Science', Printed for the British Association; rpt. in Henry Sidgwick, 1904. E. M. Sidgwick and A. Sidgwick, eds, *Miscellaneous Essays and Addresses*. London: Macmillan. 170–99.

Sidgwick, Henry, 1890. 'The Morality of Strife', *International Journal of Ethics* 1: 1–15.

Sidgwick, Henry, 1891. *The Elements of Politics*. London: Macmillan; rpt. in 1897, 1908, 1919.

Sidgwick, Henry, 1898. *Practical Ethics: A Collection of Addresses and Essays*. London: Swan Sonnenschein; rpt. in 1909.

Sidgwick, Henry, 1899. 'The Relation of Ethics to Sociology', *International Journal of Ethics* 10.1: 1–21; rpt. in Sidgwick, *Miscellaneous Essays and Addresses*, 249–69.

Sidgwick, Henry, 1903. E. M. Sidgwick, ed., *The Development of European Polity*. London: Macmillan.

Sidgwick, Henry, 1904. E. M. Sidgwick and A. Sidgwick, eds, *Miscellaneous Essays and Addresses*. London: Macmillan.

Sidgwick Henry, 1999. Bart Schultz, *et al.*, eds, *The Complete Works and Select Correspondence of Henry Sidgwick*. Charlottesville, VA: InteLex Corp.

Sidgwick, Henry, 2000. M. G. Singer, ed., *Essays on Ethics and Method*. Oxford: The Clarendon Press.

Sinclair, Upton, 1906. *The Jungle*. New York: Doubleday, Page & Co.

Singer, Marcus George, 1961. *Generalisation in Ethics*. New York: Knopf.

Sinnott-Armstrong, Walter, 2006. *Moral Skepticisms*. New York: Oxford University Press.

Skyrms, Brian, 1996. *Evolution of the Social Contract*. Cambridge: Cambridge University Press.

Smith, Adam, 1759. *Theory of Moral Sentiments*. London: Millar; Edinburgh, Kincaid and Bell; rpt. in *The Works of Adam Smith*, vol. 1.

Smith, Adam, 1776. *An Inquiry into the Nature and Causes of the Wealth of Nations*, 2 vols. Dublin, Whitestone; rpt. in *The Works of Adam Smith*, vols 2–4.

Smith, Adam, 1811. D. Stewart, ed., *The Works of Adam Smith*, 5 vols. London, Cadell; Edinburgh, Davies, and Creech.

Snare, Frank, 1991. *Morals, Motivation and Convention: Hume's Influential Doctrines*. Cambridge: Cambridge University Press.

Sobel, Jordon Howard, 2009. *Walls and Vaults: A Natural Science of Morals (Virtue Ethics According to David Hume)*. Hoboken, NJ: Wiley & Sons.

Southwood, Nicholas, 2010. *Contractualism and the Foundations of Morality*. Oxford: Oxford University Press.

Spector, Horacio, 2014. 'Hume's Theory of Justice', *Rationality, Markets and Morals* 5: 47–63; <http://www.rmm-journal.de/htdocs/latest_entries.html>, accessed October 2015.

Steinbeck, John, 1939. *The Grapes of Wrath*. New York: Viking.

Steiner, George, 1960. 'The Hollow Miracle', *The Reporter*, 18 Feb.: 36–41; rpt. in George Steiner, 1998. *Language and Silence: Essays on Language, Literature, and the Inhuman*. New Haven, CT: Yale University Press, 95–109.

Stemmer, Peter, 2000. *Handeln zugunsten anderer: eine moralphilosophische Untersuchung*. Berlin: de Gruyter.

Stemmer, Peter, 2002. 'Moralische Rechte als soziale Artefakte', *Deutsche Zeitschrift für Philosophie* 50: 673–91.

Stewart, Dugald, 1859. W. Hamilton, ed., *Collected Works*, 11 vols. Edinburgh, Constable; London, Hamilton, Adams & Co.

Strawson, Peter F., 1962. 'Freedom and Resentment', *Proceedings of the British Academy* 47: 1–25; rpt. in Peter F. Strawson, 1974, *Freedom and Resentment*. London: Metheuen, 1–25; rpt. Oxford: Routledge, 2008, 1–28.

Sugden, Robert, 2013. 'Contractarianism as a Broad Church', *Rationality, Markets and Morals: Studies at the Intersection of Philosophy and Economics* 4: 61–6.

Tainter, Joseph A., 1988. *The Collapse of Complex Societies*. Cambridge: Cambridge University Press.

Tainter, Joseph A. and Tadeusz W. Patzek, 2012. *Drilling Down: The Gulf Oil Debacle and our Energy Dilemma*. New York: Springer.

Taylor, Jacqueline, 1998. 'Justice and the Foundations of Social Morality in Hume's *Treatise*', *Hume Studies* 24.1: 5–30.

Tempier, Étienne, 1277. 'Opiniones ducentae undeviginti Sigeri de Brabantia, Boetii de Dacia aliorumque, a Stephano episcopo Parisiensi de consilio doctorum Sacrae Scripturae condemnatae 1277'. Paris; <http://hiphi.ubbcluj.ro/fam/texte/tempier_opiniones_219.htm>, accessed October 2015.

Tempier, Étienne, 1899. Rpt of Étienne Tempier, 1277. In H. Denifle and A. Chatelain, eds, *Chartularium Universitatis Parisiensis* (4 Bände), vol. 1. Paris, 543–55.

Tempier, Étienne, 1911. Rpt. of Étienne Tempier, 1277. In Pierre Mandonnett, ed. *Siger de Brabant et l'averroïsme latin au XIIIme siècle*, vol. 2. Louvain 175–91.

Tempier, Étienne, 1999. Critical edition of Étienne Tempier, 1277. 'Opiniones ducentae undeviginti Sigeri de Brabantia, Boetii de Dacia aliorumque, a

Stephano episcopo Parisiensi de consilio doctorum Sacrae Scripturae condemnatae 1277' in David Piché, ed., 1999. *La condamnation parisienne de 1277.* Paris: Vrin.

Tett, Gillian and Paul J. Davies, 2007. 'Out of the Shadows: How Banking's Secret System Broke Down', *Financial Times*, 16. Dec. 18: 33 gmt: <http://www.ft.com/cms/s/0/42827c50-abfd-11dc-82f0-0000779fd2ac.html>, accessed October 2015.

Thiele, Leslie Paul, 2006. *The Heart of Judgment.* Cambridge: Cambridge University Press.

Thomas, Keith, 2011. 'Universities under Attack', *The London Review of Books*, Online only, 28 Nov. 2011; <http://www.lrb.co.uk/2011/11/28/keith-thomas/universities-under-attack>, accessed October 2015.

Timmons, Mark, ed., 2002. *Kant's Metaphysics of Morals: Interpretive Essays.* New York: Oxford University Press.

Toulmin, Stephen, 1953. *An Examination of the Place of Reason in Ethics.* Cambridge: Cambridge University Press.

Travis, Charles, 2008. *Occasion Sensitivity: Selected Essays.* Oxford: Oxford University Press.

Truman, David B., 1951. *The Governmental Process: Political Interests and Public Opinion.* New York: Knopf.

Turiel, Elliot, 2004. *The Culture of Morality: Social Development, Context, and Conflict.* Cambridge: Cambridge University Press.

Tuschling, Burkard, 1998. 'Die Idee des Rechts: Hobbes und Kant', in D. Hüning and B. Tuschling, eds, *Recht, Staat und Völkerrecht bei Immanuel Kant. Marburger Tagung zu Kants »Metaphysischen Anfangsgründen der Rechtslehre«.* Berlin: Duncker & Humblot, 85–117.

Uleman, Jennifer, 2010. *An Introduction to Kant's Moral Theory.* Cambridge: Cambridge University Press.

Uslaner, Eric M., 2002. *The Moral Foundations of Trust.* Cambridge: Cambridge University Press.

Vallacher, Robin, Peter Coleman, Andrez Nowak, Lan Bui-Wrzosinska, Larry Liebovitch, Katherina Kugler, and Andrea Bartoli, 2013. *Attracted to Conflict: Dynamic Foundations of Destructive Social Relations.* Heidelberg: Springer.

Vallentyne, Peter, ed., 1991. *Contractarianism and Rational Choice. Essays on David Gauthier's 'Morals by Agreement'.* Cambridge: Cambridge University Press.

van der Does de Willebois, Emile, Emily M. Halter, Robert A. Harrison, Ji Won Park, and J. C. Sharman, 2011. *The Puppet Masters: How the Corrupt Use Legal Structures to Hide Stolen Assets and What to Do About It.* Washington, D.C.: The World Bank/The International Bank for Reconstruction and

Development; <https://openknowledge.worldbank.org/handle/10986/2363>, accessed October 2015.

Vanderschraaf, Peter, 2013. 'A Governing Convention?', *Rationality, Markets and Morals: Studies at the Intersection of Philosophy and Economics* 4: 131–56.

Wagner, Hans, 1994. 'Kants Konzept von hypothetischen Imperativen', *Kant-Studien* 85: 78–84.

Waldron, Jeremy, 1988. *The Right to Private Property*. Oxford: The Clarendon Press.

Waldron, Jeremy, 2005. 'Nozick and Locke: Filling the Space of Rights', *Social Philosophy and Policy* 22.1: 81–110.

Waldron, Jeremy, 2012. 'How Law Protects Dignity', *The Cambridge Law Journal* 71.1: 200–22.

Wallace, James, 2009. *Norms and Practices*. Ithaca, NY: Cornell University Press.

Watson, Donald, 2012. 'A New Dusk', The Monthly (Australia; Aug. 2012): 10–14; <http://www.themonthly.com.au/comment-new-dusk-don-watson5859>, accessed October 2015.

Watson, John, 1881. *Kant and his English Critics: A Comparison of Critical and Empirical Philosophy*. Glasgow: Maclehose.

Waxman, Henry A., et al., 2008. Hearing before the Committee on Oversight and Government Reform: 'The Financial Crisis and the Role of Federal Regulators', Second Session, 23 October 2008; US House of Representatives, 110th Congress. US Government Printing Office, Serial No. 110–209; <http://www.gpoaccess.gov/congress/index.html; http://www.gpo.gov/fdsys/pkg/CHRG-110hhrg55764/html/CHRG-110hhrg55764.htm; http://www.house.gov/reform>, accessed October 2015.

Westen, Drew, 1985. *Self and Society: Narcissism, Collectivism, and the Development of Morals*. Cambridge: Cambridge University Press.

Westphal, Kenneth R., 1989. *Hegel's Epistemological Realism*. Dordrecht: Kluwer.

Westphal, Kenneth R., 1991a. 'Hegel's Critique of Kant's Moral World View', *Philosophical Topics* 19.2: 133–76.

Westphal, Kenneth R., 1991b. 'Kant's Qualified Principle of Obedience to Authority in the *Metaphysical Elements of Justice*', in G. Funke, ed., *Akten des 7. internationalen Kant-Kongress*. Bonn: Bouvier, 1991, II.2: 353–66.

Westphal, Kenneth R., 1992. 'Kant on the State, Law, and Obedience to Authority in the Alleged "Anti-Revolutionary" Writings', *Journal of Philosophical Research* 17: 383–426; rpt. in S. Byrd and J. Hruschka, eds, *Kant and Law*. Aldershot: Ashgate, 2006, 201–44.

Westphal, Kenneth R., 1995. 'How "Full" is Kant's Categorical Imperative?', *Jahrbuch für Recht und Ethik/Annual Review of Law and Ethics* 3: 465–505.

Westphal, Kenneth R., 1997. 'Do Kant's Principles Justify Property or Usufruct?', *Jahrbuch für Recht und Ethik/Annual Review of Law and Ethics* 5: 141–94.

Westphal, Kenneth R., 1998a. 'Hegel's Solution to the Dilemma of the Criterion', in J. Stewart, ed., *The Phenomenology of Spirit Reader: A Collection of Critical and Interpretive Essays.* Albany, SUNY Press, 76–91.

Westphal, Kenneth R., ed., 1998b. *Pragmatism, Reason, & Norms.* New York: Fordham University Press.

Westphal, Kenneth R., 1998c. 'Transcendental Reflections on Pragmatic Realism', in Kenneth R. Westphal, 1998b. *Pragmatism, Reason, & Norms.* New York: Fordham University Press, 17–59.

Westphal, Kenneth R., 2002. 'A Kantian Justification of Possession', in M. Timmons, ed., *Kant's Metaphysics of Ethics: Interpretive Essays.* New York: Oxford University Press, 89–109.

Westphal, Kenneth R., 2003. *Hegel's Epistemology: A Philosophical Introduction to the Phenomenology of Spirit.* Cambridge, Mass.: Hackett Publishing Co.

Westphal, Kenneth R., 2004. *Kant's Transcendental Proof of Realism.* Cambridge: Cambridge University Press.

Westphal, Kenneth R., 2005. 'Kant, Hegel, and Determining Our Duties', in S. Byrd and J. Joerden eds, *Philosophia practica universaliz. Festschrift für Joachim Hruschka. Jahrbuch für Recht & Ethik/Annual Review of Law & Ethics* 13: 335–54.

Westphal, Kenneth R., 2006. 'How does Kant Prove that We Perceive, and Not Merely Imagine, Physical Objects?', *The Review of Metaphysics* 59.4: 781–806.

Westphal, Kenneth R., 2007a. 'Kant's Anti-Cartesianism', *Dialogue: Canadian Journal of Philosophy/Revue canadienne de philosophie* 46.4: 709–15.

Westphal, Kenneth R., 2007b. 'Proving Realism Transcendentally: Replies to Rolf George and William Harper', *Dialogue: Canadian Journal of Philosophy/Revue canadienne de philosophie* 46.4: 737–50.

Westphal, Kenneth R., 2007c. 'Consciousness and its Transcendental Conditions: Kant's Anti-Cartesian Revolt', in S. Heinämaa, V. Lähteenmäki, and P. Remes, eds, *Consciousness: From Perception to Reflection in the History of Philosophy.* Dordrecht: Springer, 223–43.

Westphal, Kenneth R., 2009a. 'Hegel's Phenomenological Method and Analysis of Consciousness', in K. R. Westphal, ed., *The Blackwell Guide to Hegel's Phenomenology of Spirit.* Oxford: Wiley-Blackwell, 1–36.

Westphal, Kenneth R., 2009b. 'Does Kant's *Opus Postumum* Anticipate Hegel's Absolute Idealism?', in E.-O. Onnasch, ed., *Kants Philosophie der Natur. Ihre Entwicklung bis zum Opus postumum und Nachwirkung.* Berlin: deGruyter, 357–83.

Westphal, Kenneth R., 2010a. 'From "Convention" to "Ethical Life": Hume's Theory of Justice in Post-Kantian Perspective', *The Journal of Moral Philosophy* 7.1: 105–32.

Westphal, Kenneth R., 2010b. 'Kant's *Critique of Pure Reason* and Analytic Philosophy', in P. Guyer, ed., *Cambridge Companion to Kant's Critique of Pure Reason*. Cambridge: Cambridge University Press, 401–30.

Westphal, Kenneth R., 2010c. 'Practical Reason: Categorical Imperative, Maxims, Laws', in W. Dudley and K. Engelhard, eds, *Kant: Key Concepts*. London: Acumen, 103–19.

Westphal, Kenneth R., 2010–11. 'Analytic Philosophy and the Long Tail of *Scientia*: Hegel and the Historicity of Philosophy', *The Owl of Minerva* 42.1–2: 1–18.

Westphal, Kenneth R., 2011a. 'Kant's Constructivism and Rational Justification', in S. Baiasu, S. Pihlström, and H. Williams, eds, *Politics and Metaphysics in Kant*. Cardiff: Wales University Press, 28–46.

Westphal, Kenneth R., 2011b. 'Self-Consciousness, Anti-Cartesianism and Cognitive Semantics in Hegel's 1807 *Phenomenology*', in S. Houlgate and M. Baur, eds, *The Blackwell Companion to Hegel*. Oxford: Wiley-Blackwell, 68–90.

Westphal, Kenneth R., 2012a. 'Norm Acquisition, Rational Judgment and Moral Particularism', *Theory and Research in Education* 10.1: 3–25; DOI: 10.1177/1477878512437477.

Westphal, Kenneth R., 2012b. 'Die positive Verteidigung Kants der Urteils- und Handlungsfreiheit, und zwar ohne transzendentalen Idealismus', in B. Ludwig, M. Brandhorst, and A. Hahmann, eds, *Sind wir Bürger zweier Welten? Freiheit und moralische Verantwortung im transzendentalen Idealismus*. Hamburg, Meiner, 259–77.

Westphal, Kenneth R., 2013a. 'Proof, Justification, Refutation', in A. deLaurentiis and B. J. Edwards, eds, *The Bloomsbury Companion to Hegel*. London: Bloomsbury Publishing, 289–302.

Westphal, Kenneth R., 2013b. 'Rational Justification and Mutual Recognition in Substantive Domains', *Dialogue: Canadian Journal of Philosophy/Revue canadienne de philosophie* 52: 1–40; DOI: http://dx.doi.org/10.1017/S0012217313000796.

Westphal, Kenneth R., 2013c. 'Hume, Empiricism and the Generality of Thought', *Dialogue: Canadian Journal of Philosophy* 52:1–38. DOI: 10.1017/S0012217313000279.

Westphal, Kenneth R., 2013d. 'Natural Law, Social Contract and Moral Objectivity: Rousseau's Natural Law Constructivism', *Jurisprudence* 4.1: 48–75; DOI: 10.5235/20403313.4.1.48.

Westphal, Kenneth R., 2013e. 'Substantive Philosophy, Infallibilism and the Critique of Metaphysics: Hegel and the Historicity of Philosophical Reason', in L. Herzog, ed., *Hegel's Thought in Europe: Currents, Cross-Currents and Undercurrents*. Basingstoke, Palgrave-Macmillan, 192–220.

Westphal, Kenneth R., 2014a. 'Hegel's Semantics of Singular Cognitive Reference, Newton's Methodological Rule Four and Scientific Realism Today', *Philosophical Inquiries* 2.1: 9–65.

Westphal, Kenneth R., 2014b. 'Autonomy, Freedom and Embodiment: Hegel's Critique of Contemporary Biologism', *Hegel Bulletin* 35.1: 56–83; DOI: http://dx.doi.org/10.1017/hgl.2014.4.

Westphal, Kenneth R., 2015a. 'Kant: Vernunftkritik, Konstruktivismus and Besitzrecht', in J.-C. Merle and A. T. G. Tivisonno, eds, *Kant's Theory of Law (Archiv für Rechts- und Sozialphilosophie,* Beiheft 143), 57–100.

Westphal, Kenneth R., 2015b. 'Conventionalism and the Impoverishment of the Space of Reasons', *Journal for the History of Analytic Philosophy* 3.8: 1–66.

Westphal, Kenneth R., 2016a (forthcoming). 'Mind, Language and Behaviour: Kant's Critical Cautions *contra* Contemporary Internalism and Causal Naturalism', in Saffet Babür, ed., *Method in Philosophy* (Istanbul: Yeditepe Universitesi Press).

Westphal, Kenneth R., 2016b (forthcoming). 'Qualia, Gemütsphilosophie und Methodologie; *oder* Wie wird aristotelische *Scientia* zu cartesianischer Unfelhbarkeit? Zum heutigen Widerstreit des Naturalismus und Cartesianismum', in M. Bykova, guest ed., *Studies in East European Thought* 68, special double issue honouring Prof. Dr Nelly Motroshilova.

Westphal, Kenneth R., 2016c (forthcoming). 'Kant, Aristotle and our Fidelity to Reason'. *Studi Kantiani.*

Whelan, Frederick, 1981. *Order and Artifice in Hume's Political Philosophy.* Princeton: Princeton University Press.

White, William R., 2004. 'Are Changes in Financial Structure Extending Safety Nets?', *BIS Working Paper* No. 145; <http://ssrn.com/abstract=901385>, accessed October 2015.

Wick, Warner, 1951. 'The "Political" Philosophy of Logical Empiricism', *Philosophical Studies* 2.4: 49–57.

Wiggins, David, 1998. 'A Sensible Subjectivism?', in David Wiggins, ed. *Needs, Values, Truth,* 3rd edn, Oxford: The Clarendon Press, 185–210.

Will, Frederick L., 1988. *Beyond Deduction: Ampliative Aspects of Philosophical Reflection.* New York and London: Routledge.

Will, Frederick L., 1997. K. R. Westphal, ed., *Pragmatism and Realism.* Lanham, MD: Rowman & Littlefield.

Williams, Bernard, 1981. 'Internal and External Reasons', rpt. in Bernard Williams, *Moral Luck: Philosophical Papers, 1973–1980.* Cambridge: Cambridge University Press, 101–113.

Williams, Melissa, and Jeremy Waldron, eds, 2008. *Toleration and its Limits.* New York: New York University Press.

Winnicott, Donald, 1964. *The Child, the Family, and the Outside World*. London: Pelican.

Wizenman, Thomas, 1786. *Die Resultate der Jacobischen und Mendelssohnschen Philosophie, kritisch untersucht von einem Freiwilligen*. Leipzig: Goeschen.

Wolff, Michael, 2009. 'Warum das Faktum der Vernunft ein Faktum ist. Auflösung einiger Verständnisschwierigkeiten in Kants Grundlegung der Moral', *Deutsche Zeitschrift für Philosophie* 57.4: 511–49.

Wood, Allen, 1998. 'Kant on Duties Regarding Nonrational Nature', *Proceedings of the Aristotelian Society*, Supplement 72.1: 189–210.

Wood, Allen, 2014. *The Free Development of Each: Studies on Freedom, Right, and Ethics in Classical German Philosophy*. Oxford: Oxford University Press.

Wright, Richard, 1945. *Black Boy*. New York: Harper & Brothers.

Zimmerman, David, 1983. 'The Force of Hypothetical Commitments', *Ethics* 93.3: 467–83.

Name Index

Subject Index

Note: Topics located by the Analytical Table of Contents are not reiterated here.

The manufacturer's authorised representative in the EU for product safety is Oxford University Press España S.A. of El Parque Empresarial San Fernando de Henares, Avenida de Castilla, 2 - 28830 Madrid (www.oup.es/en or product.safety@oup.com). OUP España S.A. also acts as importer into Spain of products made by the manufacturer.
Printed and bound by CPI Group (UK) Ltd, Croydon, CR0 4YY
14/09/2026
02216305-0001